EDUCATION AND CARE IN THE EARLY YEARS

AN IRISH PERSPECTIVE

Fourth Edition

EDUCATION AND CARE IN THE EARLY YEARS

AN IRISH PERSPECTIVE

FOURTH EDITION

Josephine Donohoe
and
Frances Gaynor

GILL & MACMILLAN

Gill & Macmillan

Hume Avenue

Park West

Dublin 12

with associated companies throughout the world

www.gillmacmillan.ie

978 07171 4975 9

Design and print origination in Ireland by

O'K Graphic Design, Dublin

Printed by GraphyCems, Spain

Illustrations on pages 86 and 88 by ODI, Oxford.

Illustrations on pages 13, 264, 292 and 293 by Rosa Devine.

Illustration on page 49 by Kate Shannon.

The paper used in this book is made from the wood pulp of managed forests. For every tree felled,
at least one tree is planted, thereby renewing natural resources.

Original cover photograph: Jayson Kingsbeer (www.kingsbeer.com).
Insert photography (*from top down*): Patrick Ward – Ireland; ad-passion.com – Romania; Jason Nelson –
USA; Shahid Siddique – Pakistan; Craig Toron – USA; Jyobish V. Nair – India; Heather Ward – Ireland.

Contents

SECTION SIX – EQUALITY AND DIVERSITY

Acknowledgments

This book would not have been written without the support of our families, friends, colleagues and associates.

Thanks are also due to all the students, children and families with whom we have worked over the years.

J.D. and F.G.

FETAC Modules and Related Chapters

*Chapter numbers highlighted in **bold** indicate the main sources of information for that module*

Level 5 Modules

Caring for Children 0–6 years	2, 4, 9, 11
Child Development	5, 6, 7, 9, 14, **Appendix 3**
Early Childhood Education	3, 4, 5, 14
Working in Childcare	1, 2, 3, 9, 12, 13, Appendix 2, Appendix 4
Children with Additional Needs	6, 7, 13
Children with Special Needs	6, 7, 13
Care Provision and Practice	3, 11, 13
Communications	12
Intercultural Studies	12, 13, 14
Intellectual Disability Studies	6, 7, 13
Legal Studies	8, 9
Social Studies	8, 9, 10, 11, 13, 14, Appendix 3, Appendix 5
Work Experience	1, 2, Appendix 4

Level 6 Modules

Child Development	5, 6, 7, 9, 14, Appendix 3
Early Childhood Programmes	3, 4, 5, 14
Social and Legal Issues in Childcare	1, 2, 8, 9, 10, 11, 13, Appendix 5
The Childcare Supervisor	2, 3, 9, 11, Appendix 5

Abbreviations Used in the Book

CCC	City/County Childcare Committee
CCS	Community Childcare Subvention
CDB	City/County Development Board
CECDE	Centre for Early Childhood Development and Education
CETS	Childcare Employment and Training Support Scheme
DEIS	Delivering Equality of Opportunity in Schools
DES	Department of Education and Skills
DHC	Department of Health and Children
DJELR	Department of Justice, Equality and Law Reform
DSP	Department of Social Protection
ECCE	Early Childhood Care and Education
ECCE Scheme	Free Pre-school Year in Early Childhood Care and Education Scheme
ECDU	Early Childhood Development Unit
ECEA	Early Childhood Education Agency
EOCP	Equal Opportunities Childhood Programme
EYEPU	Early Years Education Policy Unit
HSE	Health Service Executive
IPPA	IPPA, Playgroups and Daycare
NCCA	National Council for Curriculum and Assessment
NCCC	National Childcare Co-ordinating Committee
NCIP	National Childcare Investment Programme
NCNA	National Children's Nurseries Association
NCO	National Children's Office
NQF	National Quality Framework in ECCE
NVCO	National Voluntary Childcare Organisations
OECD	Organisation for Economic Cooperation and Development
OMCYA	Office of the Minister for Children and Youth Affairs
QE	Quality in Education mark

Important Publications

CECDE (2006)	*Síolta: The National Quality Framework for Early Education in Ireland*
DHC (2006)	*Pre-school Regulations*
NCCA (2004)	*Towards a Framework for Early Learning*

NCCA (2010)   *Aistear: The Early Childhood Curriculum Framework*
NESF (2005)   *Early Childhood Care and Education*
OECD (2004)   *Review of ECCE Policy in Ireland*
OECD (2006)   *Starting Strong*

Additional resources for *Education and Care in the Early Years*, fourth edition:

Easy-to-use online support material for this book is available at

www.gillmacmillan.ie/lecturers

To access this teaching resource on our secure website:

1.   Go to www.gillmacmillan.ie/lecturers

2.   Log on using your username and password. If you don't have a
      password, register online and we will email your new password to you.

Introduction

Since the first edition of this book was published in 1999 a wealth of material, money and time have been devoted to the subject of early childhood care and education in Ireland. Working groups, consultations, Green Papers, White Papers, reports, recommendations, committees, commissions ... tons of paper, but a lot remains to be done on the ground to significantly improve the early years experiences of children in Ireland.

However, significant changes have taken place not only in early childhood policy, legislation and accreditation but in other areas such as equality legislation and social services. This edition continues to reflect these changes.

As in earlier editions, a practical rather than a theoretical approach is taken, and exercises throughout the book are clearly linked to FETAC Level 5 assessment requirements. Activities, tasks, case studies and scenarios are interspersed at relevant stages throughout the text and are designed to provoke discussion and reinforce active learning. Many of these are suitable for use as research projects across a range of FETAC modules. Suggestions for child observations aim to facilitate the learner who is completing an observations portfolio. Resources for further reading and useful addresses are included at the end of the book. These are not exhaustive, but are aimed at the learner who wishes to explore a particular area further; the majority of the suggested resources are readily accessible on the Irish market.

High-quality early years services require trained and qualified professional workers, and in Ireland more and more options are becoming available at different levels, as demonstrated in the National Qualifications Framework (NQF). It is hoped that this textbook will be valuable to learners in all early years training, such as the FETAC Level 5 Certificate in Childcare, the FETAC Level 5 Certificate in Applied Social Studies, the FETAC Level 6 Certificate in Childcare Supervision and the CACHE Certificates and Diplomas in Early Years Work.

Although written primarily with the needs of the early childhood care and education learner in mind, the material is relevant to social studies, legal studies, intercultural studies, community and health care and equality studies. It is also hoped that this book will be of interest to parents and to early years workers engaged in continuing professional development – to anyone who has an interest in the care and education of young children in Ireland.

The authors strongly believe that the principles of quality and equality should underpin and inform all early years work and this belief is reflected throughout the book. It takes as its starting point an affirmation of the child as a unique individual with rights, who is an active agent in his/her own learning and development.

In referring to the child and the early years worker, we have used the terms 'she' and 'he' in alternate chapters throughout the book.

EARLY CHILDHOOD SERVICES

This section is designed to give an overview of issues which are of general relevance to early childhood workers. Chapter 1 gives an overview of the early childhood services, both publicly and privately funded, which are available to pre-school children in Ireland at present and describes recent policy initiatives. It also looks at employment and work in early childhood services.

Chapter 2 is concerned with the regulation of pre-school services under the Child Care Act 1991 and the Safety, Health and Welfare at Work Act 2005. Chapter 3 explores children's rights in an overall context of quality early childhood services.

1
DEVELOPMENT OF THE EARLY CHILDHOOD SECTOR

AREAS COVERED

▸ Early Childhood Services
▸ Recent Policy Initiatives
▸ Working in an Early Childhood Setting
▸ Employment Legislation
▸ The Role of the Trade Union

Introduction

Ireland provides a relatively low level of State support for early childhood services in comparison to many of our European neighbours and despite international recognition of the value of these services to children and families. A range of full-time and part-time services has emerged over the past 30 years to meet growing demand, but this has happened largely outside of any legislative framework. This chapter outlines the range of early years services currently available in Ireland and summarises the initiatives which have led to the development of those services. It looks at the work of the early childhood professional, outlines the main employee entitlements under current labour legislation and summarises the role of the trade union.

The term 'early childhood services' is used here to denote only those services concerned with early childhood care and education.

Early Childhood Services

The past three decades have seen a rapid increase in the development of early childhood services in Ireland. There were two key reasons for this:

▸   Increased participation by women in the paid labour force

▸   Recognition of the value of play and socialisation opportunities for children's development.

In recent years, women with young children have formed an increasing proportion of the paid labour force – a high percentage of women with a child under 6 years are now employed or in education – and it is now recognised that lack of childcare can act as a barrier to employment, training and education for women. Unlike several of our EU partners, Ireland has a limited State-supported mainstream early education system and does not provide a service for the children of working parents, with the result that many parents turn to the private sector to meet their childcare needs. Altogether, a high percentage of under-5s attend some form of early childhood service, whether full time or part time, publicly or privately funded.

Early childhood services fall broadly into two categories:

▸   Services aiming to meet **children's developmental needs** – playgroups, naíonraí, parent and toddler groups, Montessori pre-schools. These are known as 'sessional' or part-time services and have become the principal childcare option chosen by parents.

▸   Services aiming to meet the **needs of parents** who are employed or in full-time education or training – crèches/nurseries, workplace nurseries and family day care (childminding). These services are 'full-time'. During the Celtic Tiger years they catered for substantial numbers of children, but increasing unemployment has affected the demand for this type of service. Services are now supported by the City and County Childcare Committees and the national voluntary organisation.

City and County Childcare Committees (CCCs)

Thirty-three City and County Childcare Committees representing a wide variety of local childcare and education interests were established in 2001 to encourage and support the development of childcare locally. They offer a wide variety of services, including:

▸   Advice on setting up a childcare business

▸   Childcare information sessions

▸   Training courses

▸   Advice and support on participating in any of the schemes being rolled out by the Office of the Minister for Children and Youth Affairs (covered elsewhere in this chapter)

▸   Services to parents, such as providing information on local childcare facilities and information on parent networks.

The National Childcare Organisations

Six national childcare organisations currently receive funding to promote quality early childhood services. They are:

▶ Barnardos

▶ Childminding Ireland

▶ Forbairt Naíonraí Teo

▶ Irish Steiner Waldorf Early Childhood Association

▶ St Nicholas Montessori Society of Ireland

▶ Early Childhood Ireland, formed in 2011 by the amalgamation of the IPPA and the National Children's Nurseries Association (NCNA).

These organisations have played a proactive and supportive role in the development of quality childcare and early education services for many years. Representatives of the national childcare organisations are also members of the National Childcare Coordinating Committee, chaired by the Office of the Minister for Children and Youth Affairs (OMCYA). This allows them to feed into national childcare policy and to co-ordinate the work of their own organisations accordingly.

Sessional Services

Playgroups

Playgroups usually operate for up to three and a half hours per day and cater for children aged between two and a half years up to school-going age. Playgroups aim to promote the educational and social development of children through play and the involvement of parents/family. Privately operated playgroups are known as **home playgroups**.

Funded places may also be available in **community playgroups**, which are usually managed by local committees. Many operate out of community centres, halls or school premises and receive grant aid from local authorities or Government departments to cover costs of equipment and/or premises in addition to their own fundraising.

Playgroups are supported by Early Childhood Ireland, a voluntary body which offers advice, support and training to its members through its network of regional advisors and tutors.

Naíonraí

These are playgroups which operate through the medium of Irish. Naíonraí are supported by Forbairt Naíonraí Teo, which offers a similar service to that operated by Early Childhood Ireland.

Parent and Toddler Groups

These are aimed at providing play and socialisation opportunities to babies and toddlers within the safe and secure environment of their parent's presence. They are mostly informal, often meeting in the houses of the parents involved or in local community facilities. These are also supported by Early Childhood Ireland.

Montessori Pre-schools

These pre-schools are run according to the principles and methods devised by Dr Maria Montessori. Most operate on an academic year basis, and while the Montessori method is designed to offer a complete educational programme for the child up to 12 years, in practice in Ireland Montessori schools mainly cater for the 3–6-year age group.

The Early Start Pre-school Programme

This is defined as a compensatory/intervention programme designed to alleviate educational disadvantage and to provide more widespread access to early childhood services in economically and socially deprived areas. The programmes are based within the primary schools and avail of special grants to cover start-up and running costs as well as to develop parental involvement, thus making it 100% funded by the Department of Education and Skills. This continues to run as a pilot scheme and has never been evaluated with a view to mainstreaming.

Pre-schools for Traveller Children

Traveller pre-schools are run independently of primary schools and are mainly funded by the Department of Education and Skills. Funding is also available from the Office of the Minister for Children and Youth Affairs (OMCYA) and from the Department of Health and Children. Current policy is to phase out segregated Traveller pre-schools – fewer than 30 remain at present.

Pre-schools for Disabled Children

These services are mainly provided by voluntary organisations as part of their special school provision and are funded by the Departments of Health and Children and the Department of Education and Skills under the National Development Plan. They are linked to special education primary schools.

There is no specific funding structure in place to cover the cost of integrating children with disabilities into mainstream services. These are either met by the parents or assisted by the voluntary organisations through the provision of back-up services such as visiting teachers.

Full-time Services

Crèches, Nurseries, Day Care Centres

Since these terms are often used synonymously and in fact there is no actual difference between them, it is convenient to deal with them all under one heading. These offer full-time care for children from about 12 weeks old to school-going age. Most nurseries offer a play-based or Montessori-based curriculum for part of the day to the 3–5-year-olds, and an increasing number are responding to the demand for after-school collection and care. This means in effect that a nursery can accommodate age groups as diverse as 12 weeks old up to 10 or 12 years. Many nurseries provide hot meals and snacks throughout the day for the children; in a minority of cases this is provided by the parents.

Nurseries may be privately or publicly financed, either through fees paid by parents, subsidies paid by employers or funding from Government departments such as the Office of the Minister for Children and Youth Affairs (OMCYA). They are usually open for a minimum of 8 hours per day and aim to meet the needs of parents who are in paid employment or in education. Early Childhood Ireland supports these services.

Family Day Care

This is where children are looked after in someone else's home. Full- and part-time care is offered to a range of age groups and hours are usually by negotiation. It is by far the most commonly used form of childcare; it is equally accessible to both rural and urban families and is considered to offer the nearest thing to a home environment for a child, where she can develop a one-to-one relationship with a single adult.

The National Childminding Initiative provides supports for childminders and for people interested in becoming childminders. It is administered in local areas by the City and County Childcare Committees (CCCs), which offer initial training and support in accessing a start-up grant (Childminder Development Grant Scheme) that can be used to establish the service, buy safety equipment and toys or to make minor adjustments to the physical environment.

The *National Guidelines for Childminders* provide guidance for good practice. They contain information on:

▸ Nationally agreed guidelines for good childminding practice

▸ Notification to the Health Service Executive (HSE)

▸ Support services provided to childminders by the City/County Childcare Committees, the Childminder Advisory Officers and Childminding Ireland.

TASK
Research what early childhood provision there is in the area where you live. Group these under sessional services and full-time services. This research could be used as part of a project for Social Studies or Working in Childcare Modules.

ACTIVITY

Aim: To summarise information on early years services in Ireland in an easily accessible format.

Compile a chart which summarises the range of provision of early years services in Ireland. Use the following headings:

▸ Type of service

▸ Who it is funded by

▸ Age range catered for

▸ Whether it is full time or sessional

▸ Support organisation, if any.

Development of the Early Childhood Sector

Policy Developments

The principal policy initiatives since 1998 are follows.

1998	—	*Strengthening Families for Life – Report of the Commission on the Family* (Department of Social and Family Affairs)
	—	*The National Forum for Early Childhood Education* (Department of Education and Science)
1999	—	*The National Childcare Strategy – Report of the Partnership 2000 Expert Working Group on Childcare* (Department of Justice, Equality and Law Reform)
	—	*Ready to Learn*, White Paper on Early Childhood Education (Department of Education and Science)
2000	—	*The National Children's Strategy* (Department of Justice, Equality and Law Reform)

Strengthening Families for Life – Report of the Commission on the Family
This report focused on the needs of families in a fast-changing social and economic environment. Its recommendations on supporting families in carrying out their functions are based on an approach which:

▸ Prioritises investment in the care of young children
▸ Supports parents' choices in the care and education of their children
▸ Provides practical support and recognition for those who undertake the main caring responsibilities for children
▸ Facilitates families in balancing work commitments and family life.

The National Forum for Early Childhood Education

This was set up by the Department of Education and Science with the aim of bringing together all interested groups to engage in an exchange of views on early childhood education. It also provided these groups with the opportunity to submit their own concerns and proposals for the development of a national framework for the sector. The report of the forum was published in 1998 and informed the subsequent publication of *Ready to Learn*, the White Paper on Early Childhood Education.

The National Childcare Strategy – Report of the Partnership 2000 Expert Working Group on Childcare
The Expert Working Group on Childcare was convened by the Department of Justice, Equality and Law Reform (DJELR) in response to the crisis in childcare provision. Its membership included Government departments, social partners, statutory bodies, non-governmental organisations including the National Voluntary Childcare Organisations (NVCOs) and parents. The brief of the Expert Working Group was to develop a national strategy for the future development and delivery of childcare and early education services which would be underpinned by the guiding principles of:

▸ The needs and rights of children
▸ Equality of access and participation
▸ Diversity
▸ Partnership
▸ Quality.

The National Childcare Strategy was published in 1999 and made recommendations in relation to supports for parents, supports for providers, regulations, training, qualifications, employment, planning and co-ordination. *The National Childcare Strategy* was linked to employment policy rather than being driven by a commitment to universal provision of Early Childhood Care and Education (ECCE) as a right of all children.

The strategy was initially implemented through the Equal Opportunities Childcare Programme (EOCP) 2000–2006. The aims of the EOCP were:

▸ To provide capital grants for private childcare services
▸ To provide capital and staffing grants for community 'not for profit' providers.

This programme was facilitated by the following structures under the direction of DJELR:

▸ The National Childcare Co-ordinating Committee: This co-ordinated existing developments in the childcare field and informed national policy development.
▸ Thirty-three City and County Childcare Committees (CCCs): These co-ordinate new and existing services at local level and develop, implement and monitor county childcare plans. The County Childcare Committees offer a forum for all those involved in early childhood education and care – workers, providers and trainers – to become involved at local level in influencing policy developments which affect them.

By the end of 2006 the EOCP had delivered an estimated 37,000 new childcare places, but not necessarily for the most disadvantaged children.

The National Childcare Strategy 2006–2010 aimed to further develop and support the childcare infrastructure through the National Childcare Investment Programme (NCIP). This was a major programme of investment in childcare infrastructure, which aimed to create up to 50,000 new childcare places in both the private and community sectors. The NCIP objective was to assist parents to access affordable, quality childcare. Delivery of the programme was through the City and County Childcare Committees under the coordination of Pobal.

The NCIP aimed to:

▸ Provide 5,000 new after-school and 10,000 new pre-school education places
▸ Support quality measures for childminders and parent and toddler groups
▸ Provide support to children and families experiencing disadvantage
▸ Support training for childcare workers as a further quality measure.

The NCIP capital programme was closed to new applicants in 2010.

Ready to Learn – The White Paper on Early Childhood Education

The White Paper set out a national policy framework for early childhood education in Ireland which would build on existing provision and improve the extent and quality of service provided. The document acknowledged the value of early education both in terms of its impact on children's lives and its value to the community and to society in general. It highlighted the crucial importance of quality of provision. Particular emphasis was placed on meeting the needs of children experiencing disadvantage and children with special needs.

Among its recommendations were to:

▸ Address the area of quality and establish a Quality in Education mark
▸ Expand research
▸ Create a specialist Early Years Development Unit
▸ Establish an Early Education Agency.

An important step in fulfilling the recommendation of the White Paper and in preparing the ground for an Early Education Agency was the establishment of the Centre for Early Childhood Development and Education (CECDE) in 2002. Its aims are to:

▸ Develop a quality framework and encourage compliance with quality standards
▸ Focus on areas of disadvantage and additional need
▸ Promote research and development.

The CECDE delivered on the first of these in 2006 by launching Síolta: The National Quality Framework for Early Childhood Education (NQF). The CECDE was disbanded in 2010.

Core Developments in Relation to Children 1989–2011	
1989	UN Convention on the Rights of the Child
1991	Child Care Act
1992	UN Convention ratified in Ireland
1996	Pre-school Regulations
1998	*Strengthening Families for Life*
1998	Report of the National Forum on Early Childhood Education
1999	*Ready to Learn* – The White Paper on Early Childhood Education
1999	National Childcare Strategy
2000	National Children's Strategy
2000	National Children's Office
2002	The Centre for Early Childhood Development and Education (CECDE)
2003	Children's Ombudsman
2003	*Towards a Framework for Early Learning* (NCCA)
2005	Establishment of the Office of the Minister for Children (OMC), now the Office of the Minister for Children and Youth Affairs (OMCYA)
2006	Síolta: The National Quality Framework for Early Childhood Education Pre-school Regulations updated *National Childcare Strategy 2006–2010* National Childcare Investment Programme 2006–2010 *Diversity and Equality Guidelines* launched

2009	Free Pre-school Year in Early Childhood Care and Education (ECCE) Scheme
	Workforce Development Plan
2010	Launch of *Aistear: The Early Childhood Curriculum Framework*
	Introduction of the Community Childcare Subvention (CCS)
	Childcare Employment and Training Support Scheme
2011	Launch of Early Childhood Ireland, a merger of the IPPA and NCNA to create
	a new national support organisation for childcare and children in Ireland

Síolta: The National Quality Framework

Síolta is the national quality framework for the early childhood sector. It establishes the quality standards to which all services should aspire. Síolta means 'seeds'. It is designed to support practitioners in the development and delivery of high-quality care and education services for children aged from birth to 6 years.

Síolta can be used no matter what kind of curriculum is followed – a play-based curriculum, Montessori, HighScope or primary school. The Síolta programme is managed by the Early Years Education Policy Unit (EYEPU) within the OMCYA.

Síolta is underpinned by 12 guiding **principles** of best practice. The 12 principles underpin 16 stated **standards,** which childcare and education services work towards achieving. Services describe their own practice in each standard, make plans for improving their practice and collect a portfolio of evidence to demonstrate the progress they have made. The model then offers **signposts for reflection**, affording practitioners the opportunity to examine how they are meeting these standards (see Chapter 3 for more detail).

Figure 1.1: **The Síolta Quality Improvement Spiral**

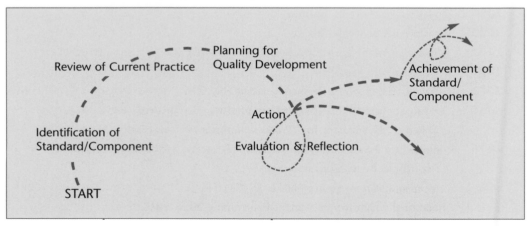

Source: Adapted from Síolta (2006).

ACTIVITY

Discuss and describe some of the ways in which early childhood care and education services can demonstrate their commitment to the principles of Síolta.

Free Pre-school Year/Early Childhood Care and Education Scheme (ECCE)

The Free Pre-school Year in Early Childhood Care and Education (ECCE) scheme is implemented by the Childcare Directorate of the OMCYA. Under the scheme, parents can avail of a free pre-school year for their children when they are aged between 3 years 3 months and 4 years 6 months in September of the relevant year. Each child can avail of the free pre-school year within one academic year only. The place may be taken within a full-time or sessional service, providing the guidelines on hours of service are adhered to.

The ECCE scheme is intended to provide children in their pre-school year with age-appropriate activities, and participating centres must adopt the Síolta principles. The age range for eligibility for the ECCE scheme spans a period of almost 17 months, which is a significant period in the developmental stage of pre-school children. Pre-school services participating in the free pre-school (ECCE) year must agree to provide an appropriate educational programme for children that adheres to the principles of Síolta. Services are supported in meeting this requirement through the assistance of Síolta Co-ordinators and by their local City and County Childcare Committee (CCC). The Early Years Education Policy Unit provides a leadership and support role.

This is the first time that direct universal funding of early education has been implemented.

Aistear: The Early Childhood Curriculum Framework

In 2010, the Department of Education and Skills, through the National Council for Curriculum and Assessment (NCCA), introduced a curriculum framework for children from birth to 6 years. The curriculum, known as Aistear (a journey), is relevant to all settings where children experience care and education, whether that is at home or in the home of a childminder, or in day care or pre-school settings.

Aistear is not a fixed or formal curriculum; it is a set of shared principles and themes that guide whatever curriculum the early childhood practitioner chooses to use, such as play-based, Montessori, HighScope, etc. Aistear recognises that there are many roads that can lead to the same destination and helps to support children's learning in a safe but challenging, stimulating and caring environment.

In Aistear, education and care in the early years are not separate. Whatever curriculum is offered, Aistear believes that early childhood care and education must support children in their:

▸   Well-being
▸   Identity and belonging
▸   Communicating
▸   Exploring and thinking.

These goals are achieved through the provision of play and take place where there are caring, supportive relationships with adults and other children. (See Chapter 4 for further information.)

The Community Childcare Subvention (CCS) 2010

The CCS is a support scheme for community-based, not-for-profit childcare services to enable them to provide quality childcare services at reduced rates to disadvantaged parents. Under the CCS, services are subvented to charge reduced childcare fees to parents who are disadvantaged or on lower incomes. Approximately 75% of parents attending these services benefit from below-cost fees as a result of the scheme. All fees are reduced pro rata for shorter hour services.

All community childcare services participating in the CCS are required to have approved fee policies in place that outline the various fee rates for parents for each of the services they provide. There are four bands of fee rates, comprised of:

(a) Parents in receipt of social welfare payments
(b) Working families in receipt of Family Income Supplement (FIS)
(c) Lower-income parents above the FIS threshold, e.g. holders of a GP Visit Card
(d) Middle- and higher-income parents.

Childcare Employment and Training Support Scheme (CETS)

In 2010, the OMCYA introduced a support scheme to meet the childcare needs of participants in training and educational courses. Under CETS, around 3,000 childcare places are funded by this office, with funding paid directly to the providers of full-time and after-school services that offer places to the children of FÁS and VEC trainees.

Participating services are paid a weekly capitation fee for each place reserved for an agreed number of weeks per· year. Services must be fully compliant with all aspects of the Childcare (Pre-school) Regulations 2006. (See Chapter 2.)

Working in an Early Childhood Setting

Early childhood professional workers are qualified to work with young children in a variety of settings, including crèches, nurseries, playgroups, primary schools and pre-school programmes. The key tasks and responsibilities of the early childhood worker are as follows.

The Childcare Worker

▶ Day-to-day responsibility under supervision for children attending the centre.

▶ Implementing and reviewing activities appropriate to individual and group needs so as to provide for children's physical, emotional, social and cognitive development.

▶ Observing all procedures as required in terms of care and control, safety and good childcare practice.

▶ Choosing, organising and maintaining equipment and materials.

▶ Contributing to compiling and updating children's records.

▶ Delegating tasks to childcare assistants.

▶ Working as part of a team.

▶ Liaising with parents.

The Childcare Assistant

▶ Undertaking routine tasks as delegated under the supervision of childcare worker/supervisor.

▶ Maintaining equipment and materials.

▶ Contributing to the updating of children's records.

▶ Working as part of a team.

▶ Liaising with parents.

Qualities of the Early Childhood Worker

As in all occupations, there are particular qualities which professional early childhood workers should strive to develop. First and foremost she needs to like children and enjoy being with them. Other qualities include the following:

▶ **Communication** – this involves being a good communicator, both verbal and non-verbal. This also means being a good listener.

▶ **Empathy** – having empathy toward others means being able to identify oneself mentally with them, to enter into their feelings in order to fully understand them. It is not the same as sympathy.

▶ **Sensitivity** – this requires being able to anticipate the feelings of others in order to be responsive to their feelings and needs.

▶ **Patience** – this means giving time to the child, parents and other team members, even when you are tempted to take over and complete a task yourself. It requires tolerance and awareness that your way of doing things is not always best.

▶ **Respect** – this comes from an awareness of the rights and personal dignity of each individual child and adult whom you come in contact with in your work. In practice, it means a non-judgemental approach to dealing with people and an appreciation of the value of their contributions.

▶ **Self-awareness** – this means being able to perceive the effect your behaviour has on other people and learning how to modify it when necessary. An early childhood worker who has a positive self-image is more likely to encourage and develop this in children.

▶ **Ability to cope with stress** – the work of the early childhood professional can be stressful. Awareness of this and finding positive ways to deal with it can ensure that it does not impact on one's work.

Working as a Professional

The National Childcare Strategy 2006–2010 identified the need to develop the skills and qualifications profile of the workforce in the Early Childcare and Education (ECCE) sector. In June 2009, a background discussion paper, *Developing the Workforce in the Early Childcare and Education Sector*, was published, followed by a consultative process, which has culminated in the development of a Workforce Development Plan for the ECCE sector. A number of County Childcare Committees are working together to develop a National Association of Childcare Professionals, which would offer support and advocacy to this sector as well as establishing a professional identity for this important work.

Employment Legislation

Early childhood workers who feel valued in their work are more likely to create a warm, supportive climate for the children and team members with whom they work. This is explored further in Chapter 3. Good working conditions and appropriate salaries are factors which help to support the work of the early childhood professional. Membership of a professional early childhood organisation also provides support through access to local and national networks, as well as to information and the opportunity to have an input into the development of early childhood policy and services.

Employee Protection

The early childhood worker has a responsibility to inform herself of her own rights and responsibilities under current labour legislation.

Ireland's EU membership has resulted in the introduction of legislation to protect the rights of employers and employees at work. State agencies to assist in resolving employer/employee disputes have also been established – these include the Labour Court, the Labour Relations Commission and the Director of Equality Investigations. Where disputes cannot be resolved through these agencies, cases may be taken to the civil courts. The main areas of protection in employment for workers are outlined below.

Contract of Employment

All full-time and regular part-time employees are entitled to receive a written statement of their terms of employment within 2 months of its commencement. A regular part-time employee is defined as one who has 13 consecutive weeks' employment and works more than 8 hours per week. Existing employees are entitled to a written statement within 2 months of requesting one. The written contract of employment must include the following.

1. Name and address of employer and employee
2. Job title
3. Job description
4. Date of commencement
5. Nature of contract, e.g. full time/part time
6. Duration of contract
7. Place of employment
8. Rate of pay
9. Method of payment
10. Hours of work
11. Holiday leave
12. Sick leave
13. Period of notice required by both parties

Local information such as pension contributions and entitlements, grievance procedures, probationary period and specific company rules may also be included. There should be two copies of the contract, each signed and dated by both the employer and employee, and a copy should be retained by both. An employer must advise an employee within 1 month of any changes in the terms and conditions of employment, apart from changes in legislation or national collective agreements.

Minimum Notice

Full-time and regular part-time employees working at least 13 weeks for an employer are entitled to receive notice if their employment is to cease. Minimum notice will depend on how long someone has been employed, varying from 1 week for those working less than 2 years up to 8 weeks for those working more than 15 years.

Employers are entitled to receive at least 1 week's notice from an employee, and both parties may receive payment in lieu of notice. The minimum notice requirement does not apply in cases of misconduct.

Holidays

Employees are entitled to 20 days paid holiday plus all public holidays for every year worked.

Maximum Working Time

Over a 4-month period, an employee should not work in excess of 48 hours per week on average.

Rest Periods

An employee is entitled to one 15-minute rest period for every 4.5 hours worked and to one 15-minute and one 30-minute break for every 6 hours worked.

Redundancy Payments

After 2 years of continuous service an employee is entitled to receive a lump sum redundancy payment, which is calculated as follows:

▸   1 half week's pay per year of service between the ages of 16 and 41 years
▸   1 week's pay per year of service over 41 years of age
▸   1 additional week's pay regardless of length of service.

Employees are entitled to 2 weeks' notice of redundancy, with time off during that period to seek other employment.

Unfair Dismissals

An employee may be dismissed if:

▸   She was not qualified or competent to do the job she was employed to do
▸   Her conduct contravenes company rules or constitutes a danger to others at work
▸   She is being made redundant.

Dismissal is considered to be unfair if it is due to:

▶   Religious beliefs

▶   Political beliefs

▶   Gender bias

▶   Racism

▶   Trade union membership or activity

▶   Pregnancy or any matter related to pregnancy or birth

▶   Sexual orientation

▶   Age.

An employee may take an unfair dismissal case through the courts, the Rights Commissioners or the Employment Appeals Tribunal. If it is found that an employee has been unfairly dismissed, the employer must reinstate the employee either to the original job or to an alternative job of similar standing, or pay financial compensation. Constructive dismissal arises when the employee has to terminate their contract, with or without notice, because of the behaviour of the employer.

Minimum Wage

All employees (except apprentices, family members and members of the defence forces) are entitled to be paid at least the national minimum wage. From January 2011 the minimum wage is €7.65 per hour worked. Employees under 18 years are entitled to 70% of the minimum rate.

ACTIVITY

▶   Read the section on children's rights in Chapter 3 and the section on discrimination in Chapter 13.

▶   Discuss in your group whether there is any justification for paying 70% of the minimum wage to people who are under 18 years. Could this constitute discrimination on the grounds of age? Why or why not?

▶   List the reasons why people under 18 years should be paid the minimum wage.

Maternity Leave

The present basic maternity leave entitlement is 26 weeks, of which at least 2 weeks must be taken before the birth and at least 4 weeks afterwards. There is an option to take an additional 16 weeks of unpaid leave. This entitlement extends to all female employees, including casual workers, regardless of how long they have been working for the organisation or the number of hours worked per week. Payment during maternity leave is normally provided through Maternity Benefit, which is a Department of Social Protection payment.

Time spent on maternity leave can be used to accumulate annual leave entitlements in the same way as if the person was in employment and the person is also entitled to leave for any public holidays that occur.

A person planning to take maternity leave must give their employer at least 4 weeks' written notice of their intention to take leave and also provide the employer with a medical certificate confirming the pregnancy. Time off work for ante-natal and post-natal care is also covered by law, as is the right to return to her original job without loss of original status or rights.

Parental Leave

This means that a parent who has been in continuous employment with one employer for 12 months can take leave without pay for up to 14 weeks in order to take care of a child up to 8 years of age. The entitlement is separate in respect of each individual child and may be taken consecutively or in blocks at any time over a 5-year period, with the consent of the employer.

Both parents have an equal, separate entitlement to parental leave and employment rights are not affected. Parental leave must be applied for in advance.

Force Majeure Leave

This is a special emergency leave which may be taken in the case of illness or accident affecting an immediate family member. It consists of 3 days in a 12-month period or 5 days in a 36-month period.

Adoptive Leave

The entitlement to Adoptive Leave at present is 24 weeks together with an option to take an additional 16 weeks unpaid. Only the adoptive mother is entitled to this leave, except in the case where a male is the sole adopter. Adoptive Benefit is paid by the Department of Social Protection and employment rights are not affected. Adopting parents are also entitled to paid time off work to attend preparation classes and pre-adoption meetings with social workers/HSE officials. As with maternity leave, 4 weeks' notice in writing must be given to the employer for both domestic and foreign adoptions.

Employment Equality Act
See Chapter 12.

Complaints/Breach of Rights
Employment law in Ireland provides protection for employees who feel their rights have been breached. Complaints, disputes and grievances regarding alleged breaches of employment rights are heard before a Rights Commissioner, who will listen to both sides before completing an investigation and issuing a recommendation. Claims under equality legislation are brought to the Equality Tribunal.

Disputes between employers and employees can also be resolved using mediation. This means that the Labour Relations Commission is contacted and appoints an independent person to meet and hear both sides. This free service is available to employees and employers, and all discussions are confidential.

The Role of the Trade Union

While workers are protected and can have their rights upheld in law, trade unions work to ensure that this continues to be the case. Unions aim to improve conditions for workers within their workplaces, to ensure that members get their entitlements and their rights and to act as representatives for their members in national negotiations such as pay deals and social partnership agreements. A trade union represents its membership on issues such as:

▸   Better pay and conditions
▸   Improved employment laws
▸   Health and safety at work
▸   Access to education for all
▸   Improving industrial relations by negotiation, conciliation and resolving disputes
▸   Supporting people who are likely to suffer discrimination at work
▸   Improving conditions for part-time workers
▸   Lobbying for fairer tax laws
▸   Campaigning for childcare services
▸   Ensuring that labour laws are properly enforced
▸   Negotiating with Governments and employers on pay deals and agreements
▸   Showing solidarity with fellow workers around the world who may experience exploitation, repression or infringement of their human rights.

The Union Representative

Workers in an organisation who are members of the same trade union usually elect a representative who negotiates with management on their behalf. A full-time official from the union is available to give support and guidance to the local representative. Issues which arise at local level are usually dealt with according to agreed grievance procedures. This means that wherever possible the representative and the employer try to sort out the difficulties. If this is not possible, the issue will be taken up at a higher level in the union, usually through the local branch. All members have the option to become involved in their local branch, which meets regularly to discuss the issues that are relevant at both local and national level.

The trade union belongs to its members. Members pay an annual subscription fee, which can be either a fixed amount or a percentage of their wage – this is usually deducted at source. Members decide (through attending or being represented at annual congress) what matters the union will deal with in the forthcoming year.

Trade unions in Ireland are usually affiliated to the larger parent body, the Irish Congress of Trade Unions (ICTU).

Benefits of Trade Union Membership

Trade unions provide the following:

▸   A national support network

▸   Solidarity with other workers

▸   A more powerful voice in national negotiations

▸   Legal representation and protection

▸   Protection of employment rights

▸   Collective efforts to improve working conditions

▸   Protection of members through the enforcement of safe work practices, pensions and entitlement issues

▸   Support of fellow members

▸   Representation at grievance and disciplinary hearings and on bullying and sexual harassment issues

▸   Group insurance schemes.

TASK

▶ **Find out:**
— Which trade union represents early childhood workers in Ireland?
— Who is the local contact?
— Are meetings held locally?
— What is the cost of membership?
— What would the benefits of membership be for yourself?

▶ **Discuss in your group**
In what ways could unionisation help to improve the general working conditions of early childhood workers in Ireland?

SUMMARY

▶ A wide range of early childhood services is available to children and families; the majority of these are operated privately.

▶ A number of policy initiatives have emerged in recent years aimed at developing and supporting the early childhood sector.

▶ Good working conditions and appropriate salaries are factors which help to support the work of the early childhood professional. Membership of a professional early childhood organisation can provide support through access to local and national networks.

▶ Trade unions work to improve conditions for workers within their workplaces and to ensure that members get their entitlements and their rights.

References

NCCA, 2006, *Aistear: The Early Childhood Curriculum Framework*, Dublin: NCCA.

Síolta, 2006, *The National Quality Framework for Early Childhood Education*, Dublin: CECDE.

2

PRE-SCHOOL REGULATIONS

AREAS COVERED

▸ Regulation of Pre-school Services
▸ Overview of Regulations
▸ Health and Safety at Work

Introduction

Early childhood care and education services are regulated by legally binding requirements. These are the Pre-school Regulations, which first appeared in 1996 and have been updated with effect from January 2007. The main purpose of these regulations is to ensure that standards are in place to safeguard the health and welfare of children in pre-school services and to promote their development through the provision of developmentally and culturally appropriate materials, experiences, activities and interactions. The regulations affect the full range of group pre-school provision, ranging from voluntary and community through to private sector full day care provision (see Chapter 1). All employers and employees are also protected at work by the Safety, Health and Welfare at Work Act 2005, which imposes duties and responsibilities on both parties to maintain safe practice.

Regulation of Pre-school Services

Part VII of the Child Care Act 1991 relates to pre-school services. In interpreting its requirements, two documents need to be considered:

1. The Child Care Act 1991, Part VII
2. The Child Care (Pre-school Services) (No. 2) Regulations 2006.

1. The Child Care Act 1991, Part VII

This provides the legal framework within which regulations can be drawn up for the supervision of pre-school services. The Act sets out two important definitions:

▸ **Pre-school child:** A child under 6 years of age who is not attending a national school or a school providing an educational programme similar to a national school.

▸ **Pre-school service:** Any pre-school, playgroup, day nursery, crèche, day care or other similar service which caters for pre-school children. These include sessional, full-time and drop-in services (see Chapter 1).

The main provisions of the Act which relate to pre-school services are as follows.

▸ Pre-school providers are obliged to notify their local Health Service Executive (HSE) that they are operating or intend to operate a pre-school service.

▸ Pre-school providers have a duty to take all reasonable measures to safeguard the health, safety and welfare of children attending the service.

▸ HSE regions are obliged to supervise and inspect pre-school services.

▸ HSE regions are obliged to provide information on pre-school services.

▸ Regulations drawn up under the Act must be complied with.

The following services are excluded from the provisions of the Act:

▸ Where children are looked after by relatives or their spouses.

▸ Where siblings or not more than three children of different families are cared for in the home of the carer, along with the carer's own children.

2. Child Care (Pre-school Services) (No. 2) Regulations 2006

There are 32 regulations, which broadly cover the areas of:

▸ Health, welfare and development of the child

▸ Notification and inspection by the HSE

▸ Recordkeeping

▸ Standard of premises and facilities

▸ General administration.

It is not intended here to give a full description of all 32 regulations, but rather to give a broad overview which indicates their range and general content. The original document (*Child Care [Pre-school Services] Regulations and Explanatory Guide*) should be consulted where exact detail is required.

Overview of Regulations

The Inspection Process

Inspection is designed to monitor and protect the health, welfare and safety of children in pre-school services and to promote their development. It ensures that services comply with all legal/statutory requirements, including the Pre-school Regulations. Inspectors are appointed by the HSE and visit the premises to view how the service is being run, taking detailed account of a wide range of aspects of provision, as set out in the regulations. The first visit is usually within 3 months of notification being received that the service is in operation, and visits after that are approximately once per year. A written report is issued to the service provider and adequate time is allowed in the event that issues need to be addressed or improvements made. A follow-up inspection is then usually carried out. The report of the inspector, known as the Outcome Inspection Report, is made available to the public by the HSE to help them make informed decisions when choosing childcare.

1. Health, Welfare and Development of the Child

This requires the provision of age and culturally appropriate opportunities, activities, experiences, interactions and materials for all children attending a pre-school service. There is a clear statement here acknowledging the value of play as a powerful learning vehicle for young children, as well as the importance of the relationships and environment they are engaged in. Reference is made here to the 'Whole Child' perspective outlined in *The National Children's Strategy* (see Chapter 1).

▶ A pre-school service is required to provide a suitably equipped first aid box for children, with recommended contents. It should be stored safely and should be taken on outings.

▶ Medicines should be clearly labelled in original containers and inaccessible to children.

▶ A person trained in first aid for children should be on the premises at all times and should accompany the children on outings.

▶ Arrangements should be in place to obtain medical assistance for a child in an emergency and written parental assistance should be in place for this. There should also be a procedure for the administration of medicine to children where required and parental consent should also be in place here.

Management and Staffing

▸ A pre-school service should have a designated person in charge and a designated deputy, one of whom should be on the premises at all times.

▸ There should be an adequate number of competent adults working directly with the children at all times. A competent adult is defined as a person over 18 years who has appropriate experience in the field and/or an appropriate qualification.

▸ At least 50% of staff should have an appropriate qualification and qualified staff should rotate between the different age groupings.

▸ There should be written policies on management, recruitment, training and staff absences.

▸ Staff, students and volunteers with access to children must have Garda clearance and two recent work references should be validated.

ACTIVITY

SCENARIO 1

Brendan is aged 7 months and has been looked after on a full-time basis by Colette in her own home since he was 10 weeks old. He is an only child. Colette minds two other children, Sarah, aged 2 years, and Mark, aged 3 years 8 months. She also has four children of her own, of which the youngest, Grace, is 8 years old and in primary school. The others range in age from 12 to 19 years and all live at home.

SCENARIO 2

Barbara is aged 3 years. She has one older brother aged 5, who is in school, and her mother works part time from home. Barbara attends a large crèche for 3 full days per week, usually for around 9 hours per day. On the other 2 days she stays at home with her mother.

Discuss:

▸ What are the advantages to the individual children and their parents of these arrangements?

▸ What are the disadvantages?

Adult–Child Ratios and Maximum Group Sizes

Full Day Care Service

Age Range	Adult to Child Ratio	Maximum Group Size
0–1 year	1:3	9
	1–3 children – one adult 4–6 children – two adults 7–9 children – three adults	
1–2 years	1:5	10
	1–5 children – one adult 6–10 children – two adults	
2–3 years	1:6	12
	1–6 children – one adult 7–12 children – two adults	
3–6 years	1:8	24
	1–8 children – one adult 9–16 children – two adults 17–24 children – three adults	

Part-time Day Care Service

Age Range	Adult to Child Ratio	Maximum Group Size
0–1 year	1:3	9
	1–3 children – one adult 4–6 children – two adults 7–9 children – three adults	
1–2 years	1:5	10
	1–5 children – one adult 6–10 children – two adults	
2–3 years	1:6	12
	1–6 children – one adult 7–12 children – two adults	
3–6 years	1:8	24
	1–8 children – one adult 9–16 children – two adults 17–24 children – three adults	

Sessional Pre-school Service

Age Range	Adult to Child Ratio	Maximum Group Size
0–1 year	1:3	9
	1–3 children – one adult 4–6 children – two adults 7–9 children – three adults	
1–2.5 years	1:5	10
	1–5 children – one adult 6–10 children – two adults	
2.5–6 years	1:10	20
	1–10 children – one adult 11–20 children – two adults	

In a sessional group, no more than 25% of children should be under 3 years and no more than 20 children should be catered for in one room.

Drop-in Pre-school Service

Age Range	Adult to Child Ratio	Maximum Group Size
Full age integration 0–6 years	1:4	24

There should be a maximum of two children under 15 months to one adult and no more than 24 children should attend a drop-in service at any one time.

Overnight Pre-school Service

Age Range	Adult to Child Ratio
0–1 year	1:3
1–6 years	1:5

Childminding Service

A childminder should look after not more than five pre-school children, including her own, and no more than two of these should be under 15 months old (except in cases of multiple births or siblings). There should be a telephone on the premises and a second person available in case of emergency. In the interests of child safety and quality care, the HSE may determine the maximum number of children to be catered for in a pre-school service.

ACTIVITY

Aim: To become familiar with the practical application of the Pre-school Regulations in relation to safety.

▶   Support organisations such as NCNA and IPPA, the Early Childhood Organisation, offer specific guidelines to their members on implementing safe practice in their centres. Find out what these guidelines are.

▶   Working in groups, draw up a specific list of safety precautions that could be applied in different areas of the early childhood environment, both indoors and outdoors.

— Write each one up as a checklist.
— Share the checklists among the group.
— Select one which could suit the environment in which you work and ask permission to use it to carry out a safety audit of one particular area.
— Evaluate the checklist afterwards, adding to it if necessary.

Behaviour Management

▶   It is strictly forbidden to inflict corporal punishment on a child in an early childhood service or to carry out any practice that is disrespectful, degrading, exploitative, intimidating, emotionally or physically harmful or neglectful to a child.

▶   Written policies and procedures should be in place to deal with challenging behaviour in a caring, constructive and developmentally appropriate way.

▶   Child protection: Within the framework of *Children First: National Guidelines for the Protection and Welfare of Children*, there should be clear written guidelines on identifying and reporting child abuse (see Chapter 9).

2. Notification and Inspection

▶   A person who intends to open and operate a pre-school service is required to notify the HSE in writing, using the format set out in these regulations. Advice, support and guidance are provided by the HSE and the service will then be inspected. The purpose of inspection is to ensure the health, safety and welfare of the children. The report should be made available to parents/guardians of children attending or planning to attend the service.

▸   In the event that a service does not comply with all regulations, a period of time is given in which to make improvements and a follow-up visit may be planned. It is considered good practice to inspect pre-school services once a year. More frequent visits may take place to provide advice and information to providers who are caring for a child with a disability or additional need. A list of pre-school services is made available to parents by the HSE.

▸   Childminders are exempt from this requirement, but may instead voluntarily notify their local County Childcare Committee or the HSE, thus availing of support and information on best practice in this way, as well as linking in to local networks.

▸   The HSE must be notified of a change in circumstances, e.g. the closure of a service.

Childminders are not obliged to go through the inspection process, but may avail of voluntary notification and inspection through their local City/County Childcare Committee.

3. Recordkeeping

The following records should be kept in a pre-school service.

▸   A register giving details of each child using the service (see Appendix 4).

▸   Details of staff, to include name, position, qualifications and experience of all staff members, and all information generated by the Garda vetting process.

▸   Staff to child ratios.

▸   Maximum number of children catered for .

▸   Type of service and age range.

▸   Care programme provided.

▸   Facilities provided.

▸   Opening hours and fees.

▸   Policies and procedures.

▸   Daily attendance records.

▸   Daily staff rosters.

▸   Details and records of medicine administered to children.

▸   Details of accidents or injuries to children.

▸   Arrival and departure times of children.

▸   Arrival times, departure times and meal break times of staff.

▸ Record of programmes, activities and opportunities offered to children, based on individual needs and interests.

▸ All accidents, no matter how minor, should be recorded and notified to parents.

All records should be updated regularly and should be available for inspection as required. Relevant information should be made available to the parent/guardian of a child proposing to attend a service.

ACTIVITY

Aim: To assess the implications of space requirements for children in the different age groups in full day care.

▸ Measure out the different spaces per child on a clear floor space, for example in the classroom, and mark with chalk.

▸ Discuss whether each seems adequate for a child in the age groups as defined below. Consider the needs and characteristics you would associate with the different groups (e.g. toddlers like to move around frequently).

▸ If the spaces do not seem adequate, suggest alternatives.

4. Standard of Premises and Facilities

▸ Pre-school services should comply with all fire safety responsibilities under the Fire Services Act 1981. Procedures to be followed in the event of fire should be displayed clearly in the premises. Records of fire drills should be maintained, as well as details and maintenance records of fire-fighting equipment and smoke alarms. Records should be open to inspection by parents, staff and persons authorised by the HSE.

▸ A copy of the Child Care Act 1991 and these regulations should be kept in a pre-school service.

▸ A pre-school premises should be suitable, sound, secure, clean, rodent proof and with adequate storage. It should be designed in a way that is suitable for use as a pre-school centre. The environment should be warm and welcoming with well-organised spaces for children and their families. It should comply with all building and planning regulations.

Space Requirements

The space requirements relate to clear floor space per child, i.e. the area available for play, work and movement. This does not include the space taken up by furniture and fixtures. Kitchens, toilets and sleep areas are not included when calculating space per child. The requirements are as follows.

Full-time and Part-time Day Care Services	
Age of Child	**Floor Area per Child**
0–1 year	3.5 square metres
1–2 years	2.8 square metres
2–3 years	2.35 square metres
3–6 years	2.3 square metres
Sessional Pre-school Services and Drop-in Centres	
Age of Child	**Floor Area per Child**
0–6 years	2 square metres

Pre-school premises should have laundry facilities and separate safe storage space for the personal belongings of staff and children. There should also be a space for storing confidential information and for staff breaks.

There should also be adequate, suitable and hygienic sanitary accommodation:

▶ Nappy-changing facilities

▶ Separate toilet facilities for adults

▶ Wash hand basins with running cold and thermostatically controlled hot water, soap and suitable hand-drying for children

▶ Safe and hygienic disposal of soiled nappies

▶ Full day care facilities should have a shower/bath facility with thermostatically controlled hot water and a designated area for sluicing soiled garments.

▶ Toilets and nappy-changing areas should not communicate directly with any occupied room except by means of a ventilated space such as a hall.

Requirements for Toilets and Wash Hand Basins		
Number of Persons	**Toilets**	**WHBs**
Every 10 toilet-using children	1	1
Every 8 adults	1	1

Equipment and Materials

There should be sufficient furniture, play and work equipment and material, bedding, towels and spare clothes for children, which should be suitable, non-toxic, hygienic and in good repair and should comply with safety standards. The play and work materials should be age and stage appropriate and should help create an accessible, challenging and stimulating environment for the children. There should be a programme and schedule for cleaning and maintaining materials and equipment.

Food and Drink

▸   There should be suitable, nutritious and varied food for the children, along with facilities for storage, preparation, cooking and serving.

▸   Appropriate eating utensils, hand-washing, washing-up and sterilising facilities should be provided.

▸   Food may be cooked on the premises or children may bring a packed lunch.

▸   Prepared food may be purchased from a supplier whose premises is registered with the HSE.

▸   Food must be stored under suitable refrigerated conditions.

▸   Pre-school services are subject to the provisions of all food safety, food hygiene and health regulations.

▸   Food and nutrition guidelines for pre-school services should be taken into account when providing meals for children. Regular and adequate food and drink should be provided, in consultation with parents. These guidelines state that children in full day care (more than 5 hours per session) should be offered at least two meals and two snacks, those in part-time day care (maximum 5 hours per session) should be offered at least two meals and one snack and those in sessional care (3.5 hours per session) should be offered one meal and one snack per day.

▸   Safe drinking water should be available to children at all times.

Safety

The health, safety and welfare of children should be a primary concern. It is required that:

▸   Heat-emitting surfaces are made safe, protected or thermostatically controlled.

▸   Hot water should be thermostatically controlled.

▸   External play areas should be made secure.

▸   Ponds, pits and other hazards should be fenced.

▸   Steps should be taken to prevent the spread of infection.

▸   Safety procedures should be in place for taking children on outings.

▸ Children should not be exposed to illness, risk or injury and there should be clear and consistent boundaries to help children keep safe. All hazards to children should be minimised.

▸ Providers should comply with all safety legislation and procedures for controlling infectious diseases.

Facilities for Rest and Play

▸ There should be adequate and suitable facilities for children to rest and play while attending a pre-school service.

▸ Children should have daily access to outdoor play, weather permitting.

▸ Sleeping facilities away from the play area should be provided for children under 2 years. This should be in a quiet, restful environment. Where there are fewer than six babies in a baby room, the sleep facility may be accommodated within the room, otherwise a separate sleep area is required. There should be an adequate supply of bed linen per child. Sofas, beanbags and buggies are not suitable for children to sleep in.

▸ Sleeping babies should be checked regularly, and a rota drawn up which takes account of who checks the babies and how often, sleeping position of babies and how information is recorded and shared with parents.

There are also regulations on heating, lighting, ventilation, drainage and sewage disposal and waste storage and disposal, as well as a requirement to have adequate insurance and to pay an annual fee to the HSE towards the cost of inspection.

Health and Safety at Work
The Safety, Health and Welfare at Work Act 2005

This Act updates and strengthens the provisions of the Safety, Health and Welfare at Work Act 1989. The updated Act takes a preventative approach to reducing accidents and ill-health at work and provides for increased fines and penalties for breaches of the legislation. Employers and employees have a duty and a responsibility to prevent accidents and increase safety levels at work.

The Act imposes duties of care on employers, employees and all who are involved in the workplace.

Employers have a legal obligation to:

▸ Manage and conduct all work activities so as to ensure the safety, health and welfare of people at work (including the prevention of improper conduct or behaviour likely to put employees at risk, including 'horseplay', bullying and working while under the influence of alcohol or drugs)

▸ Design, improve and maintain a safe place of work, with safe access and exits
▸ Use plant and equipment that is safe and without risk to health
▸ Reduce risks and prevent accidents by implementing, providing and maintaining safe systems of work
▸ Provide information, training and supervision to ensure that safety standards are met
▸ Provide appropriate protective clothing and equipment
▸ Produce and implement a Safety Statement which outlines safety procedures and emergency plans
▸ Appoint a competent person as the organisation's Safety Officer.

Employees have a legal obligation to:

▸ Co-operate with employers in matters of health and safety by following procedures and using the protective clothing and equipment provided
▸ Take reasonable care to perform their duties safely so as not to adversely affect the health and safety of others
▸ Report unsafe conditions to a supervisor or safety representative
▸ Undergo any reasonable medical or other assessment if requested to do so by their employer.

The Safety Statement

A Safety Statement specifies how the organisation will implement safe practice in the workplace. It is the responsibility of the employer to ensure that the Safety Statement is implemented. The Safety Statement should:

▸ Identify workplace hazards and levels of safety required
▸ Assess the risks arising from such hazards
▸ Identify the steps to be taken to deal with these risks
▸ Identify the resources necessary to implement and maintain safety standards
▸ Indicate necessary precautions to prevent accidents
▸ Document the names and responsibilities of safety representatives
▸ Specify the reporting procedures to be used in the event of an accident.

The statement should also contain the details of people in the workforce who are responsible for safety issues. Employees should be given access to this statement and employers should review it on a regular basis.

Protective Equipment

The employer should inform employees about any risks that require the wearing of protective equipment. The employer should provide protective equipment (protective clothing, headgear, footwear, eyewear, gloves, etc.) together with training on how to use it, where necessary. An employee is obliged to take reasonable care for his/her own safety and to use any protective equipment supplied. The protective equipment should be provided free of charge to employees if it is intended for use at the workplace only. Usually, employees should be provided with their own personal protective equipment.

Pregnant Employees

An employer should carry out separate risk assessments in relation to pregnant employees. If there are particular risks to an employee's pregnancy, for example coming into contact with rubella in the centre, the employee should be moved away from the source of risk. If this option is not possible, the employee should be given health and safety leave from work, which may continue up to the beginning of maternity leave.

Following an employee's return to work after maternity leave, if there is any risk to the employee because she has recently given birth or is breastfeeding, the risk should be removed. If this is not possible, the employee should be moved to alternative work. If it is not possible for the employee to be assigned alternative work, she should be given health and safety leave.

Health and Safety Leave

During health and safety leave, employers must pay employees their normal wages for the first 3 weeks, after which Health and Safety Benefit may be paid. Time spent on health and safety leave is treated as though the employee has been in employment and this time can be used to accumulate annual leave entitlement. The employee is entitled to leave for any public holidays that occur during health and safety leave.

Violence and Bullying in the Workplace

The possibility of violence towards employees should be addressed in the Safety Statement. For example, factors like the isolation of employees and the presence of cash on the premises need to be taken into account. Proper safeguards should be put into place to eliminate the risk of violence as far as possible and the employee should be provided with appropriate means of minimising the remaining risk, for example security glass.

An employer should have established procedures for dealing with complaints of bullying in the workplace and deal with such complaints immediately. Ignoring complaints of bullying could leave an employer open to a possible claim for damages by an employee. It is advisable for an employer to have an established grievance procedure to deal with complaints of bullying.

The Employment Equality Act 1998 and 2004 places an obligation on an employer to prevent harassment in the workplace (see Chapter 13). An employee who feels that he is the victim of bullying or harassment can also refer the matter to the Equality Tribunal.

Health and Safety and Young People

An employer should carry out a separate risk assessment in relation to an employee under 18 years of age. This risk assessment should be carried out before the young person is employed. If certain risks are present, including risks that cannot be recognised or avoided by the young person due to factors like lack of experience, the young person should not be employed.

Reporting Accidents

Incidents at work which result in minor injuries should be reported and recorded. The designated Safety Officer must also report the following events in writing to the Health and Safety Authority, using the approved form:

▶ The death of any person as a result of an accident at work
▶ The death of an employee which occurs up to 1 year after a reportable injury
▶ An accident which prevents an employee from carrying out their work for more than 3 days
▶ Injuries requiring medical treatment to a person absent from work due to work activity
▶ Work-related accidents to members of the public which require medical treatment.

If you have suffered an injury at work, you cannot seek compensation from your employer under the health and safety legislation; however, you may take a claim through the civil courts.

The Health and Safety Authority

The Health and Safety Authority (HSA) is the body which is responsible for enforcing the legislation and for securing health and safety at work. Its role is to provide the following services to employers, employees and the public:

▶ Promote health and safety at work
▶ Act as the national centre for information to employers, employees and self-employed on all aspects of workplace safety
▶ Provide guidelines on Safety Statements

- Inspect places of work and monitor compliance with legislation
- Investigate serious accidents, causes of ill-health and complaints
- Carry out research and develop new standards on health and safety at work
- Publish codes of practice, guidance and information on health and safety at work.

SUMMARY

- The passing of the Child Care Act in 1991 meant that the Department of Health and Children could now regulate pre-school services.
- The Child Care (Pre-school Services) (No. 2) Regulations 2006 set out the legal requirements and guidelines which pre-school centres must comply with under the Act.
- The HSE must now supervise and inspect pre-school services and provide information to parents on these services.
- Childminders who look after fewer than six children including their own are exempt from the notification and inspection process.
- Corporal punishment may not be inflicted on a child attending a pre-school service.
- Under the Safety, Health and Welfare at Work Act 2005, employers and employees have duties and responsibilities in relation to safe practice at work.

References

Department of Health and Children, The Child Care Act 1991, Dublin: Government Publications Office.

Department of Health and Children, *Child Care (Pre-school Services) (No. 2) Regulations 2006*, Dublin: Stationery Office.

Department of Health and Children, *Food and Nutrition Guidelines for Pre-school Services*, Dublin: Stationery Office.

Health Promotion Unit, 2005, *Keeping Your Baby Safe*, Naas: Health Service Executive.

Health Promotion Unit, 2005, *Play It Safe*, Naas: Health Service Executive.

The Safety, Health and Welfare at Work Act 2005, Dublin: Government Publications Office.

3

CHILDREN HAVE A RIGHT TO QUALITY SERVICES

AREAS COVERED

▸ Children's Rights

▸ Children's Needs

▸ Minimum Standards

▸ Quality Indicators

Introduction

In recent years, there has been a growing acceptance that children are entitled to civil and human rights independently of their parents/caregivers. This is most apparent in the UN Convention on the Rights of the Child 1989, which confers rights on children of all countries that are signatories to the convention. In Ireland, *The National Children's Strategy*, underpinned by principles of quality and equality, is our commitment to implementing the Convention.

International studies over the past 30 years have shown that participation in high-quality early years care and education programmes has long-term positive effects on the quality of life of the individual. It has a positive impact on educational achievement and social development and encourages a greater sense of responsibility and self-control in later life. Early childhood services have the potential to offer a rich learning environment to children; this potential can best be realised when there is a commitment to maintaining the highest quality in these services, based on respect for and the implementation of the rights of the child.

This chapter looks at how all the resources of the early childhood setting, both physical and human, can best be used to meet the children's needs and validate their rights. It identifies a range of factors which contribute to creating a high-quality environment and poses questions for the reader on how this can be achieved.

Children's Rights

The development of childcare policy in Ireland reflects the persistent tension between the rights of parents, the rights of children and the rights of the State to intervene in family life. The Irish Constitution does not recognise any separate rights for children; they are defined within the context of the rights of the family. The need for a referendum on children's rights is a subject of ongoing debate and is highlighted by pro-children groups such as the Children's Rights Alliance.

Laws and policies also reflect society's view on childhood and children; they are assumed to be covered by human rights generally and looked after in the context of the family. However, during the second half of the twentieth century there was an increase in the understanding of the needs of children as individuals and the recognition of the value of childhood. While the family is generally acknowledged as the fundamental unit of society and the natural environment for the growth and well-being of its members, there has been a growing acceptance that children are entitled to civil and human rights independently of their parents/caregivers. Evidence of this lies in the various international documents and charters which have been adopted.

According to the Children's Rights Alliance, the underlying assumption about the rights of the child is that society has an obligation to satisfy the fundamental needs of children and to provide assistance for the development of their personalities, talents and abilities.

The **UN Convention on the Rights of the Child 1989** (see Appendix 1) is the generally accepted instrument which confers rights on children of all countries that are signatories to the Convention. Ireland signed the Convention in 1990 and ratified it in September 1992. The 54-article Convention is essentially a **Bill of Rights** for all children and is informed by four general principles:

1. All the rights guaranteed by the Convention must be available to all children without discrimination of any kind (Article 2).
2. The best interests of the child must be a primary consideration in all actions concerning children (Article 3).
3. Every child has a right to life, survival and development (Article 6).
4. The child's view must be considered and taken into account in all matters affecting him or her (Article 12).

The articles of the Convention can be broken down into four broad areas:

1. **Survival rights** which cover a child's right to life and to basic needs such as nutrition, shelter, access to medical services and an adequate living standard.

2. **Developmental rights** which include a right to education, play, leisure, access to information, freedom of thought, conscience and religion. The adult in an early childhood centre has a duty and a responsibility to ensure the provision of developmentally appropriate routines and activities for each and every child which do not discriminate against the child on any grounds whatsoever.

3. **Protection rights** which require that children be safeguarded against all forms of abuse, neglect and exploitation. Issues covered are care and rehabilitation for children who have been abused and/or exploited, including special care for refugee children, safeguards for children in the criminal justice system and protection for children in employment.

4. **Participation rights** which encompass freedom for children to have a say and to express opinions in matters affecting their lives. Adults have a responsibility to allow children control and choice in their lives and to acknowledge and act on the feelings and opinions expressed.

In general, no one has any difficulty seeing how adults in an early childhood setting can provide for children's rights to survival and to protection. However, the area of developmental rights and participation rights may require more thought and effort. The idea of children having control and choice is a relatively new one in our society and brings with it some fears. If all children in a group setting were to choose their food, does this mean we will have to prepare several different meals? Negotiation and discussion are the means by which we agree together as a group what is acceptable, appropriate and healthy. Several studies have shown that people – children and adults alike – are more likely to compromise and co-operate when they have had a part in decision-making. Genuine respect for children is illustrated by adults' willingness to include them in the decision-making process. This is demonstrated in the Danish project Children as Citizens. The project aimed to increase the amount of influence which young children have over decisions regarding their own lives through consulting with them. In one centre, children noted that fixed times for outdoor play and mealtimes were an unacceptable adult imposition. In response the adults agreed to build more flexibility into the daily schedule, for example staggering break times and staffing the playground with one adult at all times.

ACTIVITY

Form four groups. Each group should select one of the rights areas outlined above.

▶ Under the chosen heading, make a list of specific rights which you feel all children should be entitled to, e.g. survival might include housing, water, etc., participation might include a right to choose not to participate in an activity.

▶ Give examples of situations in Ireland where children may not be enjoying these rights.

▶ Join together with the larger group and discuss similarities and differences between the different lists.

ACTIVITY

Developmental and Participation Rights in the Early Childhood Setting

List activities or ways in which early childhood workers could further children's rights in relation to development and participation in the setting in which they work. Make a separate list for 0–1 year, 1–3 years and 3–6 years.

Children's Rights in Ireland

The Child Care Act 1991 affirmed the issue of children's rights, needs and the concept of 'the best interests of the child'. While most people would accept that children's basic needs should be met, some concerns have been expressed, for example, who decides what is in the best interests of the child – the authorities, the parents or the child?

Secondly, when one considers rights at a more general level (e.g. rights to education or health services), the question arises as to whether the unequal distribution of resources in Irish society means that society is denying many children their basic rights. For example, according to the most recent figures available, nearly one in 10 children lives in consistent poverty, and one in four, or just over a quarter of a million, lives in relative poverty (see Chapter 13). Waiting lists for hospital treatments are long; in fact, anecdotal evidence suggests that waiting lists for assessment in order to be placed on treatment lists are far too long. Also, because of a severe shortage of beds in the health services, much of the hospital accommodation provided for children is inappropriate.

The commitment to a new national children's hospital is on hold, and provision for parents within existing accommodation is completely inadequate.

The introduction of sex education programmes in schools is a result of the recognition of the child's right to information and may even go some way to protecting them from abuse in the very families in which they live, but parents who are not happy about this can remove their children from such classes. Likewise, the Irish Society for the Prevention of Cruelty to Children (ISPCC) campaign to end the smacking of children by their parents has caused concern for a variety of reasons. Many still hold firmly to the belief that parents own their children and therefore have a right to decide how to treat them. In fact, they are responsible for their children and therefore have a duty to ensure that their child's rights are validated.

The UN Convention on the Rights of the Child has a monitoring system which reviews children's rights in any country that is a signatory to the Convention. A review took place in Ireland in 1998 and *The National Children's Strategy*, which was launched in 2000, deals with most of the recommendations of the review. An assessment of progress made is now underway.

The strategy is a 10-year plan and is underpinned by six core principles. All measures taken under the strategy are:

▶   **Child centred:** The best interests of the child should be served at all times.
▶   **Family oriented:** Because families are seen as providing the best environment in which children should grow up, the aim should be to support and empower families.
▶   **Equitable:** All children should have equal opportunity to access services and to participate in decision-making and planning. Those who are vulnerable or at risk should have the supports to facilitate their access and participation.
▶   **Inclusive:** The diversity of children's experience should be recognised.
▶   **Integrated:** Services, whether statutory, voluntary or both, should be co-ordinated and coherent.
▶   **Action oriented:** Services should be developed and policies implemented without delay.

ACTIVITY

▶   Brainstorm and list all the matters that affect children in an early childhood setting.
▶   Select any one item from the list.
▶   Devise ways and means to incorporate children's views and participation in decisions and policies in relation to that particular matter.

The strategy puts forward an holistic approach which recognises the child as an active participant in any process that will have an impact on his life. It has identified three clear goals:

1. **Children will have a voice in matters which affect them and their views will be given due weight in accordance with their age and maturity.** This is a core principle of the UN Convention on the Rights of the Child and should be a core principle in any establishment which cares for children.
2. **Children and their lives will be better understood; their lives will benefit from evaluation research and information on their needs, rights and the effectiveness of services.**
3. **Children will receive quality support and services to promote all aspects of their development.**

Implementation of the Goals

Goal 1

▸ Dáil na nÓg (Young People's Parliament) has been meeting once a year since 2001. Dáil na nÓg delegates are elected through local networks – Comhairle na nÓg.

▸ The Ombudsman for Children Act was passed in 2002. An Ombudsman for Children was appointed in 2004.

Goal 2

▸ A Children's Research Programme is underway, together with a unit designed to disseminate research results and information.

▸ A National Longitudinal Study of children in Ireland is underway.

Goal 3

There are 14 objectives under this goal, which include prioritising action on child poverty, children with disabilities, Traveller children, children in crises and homeless children. Recreation and play are key themes here, along with accessibility of services and supports.

The Office of the Minister for Children (OMC) was set up in 2005 and incorporates the National Children's Office, which has been operating since 2002. The National Children's Advisory Council, which is made up of representatives from all interested areas (children, the Government, the National Children's Office, social partners and researchers), is an intrinsic element of the network.

The Minister for Children and Youth Affairs was given responsibility for overseeing the implementation of the strategy and for co-ordinating Government policy on children, and submits an annual progress report about measures taken by Government departments to implement relevant actions of the strategy.

Figure 3.1: **Children's Strategy Network**

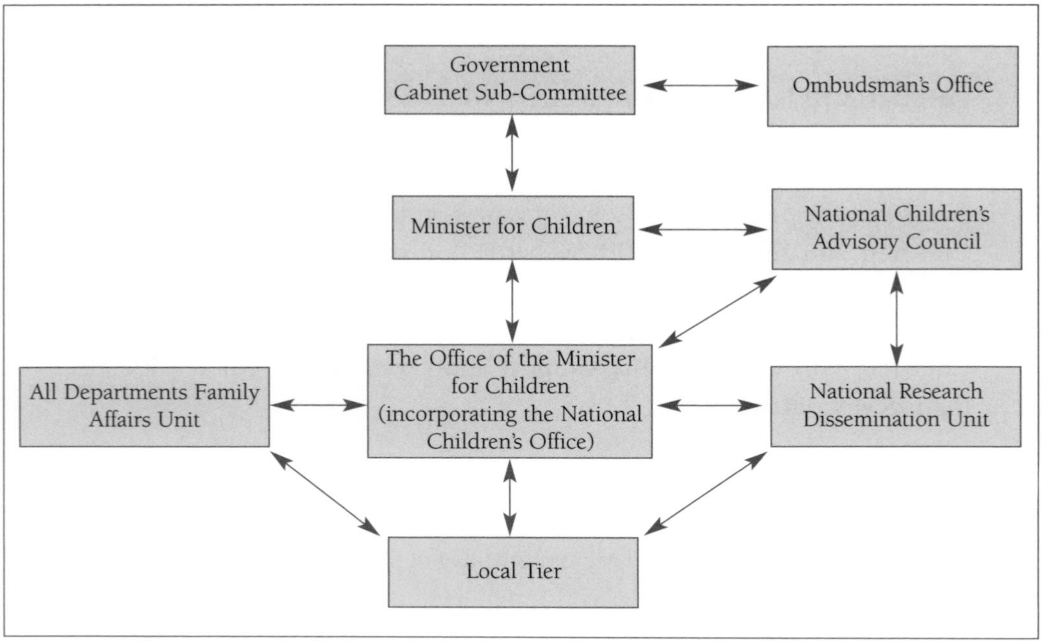

```
                    ┌──────────────────┐          ┌──────────────────┐
                    │   Government     │◄────────►│ Ombudsman's Office│
                    │Cabinet Sub-Committee│       │                  │
                    └──────────────────┘          └──────────────────┘
                             ▲▼
                    ┌──────────────────┐          ┌──────────────────┐
                    │Minister for Children│◄──────►│National Children's│
                    │                  │          │ Advisory Council │
                    └──────────────────┘          └──────────────────┘
                             ▲▼                             ▲▼
  ┌────────────────┐  ┌──────────────────┐          ┌──────────────────┐
  │All Departments │◄►│The Office of the Minister│◄►│National Research │
  │Family Affairs  │  │for Children      │          │Dissemination Unit│
  │Unit            │  │(incorporating the National│ │                  │
  └────────────────┘  │Children's Office)│          └──────────────────┘
                      └──────────────────┘
                             ▲▼
                    ┌──────────────────┐
                    │   Local Tier     │
                    └──────────────────┘
```

Source: Department of Health and Children, 2000, *Our Children, Their Lives – The National Children's Strategy*, Dublin: Stationery Office.

The Children's Rights Alliance

The Children's Rights Alliance is a national umbrella body comprising a wide range of organisations and individuals concerned with children's rights. It was formally launched in March 1995 and there are now over 60 member organisations. The aim of the Alliance is to promote the implementation of the UN Convention on the Rights of the Child in Irish laws, policies, practices and services. The key areas that are currently highlighted include:

▶ The Constitution should be changed to express recognition of children's rights.

▶ The guardian *ad litem* services (to represent children's best interests in court hearings) and the National Guidelines for the Protection of Children should both be placed on a statutory basis (see Chapter 9).

▶ The age of criminal responsibility should be raised to 12 years.

▶ The interests of ethnic minority children should be addressed.

▶ Measures should be taken to outlaw the use of corporal punishment within families.

Children's Needs

Children have a right to experience environments which meet their needs. High-quality early childhood programmes do not separate care from education or education from care. They provide warm, caring and stimulating environments for children. Children are deeply involved in their own learning, supported by a knowledgeable, observant staff in an environment structured to drive exploration and discovery. In general, there is agreement about what children need to facilitate their all-round growth and development:

▶ A social environment that provides first-hand experiences to support their meaning-making

▶ Interaction with warm, responsive staff who 'scaffold' their learning

▶ Recognition of their development and cultural context

▶ Acknowledgement of their needs, interests and cultural strengths

▶ Accommodation of their varying abilities

▶ Learning experiences that they find challenging

▶ Opportunity to explore, experiment and solve problems

▶ Opportunity to learn through making choices, being actively involved and reflecting on their experiences and actions

▶ Experiences and materials that are meaningful, varied, open-ended, real and reflect everyday life experiences

▶ Experiences and materials that reflect inclusiveness and diversity.

(taken from IPPA, Playgroups and Daycare)

ACTIVITY

In its policy on food and nutrition, a childcare centre states that 'this service believes that all children have a right to a nutritious, well-balanced diet'. List five procedures which need to be put in place to ensure that the above policy is implemented.

Minimum Standards

The first formal attempt to set down minimum standards for the operation of early years services in Ireland came with the implementation in 1996 of the Pre-school Regulations set down under Part VII of the Child Care Act 1991 (see Chapter 2). These regulations were updated in 2006 and set down the minimum standards required by law. They concentrate on aspects of the child's physical environment such as health, safety and hygiene in the early years setting as well as on the quality of the child's experiences.

High standards in the physical environment are necessary for the delivery of a high-quality childcare and education service, but these alone do not indicate that high-quality care is being provided. For example, it is possible for an early childhood centre to be adequately staffed and to meet all the requirements with regard to adult/child ratios; however, this does not guarantee that the children will receive adequate time and attention to meet all their needs, nor does it ensure that the quality of the interactions between children and adults will be positive and beneficial to the children or that their rights will be recognised.

Standards can be measured relatively easily in the areas outlined above. For example, it is not difficult to determine whether a service meets a requirement to have a specified size of premises, maximum number of children in attendance or that there are a certain number of qualified staff in attendance at any given time. But quality service provision depends on how the premises are used, what opportunities there are for exploration, discovery and learning and what the staff do throughout the day. In other words, how does the setting use all its resources to meet all the needs of all the children?

Síolta – The National Quality Framework for Early Childhood Education (NQF) 2006

The Principles

▸ Early childhood is a significant and distinct time in life that must be nurtured, respected, valued and supported in its own right.

▸ The child's individuality, strengths, rights and needs are central in the provision of quality early childhood experiences.

▸ Parents are the primary educators of the child and have a pre-eminent role in promoting his/her well-being, learning and development.

▸ Responsive, sensitive and reciprocal relationships, which are consistent over time, are essential to the well-being, learning and development of the young child.

▸ Equality is an essential characteristic of quality early childhood care and education.

▶ Quality early childhood settings acknowledge and respect diversity and ensure that all children and families have their individual, personal, cultural and linguistic identity validated.

▶ The physical environment of the young child has a direct impact on his/her well-being, learning and development. The safety, welfare and well-being of all children must be protected and promoted in all early childhood environments.

▶ The role of the adult in providing quality early childhood experiences requires co-operation, communication and mutual respect.

▶ Pedagogy in early childhood is expressed by curricula or programmes of activities which take a holistic approach to the development and learning of the child and reflect the inseparable nature of care and education.

▶ Play is central to the well-being, development and learning of the young child.

Síolta Standards

Standard 1: Rights of the Child
This means that the child is enabled to exercise choice and to use initiative as an active participant and partner in her own development and learning.

Standard 2: Environments
Enriching environments, both indoor and outdoor (including materials and equipment), are well maintained, safe, available, accessible, adaptable and developmentally appropriate and offer a variety of challenging and stimulating experiences.

Standard 3: Parents and Families
Valuing and involving parents and families requires a proactive partnership approach evidenced by a range of clearly stated, accessible and implemented processes, policies and procedures.

Standard 4: Consultation
Ensuring inclusive decision-making requires consultation that promotes participation and seeks out, listens to and acts upon the views and opinions of children, parents and staff and other stakeholders, as appropriate.

Standard 5: Interactions
Fostering constructive interactions (child/child, child/adult and adult/adult) requires explicit policies, procedures and practice that emphasise the value of process and are based on mutual respect, equal partnership and sensitivity.

Standard 6: Play

Promoting play requires that each child has ample time to engage in freely available and accessible, developmentally appropriate and well-resourced opportunities for exploration, creativity and 'meaning-making' in the company of other children, with participating and supportive adults and alone, where appropriate.

Standard 7: Curriculum

Encouraging each child's holistic development and learning requires the implementation of a verifiable, broad-based, documented and flexible curriculum or programme.

Standard 8: Planning and Evaluation

Enriching and informing all aspects of practice within the setting requires cycles of observation, planning, action and evaluation, undertaken on a regular basis.

Standard 9: Health and Welfare

Promoting the health and welfare of the child requires protection from harm, provision of nutritious food, appropriate opportunities for rest and secure relationships characterised by trust and respect.

Standard 10: Organisation

Organising and managing resources effectively requires an agreed written philosophy, supported by clearly communicated policies and procedures to guide and determine practice.

Standard 11: Professional Practice

Practising in a professional manner requires that individuals have skills, knowledge, values and attitudes appropriate to their role and responsibility within the setting. In addition, it requires regular reflection upon practice and engagement in supported, ongoing professional development (see Chapter 1).

Standard 12: Communication

Communicating effectively in the best interests of the child requires policies, procedures and actions that promote the proactive sharing of knowledge and information among appropriate stakeholders with respect and confidentiality.

Standard 13: Transitions

Ensuring continuity of experiences for children requires policies, procedures and practice that promote sensitive management of transitions, consistency in key relationships, liaison within and between settings, the keeping and transfer of relevant information (with parental consent) and the close involvement of parents and, where appropriate, relevant professionals.

Standard 14: Identity and Belonging

Promoting positive identities and a strong sense of belonging requires clearly defined policies, procedures and practices that empower every child and adult to develop a confident self- and group identity and to have a positive understanding and regard for the identity and rights of others.

Standard 15: Legislation and Regulation

Being compliant requires that all relevant regulations and legislative requirements are met or exceeded.

Standard 16: Community Involvement

Promoting community involvement requires the establishment of networks and connections evidenced by policies, procedures and actions that extend and support all adults' and children's engagement with the wider community.

Quality Indicators

It is neither possible nor appropriate to set down exact and unchanging quality standards which can be applied across the board in early years services. Each centre must formulate its own definition of quality, one which meets all the needs of the children and adults involved.

Such a definition must take account of agreed quality indicators such as those set out in Síolta – *The National Quality Framework for Early Childhood Education (NQF) 2006* – and must be arrived at through discussion and agreement with all the parties (see Chapter 1). This means that defining quality is a process rather than an end, a process which is ongoing and which involves continuous self-evaluation.

High quality in an early years service is evident in:

▸ The **ethos**, or underpinning values
▸ The **adults** and the relationships involved
▸ The **curriculum** and **the environment** within which it is offered.

1. The Ethos

This refers to the values and attitudes which underpin the service and is reflected in the policies of the setting. It is important that these are clearly articulated, implemented in practice and reviewed on a regular basis.

The essential underpinning values of quality early years services are:

▶ Respect for the child as a unique individual with rights.

▶ Acknowledgement of childhood as an important phase in its own right and not as a period of waiting for a future stage.

▶ Recognition of parents as the primary carers and educators of their children, involving a willingness to involve parents at all stages in the care and education process.

▶ Commitment to the implementation of a planned curriculum based on a sound educational philosophy and developmentally appropriate practice aimed at identifying and meeting the needs of each individual child.

▶ An interactive approach to provision that welcomes and acknowledges the importance of input from all of the partners involved – children, parents, staff and community.

▶ An acknowledgement that play is the means by which children learn; that play which is freely chosen and is process driven is as important to the child as food and drink.

▶ Recognition of the importance of keeping confidentiality with regard to children, parents and families.

▶ A commitment to equality of access and participation for children and families, valuing and celebrating diversity and challenging stereotypes, discrimination and prejudice (see Chapters 12, 13 and 14).

2. The Adults

The relationships between all those involved in early childhood services – children, staff, volunteers and parents – are critically important in the delivery of high quality. The important indicators here are:

▶ Interactions between staff and children

▶ Interactions within the adult team

▶ Partnership with parents

Interactions between Staff and Children

All areas of children's development are integrated and interdependent – physical, cognitive, language, emotional and social. It is therefore essential that children's interactions with the adults in their lives should be positive and should support their development in all areas. Such adult–child interactions are evident when:

▶ Adults interact frequently with children, speaking and listening to them at their eye level, smiling, touching and holding them.

▶ Adults are available to children – they encourage them to share experiences, ideas and feelings, they listen to them with respect and practise positive descriptive feedback.

▶ Individual staff members remain aware of the activities of the whole group by positioning themselves strategically within the room, keeping all children, as far as possible, within view.

▶ Adults try to ensure that children do not have to wait for an adult response and will show awareness of developmentally appropriate practice in their responses. For example, a baby's cry will be responded to immediately, while a 4-year-old will be verbally responded to even if she has to wait a few minutes to have the adult's full attention.

▶ Adults ensure that children are as comfortable, relaxed and happy as possible and involved in play.

▶ Adults help children deal with anger, sadness and frustration by comforting, identifying and helping children to name their feelings and use words rather than actions to solve their problems.

▶ Adults are friendly, polite and positive when communicating with children. They converse frequently with them, speaking individually to them as much as possible and asking open-ended questions requiring more than a 'yes' or 'no' response, thus encouraging language.

▶ Adults involve children in decision-making, encouraging and responding to their suggestions and comments.

Adults as Role Models

In a high-quality early childhood environment, the adults:

▶ Model good communication, both verbal and non-verbal, and appropriate ways of expressing feelings

▶ Model fair and consistent behaviour with children

▶ Value all children equally and promote anti-discriminatory practice

▸   Enjoy and value their work and that of their colleagues

▸   Demonstrate good practice in their work at all times.

ACTIVITY

Over a period of several days, carry out three observations of a child in your placement as follows.

Observation 1: Observe the child during an adult-led large group activity such as circle time or lunchtime.

Observation 2: Observe the same child during a small group activity with her peers, such as a co-operative play situation in which an adult is either not involved or only involved periodically.

Observation 3: Observe the child during a one-to-one interaction with an adult.

In each of the observations:

▸   Note the child's language interactions with the adult.

▸   In your evaluations, comment on the quality and value of the different types of interactions for the child's language, emotional and social development.

▸   Draw some conclusions based on the above.

▸   Include the observations in your child development portfolio.

Interactions within the Adult Team

The adult team works together to meet the aims of the setting and takes collective responsibility for decisions made and implemented. To function well as a team, the members must be:

▸   Motivated towards common goals

▸   Provided with the support and encouragement necessary to achieve these goals

▸   Able to communicate effectively within the team.

Effective teams:

▸   Know what is expected of them

▸   Have clearly identified roles

▸   Agree common goals for the children and the service

▸   Communicate openly and with trust

▸   Share decision-making

▸   Recognise problems and deal with them openly

▸   Co-operate and share ideas

▸   Members recognise their own and each other's strengths

▸   Meet regularly.

ACTIVITY

Role Play

You are working as part of a team in an early childhood setting which is planning an open day for parents and members of the local community. Role play the meeting to include the following:

▸   Assign roles to different members of the team.

▸   Draw up an agenda.

▸   Through discussion, reach decisions on:

— When and how the open day will be organised

— How it will be advertised/promoted

— Duties of different team members on the day

— How the children will be involved.

▸   Record the meeting for your Communications module.

The Adult Role

The effectiveness of an early years programme is determined by the skills, attitudes and commitment of the adults involved. Adults play a key role in determining the quality of the experiences of the children through:

▸   Knowledge of child development

▸   Regular, systematic observation of children

▸   Use of observation outcomes to plan for the individual in a way that links learning to the individual's needs and abilities

▸   Supporting and reinforcing the child's learning

▶   Extending the opportunities for learning inherent in a given situation

▶   Interacting with children in a way that builds trust, confidence, independence and self-esteem

▶   Respecting the children and one another.

The Work Environment

Early years workers who themselves feel valued, are confident and enjoy their work will create caring, supportive environments where children's needs can be met. This happens when:

▶   Their rights are recognised and upheld (see Chapter 1)

▶   They are trained in early childhood care and education

▶   Adult–child ratios are adequate to ensure that staff members can carry out their allocated tasks without undue pressure

▶   Roles and responsibilities are clearly defined and regularly appraised

▶   Work schedules are planned to ensure task sharing among the team

▶   There is consensus about issues to do with the day-to-day running of the centre

▶   A forum exists for resolving conflicts and solving problems

▶   A system is in place to support and supervise team members in carrying out their work

▶   Work conditions are adequate to ensure that there is a long-term commitment to the job. This includes salary structures, benefits, hours of work, a career ladder and an appreciation of their professionalism (see Chapter 1)

▶   There are regular opportunities for workers to take advantage of professional development.

Partnership with Parents

Parents as the main carers of their children have a right to be involved in a meaningful way in the care and education process in the early childhood setting. Developing a working partnership with parents will benefit the children, the parents and the centre. It builds trust and confidence on the part of the child and the parents, helps to ensure that the goals of the centre are supported in the home and that the centre supports the parents' goals for the children. (Note: Use of the word 'parent' here is meant to imply parent or carer, acknowledging the fact that many children are cared for by people other than their parents.)

High-quality early years programmes promote partnerships with parents by:

▶ Ensuring open access for parents at all times and providing an atmosphere where they are made to feel welcome

▶ Involving parents in the decision-making processes of the centre through management committees and input into policy formation

▶ Involving parents in the activities of the centre: as rota helpers, on outings, involvement in fundraising activities, sharing a special interest or expertise with the group and sharing in celebrations

▶ Providing a facility for nursing mothers

▶ Involving parents in settling in their child and encouraging them to spend as much time on this as they feel is necessary

▶ Respecting parents' wishes at all times while keeping in mind the best interests of the child

▶ Ensuring that clear systems for communicating with parents, both oral and written, are in place at all times and that there is time for both listening to parents and sharing information about the child

▶ Reaching agreement with parents on individual goals for each child and ensuring that parents are clear on how these goals are met in the curriculum of the centre

▶ Sharing all information about their child, including observations, assessments and any other written records with parents, and encouraging them to contribute to the compilation of these records

▶ Respecting confidentiality of information about parents, children and their families

▶ Encouraging participation by parents in workshops on child-related topics such as child development, play and behaviour management.

Communication with Parents

Honesty and openness should form the basis of all communication with parents. Good communication with parents helps children to sense the continuity between their home and the service. The service should encourage this communication, whether formal or informal, keeping in mind that not all parents:

▶ May be able to read

▶ May speak or fully understand the language used

▶ May have the confidence to engage in dialogue

▶ May have a lot of time.

ACTIVITY

In groups, discuss how the early childhood setting could best meet the needs of the following parents, both in terms of the service they themselves offer and in their capacity as advisors about other services available in the community.

Susan and Joe: *'Our nanny is excellent. She drops Chloë (3 years) in to the playgroup every morning and collects her at 12.30. We both have to be at work by 8.30 and Joe often works late into the evening. We rarely get to talk to playgroup staff. We'd both like to be more involved in the playgroup but it's very difficult with our work commitments.'*

Sarah: *'It's very difficult for me to leave my baby (5 months) in the mornings. I phone the nursery often during the day to find out how he's getting on and would love to call in sometimes to see him. Although I know he is being well looked after, I sometimes find myself in tears after these phone calls.'*

Seán: *'Since I split up with Jack's mother and Jack (4 years) doesn't live with me any more, I'm very conscious that he needs to have more male influences in his life. I'd like to get a bit more involved in the nursery too, but I can't face all those women!'*

Mr and Mrs Jawid: *'We came here to live 6 months ago, and Fettan (2½ years) has settled in very well to the crèche. She is now starting to speak English and we are both concerned that she is not getting enough support in this from us, as we don't speak English at home.'*

Julia: *'I wish they could take the twins (18 months) for more than three mornings a week. I really need to find a full-time job, and they get on my nerves sometimes when we're at home together all day.'*

Formal communication with parents can be facilitated by:

▸   A handbook which sets out the policies and procedures of the service, which is given to all parents as the child is enrolled (see Chapter 2).

▸   A special noticeboard for parents, used for a calendar of events, meetings, menus, etc.

▸   A standard format such as a diary for sending messages home regularly which makes it easier for parents to access information.

▸   A regular newsletter to keep parents up to date.

▶ Parents being regularly invited to meetings with staff members to discuss their child's progress, as well as group meetings to keep parents informed about new developments, policies and procedures, etc.

The everyday interactions between parents and carers are usually *informal*, but are also used to show parents how their input is valued. These include:

▶ Greeting parents by name

▶ Sharing information about the child's day

▶ Seeking advice from parents about the child

▶ Supporting parents when settling in and saying goodbye to the child

▶ Actively listening to parents' concerns about the child

▶ Acknowledging the special nature of the parent/child relationship and the intensity of feeling which this can lead to on the part of the parent.

3. The Curriculum and the Environment

Active participation and involvement in spontaneous play provide the opportunities for exploring, manipulating and experimenting which enable children to construct knowledge. Providing quality experiences for children implies an acknowledgement and acceptance of play as the medium through which they learn. This is acknowledged in the Pre-school Regulations 2006. A high-quality early years curriculum:

▶ Is based on accepted theory and knowledge about how children develop and learn

▶ Promotes the development and enhances the learning of each individual child

▶ Offers a range of learning opportunities while acknowledging that all areas of children's learning are integrated and equally important

▶ Aims to develop positive attitudes to learning

▶ Incorporates observation, assessment and recordkeeping, recognising these as essential to inform effective planning for the child as well as helping to identify best use of resources and gaps in provision.

(See Aistear, Chapter 1.)

The Learning Environment

Our physical surroundings affect how we feel, how comfortable we are, how we relate to others and how we achieve our goals. For young children, who learn by actively exploring and interacting with their physical environment, a well-organised and interesting environment is essential to enhance development and learning. In creating a high-quality environment for children, the following questions should be considered:

▶   Is the environment well designed and aesthetically pleasing and laid out in a way that promotes independence and choice for the children?

▶   Is it safe?

▶   Is it accessible to all children and adults?

▶   Is it spacious, allowing for free movement, rest and relaxation and quiet activities?

▶   Does it contain a wide assortment of clearly displayed and easily accessible equipment and materials which reflect the developmental stages and learning needs of the children?

▶   Do the materials:
   —   Interest the children?
   —   Vary sufficiently in complexity to accommodate all types and stages of play and development?
   —   Reflect a diversity of cultural interests?
   —   Promote a range of learning opportunities, e.g. creativity, language, problem-solving? (See Chapters 4, 5 and 14.)

ACTIVITY

SCENARIO

The Kidzone Day Nursery is located in a Health and Fitness Centre and caters for children aged from 1 to 7 years, offering full-time, sessional and drop-in services. Because there is limited access to outdoor space for the children, the nursery is equipped with a small gym. This is a large, airy room and contains a variety of materials for active play – large foam blocks, a ball pool, low-level balancing beams, slides and a child-sized vaulting horse.

However, the gym is mainly used as a rumpus room when children need to let off steam, and they spend around 2 hours per day in there in mixed age groups. The time is mostly spent running around, sometimes wildly, jumping up and down off the equipment and throwing the foam blocks around. Several of these are now torn and have had to be taken out of use. There have been some minor accidents too, especially to the younger children, with falling or being knocked over by older children or by flying objects.

Staff have not taken an active role in planning the use of the gym; while there are adequate numbers of adults on duty, their main roles seem to be supervisory rather than active participatory.

The manager has decided that the room will be closed down, since parents are starting to complain and staff are unhappy at the lack of structure in this area.

▶   In a small group, identify the problems that have arisen about using the gym.

▶   List the causes of these problems.

▶   Plan alternative ways to use the gym which would take account of all the children's needs as well as safety considerations.

▶   Identify specific roles for staff members in implementing the plan.

SUMMARY

▶   A growing acceptance of children's entitlement to civil and human rights has informed thinking on childhood in recent years. These rights are set down in the UN Convention on the Rights of the Child 1989, which confers rights on children of all countries that are signatories to the Convention.

▶   In Ireland, *The National Children's Strategy* articulates a rights-based approach to children's issues.

▶   Legal requirements and regulations can go some way towards ensuring that the conditions exist within which quality can be achieved.

▶   High-quality services base their provision on a knowledge of how children develop and learn, a recognition of their rights and needs and an awareness on the part of the adults involved of their own role in facilitating this.

▶   The ethos of the centre, the quality of the relationships between the adults involved and the curriculum are key factors in the development of quality in an early childhood setting.

▶   The introduction of Síolta, the National Quality Framework, and Aistear, the Curriculum Framework, will have a positive impact on the quality of early childhood care and education services into the future.

References

Department of Health and Children, 2000, *Our Children – Their Lives, National Children's Strategy,* Dublin: Stationery Office.

IPPA, 2002, *The Early Childhood Organisation, 2002, Quality – A Discussion Paper*, Dublin: IPPA.

NCCA, 2006, *Aistear: The Early Childhood Curriculum Framework*, Dublin: NCCA.

Síolta, 2006, *The National Quality Framework for Early Childhood Education (NQF) 2006*, Dublin: CECDE.

PROVIDING FOR PLAY

This section covers some of the practical aspects of planning and providing for children's play in an early childhood setting. Chapter 4 focuses on the play environment, both indoors and out, and considers some general safety issues. Chapter 5 looks at providing for play at different ages and stages and also at the role of the early years worker in this area.

4

THE PLAY ENVIRONMENT

States Parties recognise the right of the child to rest and leisure, to engage in play and recreational activities appropriate to the age of the child and to participate freely in cultural life and the arts.

(UN Convention on the Rights of the Child, Article 31)

AREAS COVERED

▸ **Aistear: The Early Childhood Curriculum Framework**

▸ **Children and Play**

▸ **The Play Environment**

▸ **The Space for Play**

▸ **Safety at Play**

Introduction

Children learn by doing, and play is what they mostly do; play must therefore involve active engagement on the part of the child with her environment in all its aspects. The more interesting the environment, the more opportunities it will offer the child to explore, discover and learn.

For a child there is no distinction between work and play – play is the child's work. Play is the child's means of discovery, learning, communication and expression.

This chapter deals with the practicalities of providing play opportunities in a safe environment within the early childhood setting. It focuses on the role of the early years worker in planning the environment for play, both indoors and out.

Aistear: The Early Childhood Curriculum Framework

Aistear is the new curriculum framework for all children from birth to 6 years in Ireland. It provides information, ideas and suggestions to help support children's learning and development during this important stage of their lives. Aistear:

▶ Is a set of shared principles and themes that underpin quality early childhood provision (see Síolta, Chapter 3) and support children's learning and development through the provision of play and learning opportunities, taking place where there are caring, supportive relationships with adults and other children.

▶ Is designed for use in all early childhood care and education settings, including the home, crèche, nursery, pre-schools, Naíonraí and junior infant classes.

▶ Recognises and celebrates early childhood as a unique period in life, when children enjoy and learn through experience.

▶ Helps adults to plan learning experiences that enable children to grow and develop as competent and confident learners, within loving relationships with others.

▶ Describes the types of learning (disposition, values and attitudes, skills, knowledge and understanding) that are important for children in the early years.

▶ Offers ideas and suggestions on how this learning might be nurtured.

▶ Provides guidelines on supporting children through partnership with parents, interaction, play and assessment.

The material in the following two chapters fits within the Aistear guidelines in that it proposes a model of provision for children that is challenging and supportive, offered in a safe, caring environment.

Principles of Early Learning and Development

Aistear is based on 12 principles, presented in three groups, which are crucial to and underpin early learning and development. The 12 principles are:

1: Children and Their Lives in Early Childhood

▶ The Child's Uniqueness

▶ Equality and Diversity

▶ Children as Citizens

2. Children's Connections with Others

▶ Relationships

▶ Parents, Family and Community

▶ The Adult's Role

3. How Children Learn and Develop

▶ Holistic Learning and Development

▶ Active Learning

▶ Play and Hands-on Experiences

▶ Relevant and Meaningful Experiences

▶ Communication and Language

▶ The Learning Environment

Each principle is presented using a short statement followed by an explanation of the principle from the child's perspective. This highlights the adult role in supporting children's learning.

ACTIVITY

Research the 12 principles of early learning and development in Aistear (www.ncca.ie/earlylearning). Pick one (e.g. the child's uniqueness) and carefully read the follow-on statements.

In each group, discuss what these tell you about your role as an adult in supporting children's learning.

Aistear Themes

Early learning and development is presented in four inter-connected themes in Aistear:

▶ Well-being

▶ Identity and Belonging

▶ Communicating

▶ Exploring and Thinking.

The themes are used to describe what children learn, such as dispositions, attitudes, values, skills, knowledge and understanding, and each is presented using four aims, which are in turn divided into six learning goals. Each theme offers ideas and suggestions for learning opportunities and experiences adults could provide for children in working towards the aims and goals of Aistear. These are called Sample Learning Opportunities and can be adapted and developed for different situations across the different age groups (babies, toddlers and young children).

Figure 4.1: Aistear

Source: Aistear (NCCA, 2006).

Guidelines for Good Practice

The Guidelines for Good Practice are listed under four headings:

▶   Building Partnerships between Parents and Practitioners

▶   Learning and Developing through Interactions

▶   Learning and Developing through Play

▶   Supporting Learning and Development through Assessment.

These guidelines describe how the adult can support early learning and development across the themes and outline a wide variety of sample learning experiences. Assessment is covered in Chapter 5.

Assessment in Aistear

With Aistear, children's learning and development are assessed using a variety of methods, including observation, conversations, setting tasks, self-assessment and testing. Evidence gathered from assessment helps the early childhood practitioner to build a profile of the child as a learner, celebrate their achievements and help them towards the next steps in learning (NCCA, 2006).

In practice, assessment of children's learning should:

▶   Be formal

▶   Be carried out over time

▶   Be carried out in the context of children's interactions with materials, objects and other people

▶   Take place in real-life contexts where children are engaged in meaningful tasks (Dunphy, 2008: 4)

Observation and assessment are covered in Chapters 6 and 7.

Children and Play

Characteristics of Play

It is essential that the adult who is providing for play should have a clear understanding and acceptance of the play process and of its importance for children's learning and all-round development – physical, cognitive, language, emotional and social. This understanding enables the adult to implement a programme which is developmentally appropriate. Play is best defined by describing its commonly accepted characteristics, which means it:

▶   Involves activity

▶   Is pleasurable and provides satisfaction to the child

▶   Is spontaneous, though it may be started by an adult

▶   Comes from within the child – you cannot make a child play, she must be a willing participant

▶   Is a process – it is the doing that is important, not the outcome

▸   There is no right or wrong way to play

▸   Children have ownership of what takes place during play

▸   Is based on what the child already knows.

ACTIVITY

Aim: To focus on the characteristics of play.

Brainstorm all the ways/games/activities, etc. you played as a child. Choose one or more of the items you have remembered and discuss which of the above characteristics of play apply to it.

The Play Environment

In the context of early years services, the play environment is where young children spend their time. It is the physical space in which they are cared for, the furniture and how it is arranged, and how the materials and equipment for play are presented in that space. Creating a play environment is an important aspect of the adult's work with young children. It is not enough to simply provide materials and equipment in an unsystematic way; children need to know where things are and be able to access them whenever they wish.

Creating a play environment involves organising space both indoors and outdoors to encourage play and exploration, as well as selecting and arranging materials and equipment in that space so as to maximise opportunities for learning and development.

When planning space for play, the basic requirements are that:

▸   There is enough space for each child

▸   Each child or group of children has a 'home base' where they can feel a sense of belonging

▸   There is access to outdoor play space, preferably attached to the setting.

Details on space requirements as defined in the Child Care (Pre-school Services) Regulations 2006 are set out in Chapter 2.

The Space for Play

Indoor Play Space

A well-designed play space should:

▶ Encourage the child to become involved

▶ Promote the child's independence and sense of responsibility

▶ Allow for decision-making by the children

▶ Acknowledge that children are different in their abilities, stages of development, stages of play, likes and dislikes and general interests

▶ Provide for spending time alone in quiet play and in groups in noisy, active play.

Involvement, Independence and Responsibility

It is important to organise play space in such a way that it enables children to do things for themselves and to take responsibility for their own activities and environment. This is encouraged through the following.

▶ Toys and materials should be stored at the child's eye level on low shelving, tables or boxes, depending on the need. For example, dress-up clothes may be stored in a box or hung up on a low-level rail; materials for cutting and gluing may be displayed on a shelf or on a table; painting materials may be stored partly on the easel and partly on a nearby shelf. Whatever the arrangement, children need to be able to see and comfortably reach everything that they need.

▶ Materials should be organised logically and located in the areas where they are to be used. For example, pencils, markers and crayons should be stored beside paper and near a table. Shelves and containers should be labelled with pictures or silhouettes to show the children where materials belong, making it easy for them to put things back when they are finished.

▶ Tables and chairs need to be light enough to be lifted and carried easily by the children if necessary.

▶ Children should be able to take charge of tasks which enter into their play – filling and emptying water at the sink, washing and drying their own hands, cleaning their utensils such as paintbrushes and playdough cutters and hanging up their paintings to dry.

▶ Coats, bags, boots and protective clothing should be accessible to the children and they should not have to wait to be given these by adults.

▶   Materials should not be moved around without consulting the children and involving them in the move. Knowing where things are leads to a sense of security and ownership of the environment, and promotes independent action on the part of the child.

Encouraging Decision-making

Children who learn how to make decisions for themselves are learning how to think for themselves – they are learning how to learn. A well-planned play environment offers children choices about how to spend their time and how to use the materials on offer.

This is evident when:

1.   Children choose for themselves how they will spend their time.

▶   There is a rich and varied supply of play materials on offer at all times which reflect the range of interests, abilities and cultures in the group.

▶   There are clearly visible and attractively displayed materials which attract the child's attention and help her decide what to use.

▶   Similar materials (for example, art materials) are grouped together, creating interest areas which help the child to focus and ensuring that everything she might need is within that area.

2.   Children choose for themselves how they will use the materials.

Developing creativity and problem-solving are of critical importance here. Exploring, discovering and devising new ways to use materials is what creative thinking is all about. Adult-devised activities which require an end product contribute nothing to this process, other than that children learn what it takes to please the adults who care for them. Children need to be engaged in the process, for example in making their own playdough and discovering what actually happens when those very different wet and dry materials are combined in varying proportions. What may seem like a disaster to the adult who has a very fixed idea of what playdough should look and feel like can offer a new window of wonder to the child, a new opportunity to make a truly scientific discovery. The end product is rarely of interest to the child who is engaged in discovering. Adults spend long summer days building sand castles on the beach with their children, only to have the whole structure gleefully knocked down and jumped upon by a laughing child!

Acknowledging Differences

Each child is a unique individual. The play environment should be designed to encourage the expression of that individuality. Each child needs to discover for herself what she can and cannot do and to feel supported in trying out new things. If she can practise these with success, she will perceive herself as capable and develop positive attitudes to learning. A well-planned physical environment acknowledges and supports that expression of individuality.

▶ Materials and equipment should be developmentally appropriate to each child. There should be a range of materials within each area, offering different sorts of challenges. For example, the area containing construction toys should have simple wooden bricks as well as more intricate connecting bricks.

▶ There should be some tables and chairs for children who enjoy working at a table, as well as space on the floor for the child who prefers this.

▶ There should be enough space for children to move around comfortably and carry materials without bumping into things and feeling clumsy.

▶ The room arrangement should be such that children with disabilities can be involved in all areas and activities. Consideration should be given to different kinds of disabilities, not just those which have to do with mobility.

▶ Cultural and language diversity should be reflected in the materials and decoration of the room. There should be a sense that diversity is valued and not just acknowledged.

▶ Interest tables and displays should reflect topics which are current (festivals, celebrations, changes in nature) as well as those which are of interest to the individual children. They should reflect what is happening in their lives and in the lives of their families and communities.

See Chapter 14 for more detailed suggestions.

Spending Time Alone and in Groups

Just like adults, children need to spend time alone as well as socialising in large and small groups. A well-planned play space takes account of this and provides:

▶ Space for group activities such as circle time, stories, music and movement sessions and eating together. These activities help children to interact with others and learn to listen to one another. There should be space for this, even if it means moving furniture around.

▶ Opportunities for quiet play, alone or in groups, in areas set aside for activities such as reading, art or table toys.

▶ Opportunities for active, noisy play, including dramatic play (home corner and dressing up), small world play (using vehicles and animals) and building blocks and bricks. These activities require more space and this needs to be taken into consideration when laying out the room. It is a good idea to partly enclose this type of space, as it helps to avoid noisy activities creeping into quiet corners. See Figure 4.2 for a sample room layout.

TASK

Aim: Planning a play space on paper helps to identify the strengths and weaknesses in a room layout.

The aim of this activity is to enable you to plan the best use of play space in an early childhood setting.

▸   Draw a plan of the play space where you are working at present.

▸   Identify which areas work well and which areas could be improved and explain why.

Outdoor Play Space

This is often thought of as a place where children can go to let off steam, but outdoor play space is that and much more. Children's developmental needs do not change because they are outdoors. A child may enjoy running around freely for a short period of time, but the outdoor space should hold special interests too, and the time spent there should offer variety, stimulation and opportunities to explore as well as fresh air and exercise. For this reason, most of the criteria for planning indoor play space will also apply outdoors.

Many of the activities which children enjoy indoors can be moved outdoors, weather permitting, e.g. playdough, paint, finger paints, books and stories, sand and water. An added bonus is that many of these can be extended outdoors in ways that are not possible indoors. Painting can be done with large buckets or bowls of water and household paint brushes (especially interesting on a hot day, when walls and paving slabs can be painted and observed as the water evaporates).

When planning outdoor play space, keep the following in mind.

▸   The Child Care (Pre-school Services) Regulations 2006 set down minimum safety requirements for outdoor play (see Chapter 2). These should be adhered to at all times.

▸   The surface should be partly grass and partly paved, if possible with impact-absorbing tiles. These are particularly important under play structures such as climbing frames or slides.

Figure 4.2: Plan of a Playroom for 3- to 6-Year-Old Children

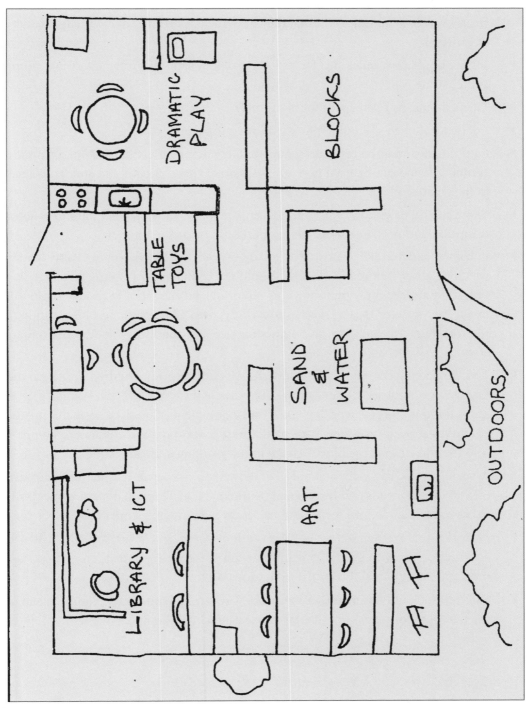

Source: Dodge, Diane T., L.J. Colker and C. Heroman, *The Creative Curriculum for Preschool*, 4th edn, Washington, DC: TSI.

▸ Some part of the outdoor area should be shaded.

▸ Space and equipment should be organised so as to ensure that the children are clearly visible at all times and that they have the opportunity to engage in a variety of activities.

▸ There should be a quiet area for activities such as sand play, digging or just sitting and chatting.

▸ There should be open space for active play.

▸ Adequate storage should be provided for equipment.

▸ Equipment should be versatile enough to allow for a variety of uses, for example a climbing frame can be used in many ways other than for climbing and lends itself to imaginative play.

▸ There should be enough equipment to ensure that children do not have to wait for turns all the time. Time spent outdoors should be utilised fully.

▸ If babies and toddlers are cared for, they need their own space. Babies enjoy watching other children at play but should not be in danger of being knocked over or hurt. Toddlers enjoy pottering and exploring and they should be able to do this in an unrestricted space, away from the potential hazard of older children. Alternatively, they may use the outdoor space at a time when older children are elsewhere.

▸ The outdoor space affords a wonderful opportunity for children to plant and nurture seeds, observe them grow and harvest their fruits. Space should be set aside for this. Strong working tools and equipment should be available to the children – trowels, watering cans, small forks, flower pots and containers, compost – so that they can actually participate in the planting and harvesting.

▸ A small part of the garden should be allowed to grow wild so that children can observe weeds, seeds and insects in a natural habitat. This will in turn attract birds to the garden and a bird feeder can be set up here in wintertime.

▸ Activities can be planned to use the outdoor space whenever possible. Themed activities to do with scientific learning such as growth, animals, insects, plants, mud and water can all be linked to outdoor play.

▸ Staff rotas should be organised in such a way that maximum use can be made of the outdoors for play – not just for an occasional half hour.

Equipment for Outdoors

The equipment provided should:

▸ *Stimulate different kinds of physical activity.*

Examples: Climbing equipment such as a climbing frame with different attachments like a rope ladder, pole, platform, chute, bridge, slide as well as balls, balancing beams and wheeled toys for pushing, pulling and riding.

▸ *Allow for children's exploration.*

Examples: Tunnel, large boxes or packing cases, water, earth and sand for digging, logs, bushes, wild garden area.

▸ *Encourage co-operative play.*

Examples: Rocking boats, skittles, dramatic play, space for group games for older children.

TASK

Observe a child at play outdoors.

▸ Note:
— What play areas the child uses
— What equipment she prefers
— How long she plays in each area
— Areas or equipment that she avoids
— Who she interacts with
— Any conflicts that arise and how she resolves these.

▸ Evaluate her stage of development and comment on how outdoor play can enhance this.

▸ Make recommendations on how the child's outdoor play experiences could be enriched.

Safety at Play

General Safety

By its very nature, play involves taking risks. In an environment where children are encouraged to play in creative ways and to take risks, there will be some element of danger. Climbing those extra few rungs to the top of the climbing frame by herself, using scissors or sitting without support for the first time all carry their own risks, but we cannot wrap children in cotton wool! What we can do is make sure that the environment we provide for them is as safe as possible while retaining its possibilities for exploration, discovery and taking risks.

ACTIVITY

Find out what these symbols mean.

This does not mean that children are wilfully exposed to danger – on the contrary, adults have to be vigilant at all times to ensure that risks to children's health and safety are kept to a minimum. When adults ensure that all measures to protect children's safety are in place, they can engage with the children instead of constantly 'policing' children's play with admonishments like 'Don't touch…!', 'Stay away from…!', 'Get down…!'

Children also need to be involved in keeping themselves and others safe – they should learn how to safely carry scissors, chairs, glass and crockery, to wash their hands properly, to open and close doors carefully, to wipe up after a spill and in general to become aware about what constitutes danger to themselves and to others.

When providing for safe but challenging play, the following general guidelines should be observed.

- All activities should be carefully supervised and correct adult/child ratios maintained (see Chapter 2). Adults should ensure that they have an unobstructed view of children at all times, particularly outdoors.

- Equipment and activities should be appropriate to the ages and stages of development of the children.

- Equipment and materials should be sturdy and well made from non-toxic materials and should conform with European safety standards.

- Equipment should be checked regularly; damaged items should be repaired or discarded.

- A strict hygiene routine should be followed for all play areas. Equipment should be washed and sterilised where possible. Particular attention should be paid to cleaning and sterilising play equipment for use by babies.

- There should be no sharp corners or points on furniture or equipment.

- Entry to and exit from indoor and outdoor play areas should be supervised closely at all times.

- Where the play area is shared with pets, stringent measures must be in place to ensure children's health and safety at all times.

- There should be safety rules about play which children participate in formulating, clearly understand and are involved in implementing.

Safety in the Indoor Play Area

- Floor coverings should be durable and of non-slip material. Loose rugs should not be used. Spills should be wiped up immediately.

- Curtain and blind cords should be inaccessible to children and cords and strings on play items such as dressing-up clothes should be too short to present a danger.

- Electrical sockets should be covered and there should be no loose or trailing leads.

- Potentially dangerous materials such as cleaning materials should be stored out of children's sight and reach in a locked cupboard.

- Litter bins should be emptied regularly.

▶ Hot drinks such as tea or coffee should not be allowed in the play areas.

▶ Paints and glue should be non-toxic.

▶ Scissors should be safe for children and stored safely after use.

▶ Small objects such as pegs and beads should be carefully monitored and should not be accessible to younger children.

▶ All early childhood workers and volunteers should be familiar with the safety policies of the setting as well as with the details of the Safety Statement and Pre-school Regulations on safety (see Chapter 2).

ACTIVITY

Aim: To familiarise yourself with the practical application of safety in the play environment.

▶ In a small group, choose an indoor activity area of a playroom, such as the art corner or the book area. Each group should choose a different area.

▶ Draw up a detailed safety checklist for that area. Present this as a checklist or a set of questions which can be ticked 'yes' or 'no'.

▶ Share the checklists among the large group, adding additional items if necessary.

▶ Ask permission to use at least one of the checklists in your workplace.

Safety in the Outdoor Play Area

▶ An adult should be assigned to supervise each area of play.

▶ Outdoor play equipment should be checked frequently for corrosion and weather damage.

▶ Walls, railings, steps and ledges should be made safe.

▶ The area should be checked before use for cat and dog faeces.

▶ The sandpit should be covered when not in use.

▶ There should be enough space between pieces of equipment to prevent children running into one another.

▶ Slides should curve at the bottom to become parallel to the ground.

▶ Slide platforms should have protective railings.

CASE STUDY

Garrymore Community Playgroup has been operating for the past 5 years. It takes place in a prefabricated building at the rear of the community centre in an urban area. Children attend for morning sessions only, from 9.30 a.m. to 12.30 p.m. each day.

The children come from all sections of the local community, which is a mixture of private rented, owner-occupied and local authority housing, set around a busy shopping area.

Funding is an ongoing problem, and while staff and volunteers are enthusiastic and committed, there is usually quite a bit of improvisation as far as equipment is concerned. Lack of an outdoor play area is a particular problem. Children are taken on walks to the local park as often as possible, but not as often as the play leader would like. Several of the children live in apartments and have no outdoor space of their own. Some of the staff are not trained. Funding has beeen accessed to improve the outdoor play facilities.

The committee of the community centre has been approached and has agreed that the playgroup may have the use of a section of the outdoor space which is free during the day. It is a tarmacadamed area, measuring around 200 square metres and well fenced in. It is sometimes used on weekend nights by young people from the nearby housing estates and on Monday mornings is often littered with beer cans, chip bags, condoms and syringes. The playgroup has decided to accept the offer, but needs some creative ideas on how to make the space suitable as an outdoor play space.

Discuss in small groups:

▶   What are the main health and safety issues which staff need to consider? List these under the headings:

—   Those which the staff can control.

—   Those which the staff cannot control.

▶   Under each heading, suggest steps which could be taken to deal with these.

▶   How could materials and equipment already in use in the playgroup be adapted for use in this space?

▶   How could the physical space be adapted to make it suitable and attractive for children? Consider the play surface, walls/fences, the need for a space to dig and grow plants, attracting wildlife and general safety.

▶   Make a list of everyday items which could be used as outdoor play equipment at small cost to the playgroup.

▶   Draw a plan of the play space as you imagine it could look when completed.

SUMMARY

▸   For a child there is no distinction between work and play – play is the child's work. Play is the child's means of discovery, of communication and expression and learning.

▸   Creating a suitable play environment is an important aspect of the adult's work with young children. This involves organising space both indoors and outdoors to encourage play and exploration, selecting and arranging materials and equipment in that space so as to maximise opportunities for learning and development and ensuring the children's safety while they play.

▸   Well-designed play space should encourage the child's involvement, promote independence, foster decision-making and accommodate differences in children's abilities, stages of development and play.

▸   Access to outdoor play space is important and time spent there should offer variety, stimulation and opportunities to explore as well as fresh air and exercise.

▸   Adults should ensure that the play environment is as safe as possible while retaining its possibilities for exploration, discovery and taking risks. Children also need to be involved in keeping themselves and others safe.

References

Dodge, Diane T., L.J. Colker and C. Heroman, 2004, *The Creative Curriculum for Preschool*, 4th edn, Washington, DC: TSI.

Dunphy, Elizabeth, 2004, *Supporting Early Learning and Development through Formative Assessment*, Dublin: NCCA.

NCCA, 2006, *Aistear: The Early Childhood Curriculum Framework*, Dublin: NCCA.

United Nations Convention on the Rights of the Child, 1989.

5

PLAY: AGES AND STAGES

AREAS COVERED

▶ Play for Babies
▶ Play for Toddlers
▶ Play for the Older Child (3–6 Years)
▶ Planning Play Activities
▶ Evaluating Play Activities
▶ Making Play Materials

Introduction

The provision of interesting and varied play materials is an important first step in facilitating children's early learning. Planning for play and supporting children's participation helps them to make best use of the opportunities offered by the environment and the materials. This chapter looks at the provision of materials and resources for play in the early years. In describing resources for play in the different ages and stages, it is not practicable to include exhaustive lists of materials and equipment. Further information can be found in the Resources section at the end of this book.

While taking account of variations in children's developmental stages, three broad age categories are covered. The term 'babies' is used to indicate from birth to around 15 months, 'toddlers' indicates from 15 months to 3 years and 'pre-school children' indicates from about 3 to 6 years.

Play for Babies

A baby comes into the world needing to find out what the world is like. Although he cannot perform the simple actions which we take for granted later on, like directing his eyes or taking his hand to his mouth, the reflexes evident at birth are quickly replaced by the planned, intentional actions that become evident as he progresses through the first year. His early experiences are sensory – sights, sounds, tastes, touches and smells.

Many of these are experienced through the feeding process, when he is held and caressed by a caring adult who talks or sings to him, making it logical that once he is able to grasp things he will want to explore them using his mouth. His mouth helps him to discern how objects feel and what they are like before he finds out what they can do. The baby cannot learn about the world just by looking at things: he must be an active explorer. As he learns simple body control, he can continue this process more actively.

Playing with Baby

Time spent playing and talking with the baby in the first year is invaluable to him since he will learn more quickly at this time than at any other period of his life. Babies learn soon after birth to prefer the sight of a human face over other objects. By looking at him, smiling and talking as you hold him and responding to his sounds, you are encouraging him to respond in turn and laying the foundations of human communication skills. Later on, this interaction will include simple games, finger rhymes and looking at books together. These simple activities are essential for further developing communication skills, and the baby learns about the whole process of listening, waiting, responding – the turn-taking that is a necessary part of acquiring language. Play in this way takes place while the baby is feeding, being changed or bathed. It becomes part of the normal routine of adult–baby interactions.

TASK
Observe a baby's responses to an object which has been placed near him. Describe in detail actions such as touching, grasping, hitting and mouthing. Write up the observation using the format suggested in Chapter 7 on page 131.

The First Year

Play for babies in the first year should include a whole range of experiences in a form that is appropriate to them. Babies need stimulation which involves interaction with others, mainly adults, and they need opportunities to explore things by themselves. A baby's play during this stage is defined as solitary or isolate play, which means that he does not play in a sociable way or interact with others while at play; he plays alone.

With adults, babies can play simple games, look at books, get involved in rhymes and songs or enjoy simple trips outdoors. Games, rhymes and songs played together with actions, such as Round and Round the Garden, Roly-Poly and This Little Piggy, all offer a chance for one-to-one activity involving pleasant physical contact and language. Time spent looking at books and telling stories helps the baby to associate these with a warm loving feeling, are calming and relaxing and stimulate language. Spending time outdoors stimulates the baby visually, and he will often be fascinated by things which adults no longer notice, such as leaves moving in the wind, flickering shadows or birds in flight. This is particularly relevant for the younger baby, whose body position when lying back in a chair gives him a different angle on the world outdoors.

All of these provide for the vital interactions through which babies develop a sense of security, language, responsiveness to others and to their environment. Variety is important for a baby, and while he will enjoy the familiar, he may become bored. He needs a range of experiences and things to look at and explore – new songs, different rhymes and several kinds of objects.

Exploring Objects

Babies enjoy being presented with simple objects to explore. Examples appropriate to the different ages are set out below.

0–6 Months

▶ A piece of card with one primary colour placed within his field of vision will help a new baby to focus.

▶ Objects hung above where he is lying will provide visual stimulation. For example, mobiles made from coloured card or other light material will move in the air and attract his attention.

▶ Household objects such as cotton reels, clothes pegs or things that rattle or ring can be strung together on strong elastic within the baby's reach. These will encourage hitting and grabbing, and when one object is pulled it can set the whole lot dancing. This means that the whole selection can be changed often, giving plenty of variety.

▶ A baby can also hold onto objects such as rattles during this period, and will bring them to his mouth to explore.

Sensory Learning

Satisfying his curiosity at this stage needs careful consideration, and there is a wide range of equipment on the market for this purpose, in different sizes, colours and patterns with a variety of price ranges. A closer examination reveals, however, that most of this material is concerned with stimulating the visual sense, and to a lesser extent the sense of hearing. It is predominantly made from plastic, in very bright primary colours. In adults, the visual sense is so dominant that it gives us a lot of initial information about objects and we do not need to handle and mouth them in the same way that babies do to find out what they are like. These brightly coloured plastic toys appeal to the adult sense of what a baby will enjoy because they are visually very attractive.

Babies, however, are developing all their senses, and during this stage their mouths give them more information about an object than their eyes can. Even if a child has a wide selection of bright plastic rattles to choose from, the information he receives about them will be broadly similar, since one plastic rattle tastes pretty much the same as another.

What the baby needs is a range of objects which vary in texture as well as colour. Examples are:

▶ Rubber rings

▶ Wooden spoon

▶ Large curtain rings

▶ Clothes pegs

▶ Keys on a large ring

▶ Spoons

▶ Rounded lids

▶ Fabrics in different textures.

These everyday objects can be changed often in order to prevent boredom, and of course what might appear ordinary and familiar to the adult is new and exciting to the baby.

6–12 Months

Once the baby can sit up, household objects can be collected into a basket for selecting, investigating and discovering. This is known as the Treasure Basket.*

The **Treasure Basket** is a medium-sized, low, round or oval rigid-sided basket which contains up to 100 natural and household objects. These can range from a pine cone, a lemon or a shell to a leather purse, a velvet jewellery box or an egg whisk – the only rules are that the objects should be non-synthetic and that the adult should feel comfortable about what is put inside. All objects should be checked for safety.

The Treasure Basket provides a rich sensory experience for the child. For example, the inclusion of a lemon in the basket can offer opportunities for the baby to discover weight, smell and texture as well as colour. The Treasure Basket offers choice and variety and encourages exploration and independent activity. A 6- to 9-month-old baby may spend up to an hour exploring the objects in different ways – mouthing, sucking, handling, waving, banging. Some babies will spend a long time exploring one object, while others will select and discard one after the other, constantly rummaging for something new. Each is meeting his own need, and when more than one baby is using the basket at the same time, there will also be some level of social interaction as they show awareness of one another's presence.

The presence of the adult is also important here to give a sense of security to the child and freeing him to learn. The adult should, however, resist the temptation to intervene, as this can distract the baby from following his own ideas and will change the play from exploration to social interaction.

Toward the end of the first year, play changes again, and this is linked to the child's development of new physical skills such as crawling and standing and the ability to use finger and thumb in a pincer grip. These developments in themselves take up a lot of time, and often the objects used will be connected to this newfound mobility, e.g. following a rolling ball, pulling himself up toward an object which is out of reach or picking up small objects off the floor. His primary play requirement now is for a safe space in which to move around freely.

Play at this stage typically includes the following.

▶ **Dropping objects voluntarily** – this involves practising a new skill and becomes a favourite occupation for a while. Objects to drop could include some that are heavy and light, roll and stay still. A large container to drop things into is also useful.

▶ **Emptying and filling** – posting boxes are often offered at this stage, but the different hole sizes make them somewhat complex. Typically at this stage, a baby will take off the lid and fill and empty the box over and over again. Simple variations on this theme can be offered, such as a saucepan and some oranges, or an egg carton with empty cotton reels.

* The Treasure Basket and heuristic play were devised by the late Elinor Goldschmied and are described in her book *People Under Three: Young Children in Day Care*, published by Routledge.

▶   **Discovering cause and effect** – the baby enjoys a sense of power on discovering that his own actions have caused a particular reaction and that he can cause it to happen over and over again. Examples here are toys which respond when a lever is pressed or a string is pulled. He enjoys repeating these actions and in the process develops new skills and refines finger movement.

Play for Toddlers

The play needs of a baby change as he becomes mobile. Many of the objects which he enjoyed in the first year will continue to interest him, although he will probably use them differently. His main focus with objects now is not so much to discover what they are like as what he can do with them, for example, whether they will fit, bang, bounce, slide, roll or move – the possibilities are endless. Play provision for toddlers should be based on meeting this need as well as on a recognition of their stage of social play, which is moving from *solitary* to *parallel* play. This means that the child will play alongside and will observe others at play.

When providing play for toddlers, the following should be kept in mind.

▶   The room should be laid out in such a way that children can move around easily, see what choices are on offer and make decisions about what they do. Toys should be easily accessible on low-level shelving or in boxes or by placing larger toys on the floor.

▸ The toddler's need to move around constantly should be respected and toddlers should never be expected to sit for long periods at a table. Sitting down to play for a toddler usually means sitting on the floor.

▸ Toddlers engage in solitary and parallel play and have not yet reached the developmental stage to understand sharing and turn-taking. For this reason, several of the same popular toys should be provided so they do not have to wait or take turns; in this way, conflicts between children can be minimised.

▸ There should be opportunities for active, large muscle play both indoors and out. Practising newly acquired skills such as climbing should be safely encouraged by the inclusion of small climbing equipment, ramps and steps. Push and pull toys as well as ride-on trucks and cars should also be freely available.

▸ Experimentation with materials should be encouraged. This includes the provision of natural materials like sand, water, playdough and paint and finger paints. Art materials such as large crayons and large pieces of paper should be available.

▸ Adults should never expect toddlers to use templates, colour in pictures or produce finished 'art products' and should respect the process involved for the child in using materials, rather than expect an end product.

▸ Toddlers also need play with adult involvement, e.g. reading and telling stories, making music, looking at pictures, finger plays, rhymes and puppets. These activities provide the adult with opportunities to observe and support the child's learning and development.

Heuristic Play

The term 'heuristic' derives from the Greek '*eurisko*', implying discovery. Heuristic play* offers opportunities for toddlers to explore objects and make discoveries within a safe environment. As with the Treasure Basket, commercially bought toys are never offered to children during a heuristic play session; rather, a range of everyday objects is used to enable children aged around 12 to 20 months to do what they enjoy best – filling and emptying, slotting, selecting and discarding, recognising differences and similarities, building and balancing. Instead of the individual objects available in the Treasure Basket, there is a collection of each kind of object, as many as 40 or 50 of each. Material is abundant, so conflicts between children are rare. Again, the adult does not become involved in this play, but sits nearby to support, supervise, name, set out materials and observe. Heuristic play materials are referred to in Síolta (standard 6.54) as open-ended, real-world materials. They include:

▸ **Large containers** of all shapes and sizes, such as biscuit tins, cans, plastic bottles, egg boxes, cardboard and wooden boxes.

* The term 'heuristic play' was devised by the late Elinor Goldschmied.

▶ **Objects which roll**, such as small balls, pom-poms, tubes, reels and rollers.

▶ **Assorted objects** such as lengths of chain, jar lids, pine cones, ribbons, keys, ring bracelets, curtain rings and kitchen roll rods.

All of these objects can be explored in an open-ended way with no right or wrong result, in contrast to many commercial toys. For example, bracelets can easily be slotted onto and taken off the kitchen roll rod, in contrast to the shop-bought 'rings on a peg' where graded rings will only fit in a particular order. Pine cones or shells can be put into and taken out of cans without having to first fit them through a certain shape of slot. With heuristic play the child cannot fail because there is always more than one way of doing something.

Play for the Older Child (3–6 Years)

Planning for children in this age group should recognise that play is now becoming shared or co-operative, which means that increasingly during this period the child enjoys playing with others and has the linguistic ability necessary for negotiating in play. Play materials should be provided in clearly defined interest areas where similar types of activities and resources are grouped together, for example:

▶ Dramatic play

▶ Sand and water area

▶ Book corner

▶ Table toys

▶ Art area

▶ Interest table.

When organising the indoor play space for 3–6-year-olds, the following should be kept in mind.

▶ Each area of play, or interest area, should be clearly defined using tables, shelves or different floor coverings, and as far as practicable should be cut off from other areas.

▶ Noisy and quiet activities should be kept separate and as far apart as possible. Similar activities should be grouped near to one another, e.g. the book area near to the area

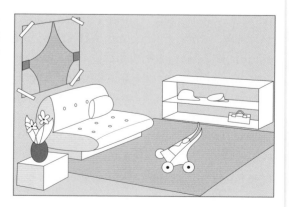

used for drawing, colouring, cutting and pasting. Both involve quiet concentration on the part of the child.

▶ Practical resources should be used to their best advantage, e.g. the art area and the water play area within easy reach of running water and the book corner near a window.

▶ It is best to arrange furniture and equipment in such a way that children are discouraged from running in the room.

▶ Adults and children should not have to pass through the interest areas to get to somewhere else, so interruptions to play are minimised.

▶ Each area should be clearly visible to the adults while giving children the sense of security that comes from being in a small, enclosed space.

The room plan on page 75 shows how these could be incorporated into a play area.

Interest Areas

The Dramatic Play Area, or Home Corner

Pretend play provides an opportunity for children to make-believe, role play and dramatise while planning, solving problems, using imagination, developing creativity and language and refining social and physical skills.

The home corner should be in a clearly defined area of the room and should as far as possible resemble some areas of the home, since children's play in this area is based on familiar themes and home life is familiar to all. This does not exclude the possibility of adding materials which will extend this play – dressing-up clothes can reflect a variety of occupations, both male and female, and the area can easily become a hospital, shop, car, train or a scene from a favourite story by the addition of suitable extra materials.

Equipment in the dramatic play area should include:

▶ **House equipment:** For example, furniture, kitchen equipment, variety of dolls and doll equipment, keys, large unbreakable mirror, telephones, ironing board and iron.

▶ **Dressing up:** A variety of clothes, shoes, hats, jewellery, handbags, purses, wallets, briefcases and large scraps of material in different fabrics which can be adapted for various uses such as cloaks, robes or shawls for carrying baby dolls.

▶ **Additional materials:** To facilitate play in a shop, hospital, post office, train, aeroplane, boat or specific roles like mechanic, cook, teacher.

▶ **Small world play:** Farm, zoo, doll's house, garage, small figures of animals and people.

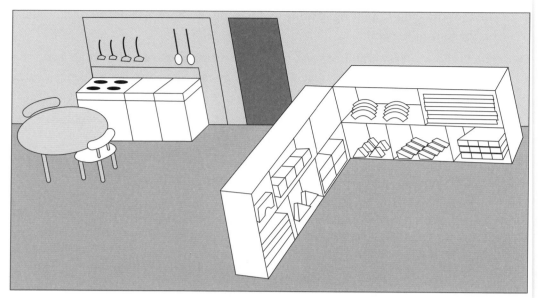

Dramatic play and block play located near one another

The Sand and Water Area

Sand and water are familiar, soothing, relaxing, natural materials which are inexpensive to provide and offer opportunities for children to explore and learn, make discoveries and solve problems. Although separate activities, they are related. They can be played with alone or combined. Dry sand can be poured, sifted, raked and scooped into containers; water can be poured, filled, splashed, bubbled and used to float objects. When combined, a third element emerges – wet sand, which can be used differently again. It can be built, shaped and moulded and will change its texture as more water is added.

Play with sand and water provides an opportunity for children to safely explore the properties of natural materials and to experience their calming, therapeutic effects. In doing so they can discover important mathematical and scientific principles, make plans, investigate and solve problems, understand cause and effect and develop language as well as social and physical skills. While each should have its own distinct space, the two should be near enough to one another to combine easily when necessary.

The floor covering should be non-slip and easily wiped. Equipment for play should be stored in suitable baskets or basins and not in the sand and water containers, as they can become easily cluttered and this can disrupt play. Children may need protective clothing in this area. If so, hooks can be provided at their level for storing these items.

Sand can also be provided on baking trays or in basins to encourage small world play. These can be set up on a separate table and should be seen as supplementing rather than substituting for the main provision.

Equipment for sand play should include:

▸ Sand and water trays, storage baskets for materials, dustpan and brush

▸ Sand – silver, coral or play sand

▸ Containers – buckets, plastic pots, empty cartons of different shapes, beakers, bun tins

▸ Sand wheel, shovels, scoops, spoons, rakes, sieve, funnel

▸ Weighing scales and measuring cups

▸ Shells, stones, twigs, leaves, small vehicles, play people.

Equipment for water play should include:

▸ Many of the items listed above are also suitable for water play

▸ Bottles and bottle tops, dolls for washing, spray bottles, siphon, boats

▸ Straws, plastic tubing, corks, sponges, objects that sink and float

▸ Protective clothing.

The Book Area

Books should be part of every child's experience and the early childhood setting can ensure this by:

▸ Providing a wide range of high-quality books

▸ Ensuring these are accessible to children

▸ Presenting them appropriately

▸ Using them regularly

▸ Being seen to value them.

The book area should be quiet, comfortable and well lit, with a variety of books clearly visible and accessible to the children. It is a place where children can take 'time out' from busier, noisier activities and where they may choose to spend time alone.

Books offer children an enjoyable way to:

▸ Gain information about specific subjects

▸ Deal with difficult events and transitions in their lives

▸ Acquire new ideas

▸ Discover different forms of literature, such as stories, poems, rhymes and fairy tales

▸ Lose themselves in other worlds

▸ Find out about other people, countries and ways of life

▸ Develop visual understanding and pay attention to detail.

Books stimulate imagination and help develop understanding of how other people act and feel. Through using books, children develop familiarity with the written word and its symbolic role. They develop an appreciation of the sequence in a story – the concepts of beginning, middle and end. Stories can be enjoyed alone or in groups. Enjoyment of books and stories in the early years lays the foundation for lifelong pleasure in reading. Membership of a public library provides access to around 20 books on special loan for playgroups and nurseries. This means a constant supply of books as well as a regular outing for the children and the chance to make choices for themselves about what they read.

ACTIVITY

Aim: Books for children should be chosen with care. This activity aims to help you draw up and test ways of choosing books for the different age groups. It will be useful to have read Chapter 14 before carrying out the activity.

▶ Draw up a checklist which would help you to choose books for:
— Babies
— Toddlers
— 3–6-year-olds.
▶ Include the criteria for promoting positive images set out in Chapter 14.
▶ Visit your local library to check out the children's books.
▶ Select one book for each age group above and use your checklist to critique them. If the books seem suitable, note the author, year of publication, title and publisher.

Equipment for the book area should include:

▶ Books!
▶ Low-level shelves, placed at a right angle to each other, can be used to form a semi-enclosed space.
▶ Books should be displayed with the front rather than the spine facing out.
▶ There should be comfortable seating, with space for an armchair, beanbags, cushions and room to manoeuvre a wheelchair.
▶ Remember that younger children will enjoy books which:
— Reflect their life experiences and interests

- — Feature characters with whom they can identify
- — Have a simple plot
- — Are expressed in engaging language with lots of repetition
- — Contain clear, well-executed illustrations, filled with detail
- — Are well constructed, robust and easily handled.

▶ In addition, older children will enjoy.

- — A more complex plot
- — Humour
- — Imaginative sequences
- — More detail in the story
- — Factual books.

▶ Books for all children should challenge stereotypes – see Chapter 14 for further information.

▶ Books should be changed regularly, reflecting the changing interests of the children, while keeping old favourites available.

▶ Reading and telling stories with children is an important feature of book provision in the play area and should be incorporated into individual and group activities every day.

Table Toy Area

This area is set aside for play with toys which are suited to being used at a table, though many of them can be used on the floor equally well. Table toys can be grouped into two types:

▶ Toys which are self-correcting, such as jigsaw puzzles

▶ Toys which are open-ended, like Lego bricks, threading cards or pegboards.

Play with table toys helps children to:

▶ Develop concepts of colour, size and shape

▶ Group, match and pair objects

▶ Develop creative ways of using materials

▶ Refine hand–eye co-ordination and visual discrimination

▶ Learn how to work in co-operation with others through shared projects

▶ Develop concentration.

Equipment in this area should be stored on open shelving near the tables and some floor space should be allocated for more expansive projects. There should be a clear system to make it easy for children to return the materials to the correct place – plenty of shelf space so that materials are not stacked on top of one another and a system of labelling and silhouettes to indicate where each item goes.

When selecting materials for this area, keep the following in mind.

▶   Children using this area will be at different developmental stages and materials should reflect this.

▶   Both self-correcting and open-ended materials should be available.

▶   Materials need to be of high quality to endure constant usage.

▶   Materials such as puzzles should challenge stereotypes and reflect an anti-bias approach (see Chapter 14).

Equipment in the table toy area should include:

▶   Jigsaw puzzles, both interlocking and tray types, in a variety of sizes

▶   Lotto games

▶   Matching cards

▶   Pegs and pegboards

▶   Threading aids

▶   Table bricks, such as Lego and wooden bricks

▶   Activities for sorting, grouping and pairing objects using shells, pasta, buttons.

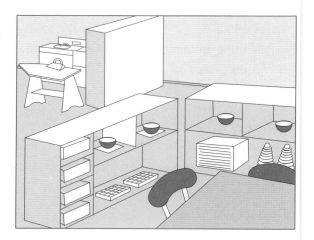

The Creative Play Area

Creative play can be taken here to mean all the activities which involve children in working with paint, paper, pencils, crayons, markers, scissors, glue, junk materials, playdough and clay. All of these involve children in a process of exploration and discovery – about the materials, the tools and about themselves. They can:

▶   Represent their ideas creatively

▶   Learn about cause and effect

▶   Observe changes in properties of materials

▶ Become familiar with colour, shape and texture

▶ Compare and contrast

▶ Solve problems

▶ Make choices and develop an aesthetic sense

▶ Develop fine motor skills and hand–eye co-ordination

▶ Use tools with increasing expertise and intention.

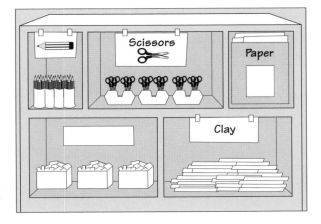

Children should feel in charge of their own activities here. A layout which enables this includes easy access to a range of materials, space and time to carry projects through and facilities for children to independently clean themselves and their environment. Constant replenishing of materials means that activities can be ongoing.

Adults should not direct children in what they may produce – play in this area is about process, not end product. If a child is working towards an end product, it should be of his own choosing.

The creative play area should take up a large part of the room, since it incorporates many different kinds of activities. Space can be divided up for the different kinds of activities, for example drawing and colouring can be near the quieter table toy area, while messier play can take place near the sand and water.

The creative play area should include:

▶ Space set aside for painting, containing double-sided easels, and space for table painting and finger painting if children prefer this

▶ Storage for painting materials

▶ Tables for clay and playdough, along with storage for tools

▶ A table for junk modelling and storage for materials

▶ A table for drawing

▶ Protective clothing on low-level hooks

▶ Thermostatically controlled hand washing and drying facilities accessible to children

▶ A facility for drying paintings, clay models and junk models.

Equipment for the creative play area should include the following.

Painting

▶ Paper – different sizes, textures and colours.

▶ Paint – non-toxic poster and powder paint in primary colours, black and white. Children discover other colours through their own exploration.

▶ Non-spill pots.

▶ Brushes – variety of bristle sizes, blunt tipped.

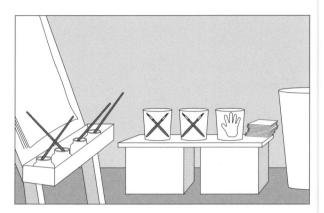

Drawing and Colouring

▶ Large and small crayons.

▶ Pencils, both coloured and plain, and pencil sharpeners.

▶ Markers.

▶ Paper – different sizes, textures and colours.

Modelling

▶ Safety scissors, sharp enough to cut with.

▶ Non-toxic glue.

▶ Variety of scrap materials, e.g. paper, card, fabric, three-dimensional objects, wood shavings, feathers.

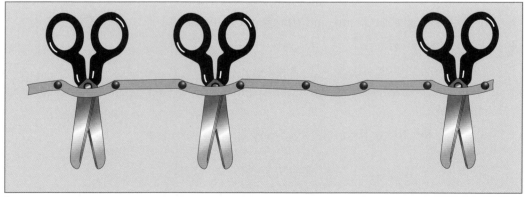

Storing scisssors

Playdough and Clay
▶ Ready-made playdough.
▶ Ingredients for children to make their own playdough.
▶ Recipe for playdough (see page 104).
▶ Clay.
▶ Working tools for cutting, rolling and making impressions.

Interest/Discovery Area

These are used to display articles relating to themes or topics dealt with on an ongoing basis, e.g. seasons and festivals, concepts such as movement and colour or practical topics such as transport or food.

The interest table can include items brought from home, from outdoors or from within the nursery or playgroup. It is a useful way to help children develop observation skills and creates a link between home and the centre.

Interest tables should be eye-catching, relevant and attractive to the children and they should feel that all their contributions to the display are valued.

Information and Communications Technology (ICT)

Children should have access to a range of ICT and digital technology in the ECCE environment. It provides the opportunity to access educational software to enhance and build on traditional methods of learning. Children can manipulate objects on screen in a fun way without fear of failure. They can experiment, repeat activities, discuss what they are doing and collaborate with peers and adults in a variety of new challenges that will extend and transform their learning.

Screen time should be limited and should not take the place of actual hands-on learning, but rather complement it. This should also be located in a quiet area.

Planning Play Activities

In a well-planned environment, children will practise skills they have learned while also trying out new skills. The sense of achievement and enhanced self-esteem that comes from mastering a skill brings confidence, a willingness to take risks and the ability to face new challenges. Children show most interest and concentration while engaged in child-initiated activities, but there is still a place for adult-initiated activities where specific skills and ways of using materials can be introduced. Activities are planned by the observant adult to extend learning and to encourage the child.

When planning for specific activities, remember to:

▸ Discuss with supervisors how this fits into the centre's curriculum planning (Aistear).

▸ Use knowledge of child development to plan activities which are developmentally appropriate.

▸ Be aware of what the child's existing skills are so that these can be reinforced and extended. This information is gained through regular observation of the child at play (see Chapters 6 and 7).

▸ Consider whether the activity will lay the foundations for future learning. Pouring sand in and out of containers is relaxing and refines hand–eye co-ordination, but it also develops mathematical and scientific concepts such as weight, shape, volume and capacity, texture, gravity and problem-solving.

▸ Consider whether the activity is best suited to an individual child or a group. Activities such as stories, rhymes, songs and music-making are suitable as group activities. Small groups generally work better than large ones, since each individual has the opportunity to participate.

▸ Take account of the space available for the activity and ensure that children are not restricted.

▸ Allow enough time to carry the activity through to the end. This includes preparation and tidying up time and children need to be involved in both.

▸ Check that staffing levels are adequate. Adults should be able to give their full and undivided attention to the activity.

▸ Check in advance that all necessary materials are available and in good order.

▸ Ensure that activities and materials used reflect an awareness of equality issues (see Chapter 14).

▸ Consider the health and safety of the children at all times.

▸ Link in to a current theme or topic if there is one.

Evaluating Play Activities

The cycle of 'Plan-Do-Review' is the basis of the planning process. Having observed and assessed the child's developmental and learning stage, an activity may be planned to reinforce or support this. The activity is carried out and should then be evaluated by the adult. Activities should be evaluated in terms of Aistear and the curriculum planning of the centre.

Evaluating the Adult Role

Adults guide and help children to make choices and decisions about their play, providing the scaffolding or framework within which learning can take place.

Evaluation of the adult role should consider all of the points on the checklist for planning as previously outlined. It should also:

▶ **Assess** what has been learned from planning and carrying out the activity:

— About the child or children

— About oneself – strengths and areas where there is room for improvement.

▶ **Identify** what could be done differently if doing the activity again, and why.

▶ **Recommend** follow-on activities which would further extend the child's interests, learning and development.

TASK

Aim: To apply the principle of Plan-Do-Review in early childhood practice.

▶ Observe a child at play. Use the information in Chapter 6 to help you decide on the most appropriate method.

▶ In your evaluation, assess what learning is evident in the play.

▶ Draw up a detailed activity plan for the child based on your assessment.

▶ Carry out the activity.

▶ Evaluate the plan in terms of the child's learning, the curriculum and your own role.

Making Play Materials

Even with a wide range of play materials available on the market, there are several reasons why early childhood workers need to be able to assemble their own on occasion.

▶ Cost – an item can often be made for a fraction of the cost of buying it, e.g. a simple mobile for a baby or finger puppets to aid in storytelling.

▶ The need for variety and change – interest is maintained when new material is frequently made available.

▶ Extending learning – e.g. a collection of household items can be assembled to extend learning about the properties of water.

▶ Catering for specific interests – e.g. if a child enjoys spending time dressing and undressing dolls, additional simple clothes can be made from scrap material.

▶ Availability – items which are not locally available can often be reproduced, e.g. matching cards, simple percussion instruments.

▶ Personalising a play item – e.g. a book about a particular child can be made from photographs.

Making play items does not usually require any specific skills on the part of the adult; it is more often about assembling things than actually making from scratch. Early childhood workers often tend to collect scrap materials for children's use and many of these can be converted into usable items. Examples of these are fabrics, paper, ribbon, wool, string, plastic bottles, yoghurt cartons, tins with lids – in fact, almost anything that is safe. Some materials will need to be bought, e.g. clear contact, different kinds of paper and glue as well as basic equipment such as a craft knife, steel ruler and sharp scissors.

The following are examples of play materials you could make.

To Develop Sensory Discrimination

▶ Fabric box with matching squares of different textures

▶ Mobile

▶ Matching sound boxes.

To Develop Language

▶ Wall frieze

▶ Books

▶ Puppets – sock, finger, wooden spoon, felt, paper bag.

To Develop Imagination and Creativity

▶ Doll clothes

▶ Collection of props for dressing up – jewellery, hairdressing props, post office

▶ Collection of painting tools – sponges, corks, string, feathers.

To Develop Physical Co-ordination

▶ Threading aid made from pasta or large buttons

▶ Tiddlywinks

▶ Skittles made from empty plastic bottles.

To Develop Rhythm and Make Music

▶ Drums – coffee or biscuit tins covered with contact

▸ Tambourine – pie plates filled with grains or rice and taped together

▸ Maracas – small plastic bottles containing seeds, pasta, sand.

ACTIVITY

Aim: To assess the play value of commercial and home-made play materials.

▸ Using some toy catalogues, work in small groups to list toys which would be suitable for children aged 6 months, 9 months, 2 years, 3 years and 5 years.

▸ Based on the information in this chapter, draw up a list which you could use to assess the suitability of some of the items you have chosen.

▸ Assess the items using your list.

▸ For each item chosen, suggest an alternative that could be easily made or assembled either from household articles or from junk/scrap material.

Recipe for Cooked Playdough

You will need 1 cup each of plain flour, water and salt and 1 tablespoon of cream of tartar ('Bextartar'). Mix all the ingredients together in a heavy-bottomed saucepan and cook over a very low heat, stirring gently all the time, until the mixture leaves the sides of the saucepan and comes together into a ball. Remove from the heat and leave to cool a little, then knead the mixture until you have a lovely soft, shiny lump of playdough which is not at all sticky. Once cool, this can be stored in an airtight container for quite a long time. Enjoy!

SUMMARY

▸ When providing play activities for babies in their first year, adults should ensure that they meet the need for stimulation, which involves interaction with others, particularly adults, and exploring things by themselves.

▸ Toddlers focus mainly on what objects can do, so provision for their play should focus on meeting this need.

▶ Play for children in the 3 to 6 years age group should be based on the provision of clearly defined interest areas, where similar types of materials are grouped together and children can freely choose what they want to play with.

▶ In the early years environment, specific activities may be planned to extend children's learning. These activities should be evaluated both in terms of their effectiveness in meeting curriculum objectives for the children and of the adult's own role.

References

Dodge, Diane T., 2002, *The Creative Curriculum for Early Childhood*, Washington: Teaching Strategies Inc.

Goldschmied, Elinor and Sonia Jackson, 1994, *People Under Three: Young Children in Day Care*, London: Routledge.

NCCA, 2006, *Aistear: The Early Childhood Curriculum Framework*, Dublin: NCCA.

Riddall-Leech, Sheila, 2009, *Heuristic Play: A Practical Guide for the Early Years*, Leamington Spa: Step Forward Publishing Ltd.

SECTION THREE

CHILD OBSERVATION

This section examines the subject of child observation, which is an essential professional skill for work with young children in an early childhood setting. Chapter 6 looks at what child observation is and outlines a range of observation methods. It gives examples for each of the methods described, analyses the advantages and disadvantages of each and suggests a format to use when writing up an observation.

Chapter 7 looks at completing an observation, interpreting the information gained and writing it up. It also examines observation as a tool for assessing children's learning and development through a child study. Suggestions are included for presenting an observations portfolio for assessment.

6

INTRODUCING CHILD OBSERVATION

Introduction

Assessment is one of the four areas of practice covered in *Aistear: The Early Childhood Curriculum Framework*, which defines assessment as 'the ongoing process of collecting, documenting, reflecting on and using information to develop rich portraits of children as learners in order to support and enhance their future learning'. Observation is one of the essential elements of professional assessment in early childhood settings. It provides the key to understanding a child's development, play and behaviour and forms the basis of future planning for the child. A wide range of observation methods can be used and it is important to be familiar with these. The method chosen will depend on the aim, the subject and the time available to the observer. In this chapter, the most commonly used observation methods are described (narrative, time sample, event sample, checklist, flow chart, histogram), their advantages and disadvantages are considered and an example of each is given.

What Is Child Observation?

Child observation is a professional skill which early childhood workers need to practise and perfect in order to enhance the quality of their work with children. Watching and listening to children is a routine part of early childhood care and education. We do this for several reasons:

▶ To ensure their safety

▶ To pay attention to meeting their different needs

▶ Because it can be informative, interesting or even amusing to listen to their conversations

▶ To understand behaviour

▶ To report back to parents at the end of the session

▶ To make provision for play

▶ To keep ourselves informed in a general way about the child's developmental progress.

There is an important difference, however, between watching and listening in this informal way and actually observing children in a formal, structured way. There is no doubt that in the busy environment of an early childhood setting, the adults can become so involved in routine work that they miss the opportunity to really take in what children are doing. Yet if we do not learn how to observe children properly, we will have little more than vague memories to guide us when we need to interpret a child's behaviour or play, assess a child's development or plan their curriculum.

The concept of developmentally appropriate practice means that our work with children is based on our knowledge of each individual child and awareness of different stages of development. This information is gained through observation.

For observations to be effective, the observer needs to know:

▶ Who is being observed

▶ Why she is being observed

▶ When the observation will take place

▶ Where the observation will take place

▶ What format will be used to record the information

▶ How the information will be interpreted

▶ How the information will be used.

The observer sets time aside in which to observe a particular child and focuses her attention on that child only during that time. The information is recorded accurately by the observer and will subsequently be used to help assess the child's developmental progress and for planning the adult's future work with the child while using certain observation methods. The observer does not participate or interact with the child during this time, since it is likely that the child's awareness of being studied may cause unnatural or unusual behaviour and influence the outcome of the observation.

ACTIVITY

Aim: To help you identify situations where observation would be useful or informative.

▶   In the large group, spend 1 minute brainstorming the things you would be interested to observe about children.

▶   Chart up the information.

▶   From this, compile your own list of what might be useful or achievable for you.

Descriptive Writing

Accurate and objective description is the key to effective observation. It is a skill that needs plenty of practice to perfect. This is one of the reasons why early childhood workers are usually required to complete a portfolio of observations while training.

Accurate Description

Everyday speech is rarely totally accurate, yet we are usually able to interpret what people are saying because many of the inaccuracies are accepted within society. For example, it is quite common to hear phrases such as 'I don't believe you!' or 'I nearly died!' used in everyday speech. While these are accepted common usage, it is essential that a more scientific approach is adopted when recording observations. The most common inaccuracies here have to do with assumptions made by the observer. Early observations are likely to contain such phrases as 'She is looking **at** the teacher' or 'She is pointing **at** the toy'. It is more accurate here to replace the word 'at' with '**toward**' or '**in the direction of**', since these do not make any assumptions about what is happening. It is easy to assume that you know what a child is looking at, but in fact you probably do not – she might appear to be looking at the teacher, while all the time she is watching a tiny speck of dust floating in the air!

The more information you have, the better equipped you are to make an assessment afterwards. It is important to note the small details and not to assume that these are unimportant. For example, if you are observing a child using a pencil, note which hand she is using as well as the details of her activity. While observing, use the present tense, as this helps to ensure accuracy. Even an hour later, you may have forgotten many important details.

Figure 6.1: Accurate Description

✓	✗
J is sitting at the table, holding a book in her left hand.	J was sitting at the table. She was holding a book.
She smiles and talks to herself as she turns the page.	She seems happy as she turns the page.
C is looking towards her.	C looked at her.
She is moving in the direction of the display table.	She walks over to the display table.

ACTIVITY

Aim: To help you to judge the accuracy of your description.

▶ Working with a partner or in a small group, spend around 5 minutes observing and recording in one or more of the following situations:

— An area where several people are gathered, e.g. the college or workplace canteen

— Watching part of a TV programme such as a soap opera

— One of the group acting out a simple role play such as entering the room, moving toward the window, picking up an object, etc.

▶ Try to accurately describe body movements, facial expressions and, if possible, language.

▶ Take turns reading your descriptions to one another.

▶ Discuss areas where the descriptions seem to match and where they do not.

▶ Do your descriptions contain interpretations?

▶ Compare notes with the rest of the group.

Confidentiality

Respecting the confidentiality of information gained when carrying out observations is an acknowledgement of the rights of the child and the family not to have information about them used or made available to others in any way. This means that in practice:

▶ Permission is requested from the parent or primary carer before starting to observe a child and an explanation is given as regards who is involved and who will have access to the information gained. In the case of a learner who is observing, this is usually done through the workplace supervisor. It is still the responsibility of the observer, however, to ensure that the permission is in place. This is clearly stated on all observations.

▶ The name of the child or the name of the centre where the observation has been carried out is never given on the observation of a student or learner. Abbreviations such as TC (Target Child) or the child's initials are used.

▶ All learner observations are signed by the learner and parent or workplace supervisor before being submitted for assessment.

▶ Observations are not discussed with outsiders. Any discussion which may be considered appropriate is carried out either with parents, in the workplace with colleagues or in certain classroom contexts, e.g. in a discussion of what has been learned from carrying out a particular observation. It is essential that there is group agreement that information discussed in this way during class time is not referred to outside that context, and that even in the classroom situation the child's anonymity is preserved.

Carrying Out an Observation

Having established through discussion with parents/management and co-workers that you are ready to get started on your observations, there are a number of practical issues which need to be considered. These are:

▶ Finding time and establishing a routine for observing

▶ Identifying the necessary equipment and taking notes

▶ Writing up the observation (dealt with in Chapter 7).

Finding Time

Developing observation skills is an ongoing process and needs to be integrated into the daily routine of the early childhood worker and into the practical work experience of the learner.

It is very important that the issue of setting time aside for observing is clarified at an early stage between all the parties concerned, be they learners, staff, volunteers, supervisors or course tutors, so that everyone can be quite clear about what is expected from them. It can happen that a learner or early childhood worker becomes so caught up in day-to-day routine tasks that time spent observing is seen as less important than time spent on other activities. However, the value of time spent observing is well documented in terms of the insights it provides into the individual child.

From the point of view of the learner, the best approach is to establish a routine right from the start of each work experience placement. This should be negotiated with the work placement supervisor, as should an agreement on a routine for handing over the completed work for reading, discussion and signing. It is not recommended that you observe at the same time every day, since observations should cover the whole range of experiences that make up the child's day – arrival, free play and structured play times, both indoors and outdoors, care routines such as nappy changing, preparation for sleep-time and transition times such as preparing for mealtime or going home.

Taking Notes – Necessary Equipment

The most essential tools for carrying out observations of children are your eyes and ears! Most often, the only other piece of equipment you will need is a notebook and a pencil. Learners should make sure to take these into placement every day, since opportunities to observe often present themselves unexpectedly. Observations can be carried out on individual children or on groups, but the essential skills are mastered by focusing first on the individual. This is known as the 'Target Child' approach, first developed by the Oxford Pre-School Research Group. The following shorthand code may be helpful for recording information while observing, or one can devise a code unique to themselves.

TC	=	Target Child (the child who is being observed)
C1	=	Another Child
C2	=	Another Child
A1	=	An Adult
A2	=	Another Adult
→	=	Speaks to

Examples of how these can be used in noting use of language:

TC	→ C1	'I'm the father and you're the mother'
C2	→ TC	'You're not coming to my party'
A1	→ TC	Comforts him
TC	→ A1	'Will you tie my apron please?'
A2	→ Group	Announces milk time
A1	→ TC + C1	Reads a story

Mastering codes such as these (or devising your own) will help you to capture as much detail as possible and they can be used in all of the observation methods outlined in this section. It is important when using a code to clearly identify this on the observation and to provide the code key for the benefit of the reader.

Observation Methods

The Narrative Method

At its simplest, this involves recounting exactly what the child is doing and saying while being observed. The narrative observation is written in the present tense and involves setting time aside to watch and listen carefully for the designated period, which can be anything from 5 minutes to half an hour. This written record of the child's activity is recorded in rough form and written up as soon as possible afterwards. It is important that each observation session records everything the child does or says in minute detail. Thus, even if you want to observe the child's language you will describe any physical or other activity that may take place while you are observing.

Observing at the sandpit

> **Example of a Narrative (see Appendix 4 for an example of a full narrative observation)**
>
> TC is standing at the sand tray, holding a sieve with her right hand and a spoon in her left full palmar grasp. Both her feet are planted firmly on the floor. Bending slightly forward at the waist, she is scooping sand up in the spoon and raising her left arm and is pouring the sand through the sieve.

A shorter form of the narrative is the snapshot observation or anecdotal record, used to give a brief account of a specific incident. This is recorded as or soon after it occurs. While anecdotal records may be short, they can be collected in a series over a period of time and are used to build up a picture of the child. This method could be used, for example, over a week to observe a child settling in on arrival in the nursery or playgroup. At the end of that time, all the anecdotes are put together in sequence and the information is evaluated. Anecdotal records may also form the basis of a child study.

Uses
▶ When beginning to develop observation skills, as it trains the observer to be observant!
▶ When it is possible to set time aside without interruption, e.g. in the case of a learner who is on work experience placement, or when there are enough staff in the room to allow for one person taking time out.

Advantages of the Narrative Method
▶ It trains the observer to become aware of the small details of a child's actions, interactions and language.
▶ No unusual equipment is necessary – just pen and paper, eyes and ears.
▶ It gives a comprehensive and detailed record to the observer. It is non-selective in that the observer writes down everything that she has seen and heard the child do and say, rather than picking out specific actions to note.
▶ The observer starts out with no preconceived ideas or expectations about what will occur; the observation is recorded in a naturally unfolding situation.

Disadvantages of the Narrative Method
▶ It can be difficult to catch everything which occurs during the observation time, particularly during the early stages when the observer is not skilled and will not have developed a system of note-taking or codes for speed writing.
▶ It may give an atypical picture of the child, since it does not take into account factors such as tiredness, hunger, time of day or other factors that may influence

how a child behaves at a particular time. For this reason, it is very important to note as much relevant preliminary information about the child as possible.

▸ Because the observation time is limited, an incident may be taken out of context and therefore may be misinterpreted.

▸ It can be difficult for the observer to find periods of completely uninterrupted time during a busy daily schedule.

Time Sampling Method

A time sample observation gives a picture of a child's activities, social group and language interactions at fixed periods throughout a session.

Figure 6.2: Time Sample to Discover More About a Child's Activities in the Playgroup

Time	Actions	Social Group	Language
9.30	Sitting on floor completing a jigsaw puzzle.	C	Hey – look! This bit looks funny here! Give me that!
10.00	Working on puzzle. Pointing towards unfinished edge.	C	Put it there! Put it there – No...there!
10.30	Sand tray. Plunging both hands into sand and churning it up.	E D	I'm going to pour some into this (cup).
11.00			
11.30			
12.00			
12.30			

(The child is observed every 30 minutes over a 3-hour session.)

Since it is not always possible to observe continuously, this method enables the observer to take notes at pre-set regular intervals using pre-set headings, such as:

▶ **Actions** (what the child is doing)

▶ **Social Group** (who the child is with)

▶ **Language** (what the child is saying).

It is important that the time set for the observation is decided in advance, and can be for as little as half an hour or as long as a full day, depending on the aim of the observation. For example, an observation of a child's spontaneous play could be carried out over half a day, while a 30-minute observation could be used to discover something about the child's interactions with other children. The observation intervals are also decided in advance, e.g. you could decide to observe the child at 10-minute intervals for an hour, or at half-hour intervals over a 3-hour period. This would give a sample of the child's activities during that time.

Uses

▶ When there is a concern about a child who appears quiet or withdrawn, the time sample will provide evidence to either back up or disprove the concern. (It is important that this concern should be clearly stated at the beginning of the observation.)

▶ When there is a lot of activity, making it difficult for the observer to focus on a child for a long uninterrupted period.

▶ To observe a child's spontaneous play.

▶ To assess language and social development.

Advantages of Time Sampling

▶ It gives a good overall picture of a child's activities over a period of time.

▶ It can be completed without much interruption to the daily staff routine.

▶ There is a specific focus on the child's social interactions and language.

Disadvantages of Time Sampling

▶ The observer may miss out on specific behaviours which may be important to note.

▶ It is possible to forget to take the sample in a situation where the observer is busy with other tasks (a kitchen timer can be useful here!).

ACTIVITY

Make a list of examples of when a time sample observation could be useful in an early childhood setting.

Event Sample/Frequency Count Method

An event sample observation records events involving a particular child whose **behaviour is causing concern**. It is used to study the frequency of particular behaviours and the conditions under which they occur. This observation is carried out over a number of sessions or days.

The adults first need to define what their concerns are about the child's behaviour before carrying out the observation. Examples could include aggressive or disruptive behaviour such as hitting, biting, kicking or using aggressive language.

The observer documents the behaviour as it occurs, rather than at pre-set intervals as in the time sample. Influential factors such as time of day, social group, whether or not the behaviour was provoked, the antecedent (what happened just before the incident) and consequences of the behaviour are also recorded. This shows at a glance how frequently the behaviour occurs and under what conditions. Event samples can often show surprising results. A child who has been observed over several sessions may well show fewer incidents of unacceptable behaviour than the adults expected. There may be also be evidence of provocation by another which had hitherto gone unnoticed.

Figure 6.3: Event Sample

Date	Time	Duration	Provoked/ unprovoked	Who with	Antecedent if known	Description of behaviour	Consequence
Jan 3	9.20	30 secs	UP	Alone	None	TC walks over to the bricks and sweeeps them onto the floor. Kicks them around.	A goes to speak to him. Asks him to pick them up. TC begins to cry.
Jan 3	10.05	1 min.	P	FJ	J has pulled the bowl of crayons over to herself. They had both been using them out of the same box.	TC pulls the crayons back. Reaches over and grabs J's picture, tears it up. Pushes her in the chest.	J cries. A walks over to comfort J. Asks TC why he has torn the picture. Tells him to leave the table.

> *Example*
> Event sample (Fig. 6.3) to document the behaviour of TC, aged 2 years 11 months.
> CONCERN: TC has been attending the nursery for over 2 years. He has recently begun to act aggressively toward some of the other children; in particular there have been incidents with pulling hair, grabbing toys and kicking. Several children have become upset as a result of these.

Uses

▸ To collect information when there is concern about aggressive or disruptive behaviour

▸ To help adults interpret children's behaviour in its overall context

▸ To form the basis of planning to manage the behaviour.

ACTIVITY

SCENARIO

TC is aged 3 years and 8 months. She started in playgroup 3 months ago and attends five mornings per week. She had previously been minded by her granny all day while both her parents were at work; now she goes there in the afternoons. She has a brother aged 7 months who is still minded by her granny.

TC appeared to settle in well at first, but things have changed over the past month or so. She cries every morning on arrival and regularly gets into a fight with another child within the first half hour. During the session she frequently fights with other children over different things, kicking, hitting, screaming at staff and children and pulling hair; this often ends in tears all round.

Staff are concerned about this and have decided to observe TC using the event sample method.

▸ **In a small group, discuss the advantages of using an event sample observation in this situation.**

▸ **How could this observation method help staff to learn more about TC's behaviour?**

▸ **What further information could be useful to staff when preparing to observe? Consider family factors here.**

Advantages of Event Sampling

▸ It helps to isolate the behaviour which is causing concern.

▸ It clarifies the context in which the behaviour occurs – who else was involved? What was the antecedent? Was the incident provoked? In this way, the behaviour rather than the child is seen as the problem.

▸ It helps to clarify whether or not the adult's concern was justified.

▸ It can show significant patterns in behaviour occurrences, e.g. time of day (are tiredness or hunger relevant?), which adult is present, which children are involved.

▸ It can help the adult to develop strategies to support the child.

Disadvantages of Event Sampling

▸ It is time consuming.

▸ The child may notice that her behaviour is becoming a focus of attention, potentially causing further occurrences.

▸ As there is no time limit, it is possible for the adult to influence the outcome by allowing the observation to continue until she observes what she expected in the first place.

▸ The observation record takes no account of external or family factors which may influence the child's behaviour. However, background detail should do so.

Checklist Method

A checklist is a bit like a shopping list! It shows at a glance a range of skills or behaviours, arranged in a logical order on a list, which the observer ticks off if and when they are observed.

Checklists are drawn from recognised developmental guides (accessible in most good child development textbooks) and the source should be clearly referenced at the end of the checklist.

The skills or behaviours listed will be easily observed, e.g. physical or social skills. In addition to ticking off items on a list, the observer may indicate what evidence there is to justify the item being ticked. For example, if a tick has been placed beside 'Plays parallel to others using similar materials', the evidence could be 'Sat beside P using Duplo™ from a pile in the centre of the mat'.

It should be possible to take in the information on a checklist at a glance. The completed checklist should indicate only those behaviours which have been observed. If it is not possible to observe certain behaviours, e.g. something which is not a feature of the child's day in nursery or playgroup, such as going to bed or certain mealtime rituals, these items should be indicated by some agreed symbol (e.g. N/O for not observed) rather than being left blank. As with all codes, this should be explained to the reader. It is possible to transfer data collected in a narrative observation onto a checklist if it is necessary to store and share the information in an easily accessible format.

Guidelines for Preparing a Checklist Observation

▸ Items listed should be short and descriptive using non-judgemental language (e.g. 'jumps over a 10-centimetre high object' rather than 'jumps high').

▸ Items listed should be positive (e.g. 'separates from parent with difficulty' rather than 'clings to parent').

▸ The checklist should be easily understood by all users.

▸ Checklists should be drawn up objectively and not based on knowledge of a particular child.

Uses

▸ When it is only necessary to find out whether a behaviour or skill is present rather than the degree to which it is present.

▸ When focusing attention on a specific area of development.

▸ When accurate baseline information is required, e.g. to record the skills of a child who has just started attendance at a service.

Figure 6.4: Checklist: Social Development. Age: 18 months
Put a ✓ for skills you have observed. Write N/O for skills you have not observed. Leave all others blank.

Skill		Evidence	Date
Plays contentedly alone	✓	Played on the kitchen floor for 10 minutes with some blocks	22/10/10
Is eager to be independent	✓	Said 'me do it' and tried to put on wellies	22/10/10
May indicate toilet needs by restlessness	N/O		

Source: Meggitt (2006: 59)

Advantages of Checklists

▸ They are quick and easy to use and give information at a glance.

▸ The observer is not limited to a short space of time to gain the information; the observation can be carried out over several days.

▸ Checklists can be completed in a variety of situations, both indoors and out.

▸ No specialised equipment is needed by the observer.

▶   Through regularly consulting developmental guides and the application of theory into practice, the observer becomes familiar with the range of normative development and its limitations.

Disadvantages of Checklists

▶   The information given is very limited. Checklists lack detail on duration of activity and behaviour and there is no description. Since they do not record everything that happens, they may leave out important information.

▶   It is possible that if a checklist is drawn up with a particular child in mind, the list will only include those skills or behaviours which the observer is sure the child will 'score' positively on.

▶   It is tempting to view a checklist as a kind of test which a child has to pass; the observer should not place a tick against items which she has been told the child has done or which she seems to remember having seen at an earlier stage.

ACTIVITY

Aim: To draw up a series of checklists for practical use.

▶   Use a developmental guide to draw up a checklist which could be used to assess an area of development in a specific age range, e.g. physical development of a 3-year-old.

▶   Use the guidelines on preparing a checklist observation on page 120.

▶   Different checklists can be drawn up ranging over a variety of ages and areas of development and these can be shared among the group.

▶   Use one of the checklists to carry out an observation in your workplace. In a subsequent session, evaluate how useful it was in helping you to gain insights into the child observed. Include this in the 'Personal Learning' section of the observation.

Movement or Flow Chart Observations

A flow chart depicts the movements of a child through the play area over a specified period of time. The information is shown on a plan of the room or play area. Lines and arrows are drawn onto the plan, indicating the child's movements and giving the time of each. It is sometimes known as a 'trail' or 'tracking' observation.

It shows the child's use of the available space and equipment/materials and indicates her play preferences. It can form the basis of an observation of an individual child or an analysis of the use of the play space.

Uses

▸   To show a child's use of play space and materials

▸   To plan for play provision.

Figure 6.5: Flow Chart Showing a Child's Use of Play Area During a Morning Session

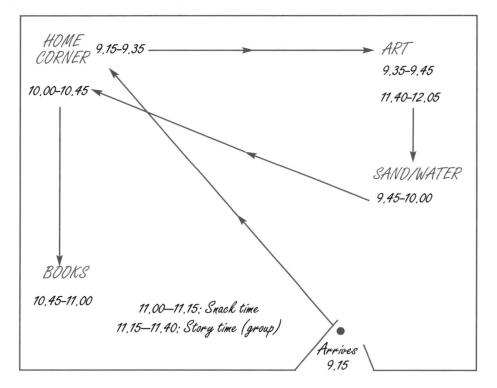

Self-initiated activity:	
Sand/water	15 minutes
Art	35 minutes
Home corner	1 hour 5 minutes
Alone in book area	15 minutes
Adult-initiated activity in group:	
Story time	25 minutes
Snack time	15 minutes

The flow chart gives a general picture of how the child has spent her morning in the playroom. The information can be summarised easily from the plan.

Advantages of a Flow Chart

▸ It is useful for showing the play preferences of the child.

▸ It shows the extent to which different areas or equipment are being used.

▸ Different children can be observed on different occasions to show the play preferences within the group.

▸ It can be used in combination with other observation types, e.g. narrative, to build up a picture of a child's activity.

Disadvantages of a Flow Chart

▸ The information collected is very general. For example, even if you know that a child has spent 1 hour in the home corner, you have no information on what she actually did there, with whom she played or spoke to. It is not possible to make any kind of assessment of the quality of the child's experiences when using this method.

▸ It takes a considerable amount of the adult's time to complete, as the child's movements have to be followed and recorded.

▸ The information can be difficult to interpret if the child is very active and moves constantly from one activity to another.

TASK

▸ Draw up a plan of a play area in your workplace.

▸ Observe and record a child's movements during a play session using a flow chart.

▸ Evaluate the observation.

▸ In the section on 'Personal Learning', evaluate the observation method.

Bar and Pie Charts/Histograms

Information about a group of children can be shown on a pie or bar chart. It is useful when compiling information about the group or the centre for use by the staff team, parents or managers.

Bar and pie charts can be used to collate information on topics such as:

- Which piece of equipment in the play area is most in demand at a given time.
- The nutritional content of the children's lunch boxes.
- Are there significant differences in the play choices of boys and girls at different ages?

This information can be collected over a period of time and used in overall assessments of the centre's policies. For example, early childhood workers may be aware in a general way that dairy products are not appearing regularly in the children's lunch boxes, but may not be sure of the full extent of this. An observation carried out over a 5-day period and presented on a chart can give concise information about this. This could then lead to a discussion with parents of the need to include dairy products in the child's diet and why, a promotion of dairy products on the noticeboard or a series of activities with the children on the same theme.

Figure 6.6: Collecting Information on Children's Play Choices

Child		Equipment						
		Lego	Dolls	Farm	Kitchen	Blocks	Puzzles	Sand
Patrick	m	✓		✓			✓	
Amy	f		✓	✓		✓		✓
Sinéad	f		✓	✓		✓		✓
Conor	m	✓					✓	
Jack	m	✓		✓			✓	✓
Katie	f		✓				✓	
Alice	f	✓		✓			✓	
James	m	✓			✓	✓	✓	✓
Awor	f					✓	✓	
Sophie	f					✓		✓
Ngor	m	✓	✓		✓		✓	✓
Emma	f	✓		✓			✓	✓
Adam	m	✓			✓	✓	✓	

Uses

- To assess in a general way whether the provision is working effectively for all the children and parents involved.
- When easy-to-read information is needed, e.g. to present at committee or parent meetings.

Example

The aim of this observation is to record the play choices of a group of boys and girls aged between 3 and 4 years and assess whether there are any significant differences between the sexes in their choices.

The children are observed over a period of 1 week and rough notes are taken about who played with what. A simple way to do this would be to list the children's names, indicating whether they are male or female, list the equipment being observed and place a tick against the child's name whenever a particular piece of equipment is used. The notes would look something like those in Figure 6.6.

The information can then be presented using a pie chart to show the overall picture and bar charts to show the gender preferences.

Figure 6.7a: Pie Chart: Play Choices – All

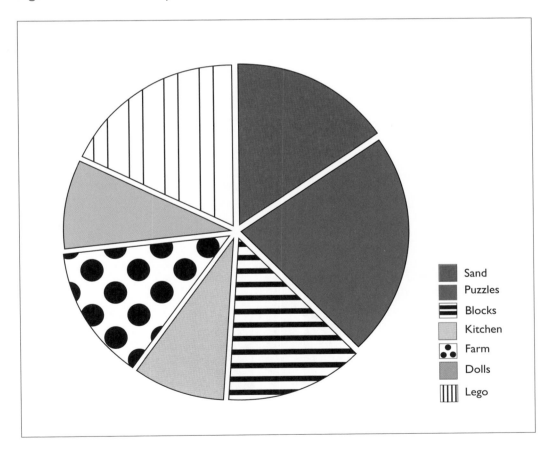

Figure 6.7b: Bar Chart: Play Choices – Boys

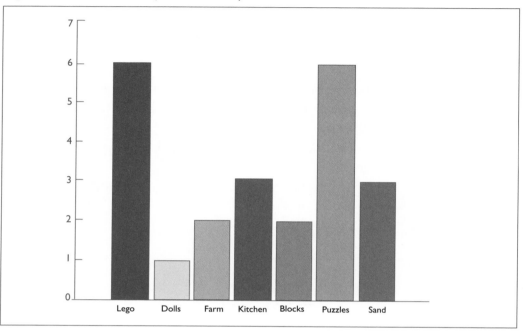

Figure 6.7c: Bar Chart: Play Choices – Girls

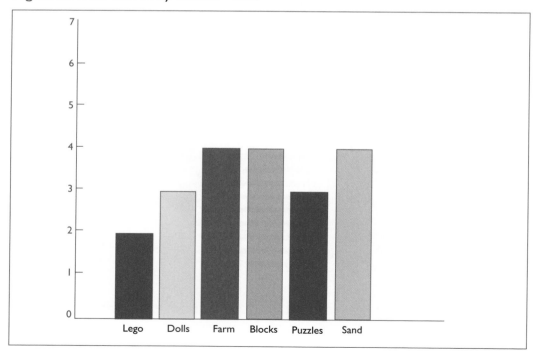

TASK

Aim: To use bar chart and pie chart observations to compile information about an early childhood centre

Plan and carry out an observation of this type at work. Discuss possible themes with your supervisor in order to make sure that the completed charts will be of use to the centre.

Audio/Visual Observations

Recording is a useful way of capturing the richness and complexity of a child's language when it is not practical to attempt to write it all down.

Some important points to note when using a recorder are as follows.

▶ Children have a right to know that you are recording them and to be involved in the discussion about this.

▶ The child should feel comfortable in the presence of the recorder; it is not unusual for children (as with adults) to overreact to being recorded, giving an atypical picture to the observer.

▶ Permission should be sought from the parents, who should clearly understand why this observation method is being used.

▶ As with all observations, preliminary information, including the purpose of the recording and where it took place, should be entered on an attached sheet along with the evaluation. For learners who are completing an observations portfolio, this information should be included in the file.

The above also apply when using film, and in addition the observer should note the following.

▶ Filmed recordings can be useful when a detailed observation is required in special cases, e.g. if there is a serious concern about a child's behaviour and specialist help is being sought.

▶ It is not possible to protect the identity of a child on film. This should always be clarified with parents/carers when seeking permission to carry out the observation and it is not recommended that a learner would seek to use this method at all for training purposes where the film would be made available to people outside the service.

SUMMARY

▸   Child observation is an essential skill for working with young children. It involves careful, systematic watching and listening to a child for a specified length of time and with a particular aim or purpose in mind and accurately recording what the child does and says during that time.

▸   Observation enables the early childhood worker to assess a child's developmental progress and to interpret needs, interests and behaviours. It helps in planning to meet these identified needs through evaluating workplace provision, routines and procedures, and provides accurate records for sharing with parents and, if required, with other professionals.

▸   Confidentiality should always be maintained.

▸   Several observation methods are commonly used for recording information about children's play and development. The method chosen depends on the aim, the subject and the time available to the observer. There are advantages and disadvantages to each of these. Learners need to practise using different methods in order to refine their skills.

References

Meggitt, C., 2006, *Child Development: An Illustrated Guide*, 2nd edn, Oxford: Heinemann.

7

OBSERVATION IN PRACTICE

AREAS COVERED

▶ Why Observation Is Important
▶ Writing Up the Observation
▶ Interpretations and Judgements
▶ Observation as Assessment – A Child Study
▶ Presenting a Portfolio of Observations

Introduction

This chapter describes how an observation may be written up. It examines the interpretation of information gained through observation and looks at observation as a tool for assessing children's learning and development through a child study. Guidelines on presenting a portfolio of observations for assessment are offered in accordance with the requirements of the FETAC Level 5 Certificate in Childcare. The activities suggested in the chapter may be used as a basis for compiling such a portfolio.

Why Observation Is Important

It is through carrying out observations that you will be able to relate the theoretical to the practical elements of your training course – in fact, this is where much of the theory comes alive and is memorable, simply because it becomes evident in the behaviour and play of individual children with whom you are working. Observation reveals to us and helps us to understand and interpret the varied and complex ways in which children play, develop and learn.

Systematic and regular observation enables the observer to:

▶ Make assessments of children's developmental progress and maintain accurate written records for use within the workplace setting, for sharing with parents and, if required, with other professionals.

▶ Record interactions between the child, other children and adults.

▶ Interpret and assess a child's needs, interests and behaviours.

▶ Plan a high-quality curriculum for the child based on the outcome/analysis of the observation.

▶ Assess workplace routines on an ongoing basis to determine how they meet the changing needs of the children.

▶ Determine the effectiveness of curriculum provision and room and equipment layout.

▶ Initiate and maintain practice which is developmentally appropriate.

Observation should therefore be seen as part of a cycle which includes the following:

▶ **Observation:** Observe the child while engaged in activity.

▶ **Analysis:** Evaluate the outcome, identifying skills, strengths, difficulties and needs.

▶ **Planning:** Plan experiences to consolidate and extend existing areas and help develop others.

▶ **Implementation:** Carry out the plans.

▶ **Observation:** Observe the child again and evaluate the outcomes, starting the cycle anew.

Figure 7.1: Observation Cycle

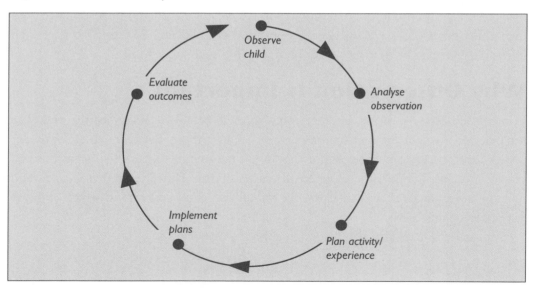

Writing Up the Observation

When writing an observation it is advisable to use a format which clearly sets out the necessary background information and clarifies for both the observer and reader who is being observed, where and why. This could contain the following information.

1.	Observation number	10.	Child observed
2.	Date	11.	Brief description of the child observed
3.	Method and media used	12.	The observation aim and rationale
4.	Time started/finished	13.	The observation
5.	Number of children present	14.	The evaluation
6.	Number of adults present	15.	Personal learning gained
7.	Permission obtained from	16.	Recommendations
8.	The setting	17.	References and bibliography
9.	The immediate context	18.	Signatures

Observation Number and Date (1, 2)

When observations are carried out regularly in an early childhood setting as part of care and education practice, it is important that they are numbered and dated, as this can help to give both staff and parents a picture of a child's progression within a particular area and can clearly indicate a sequence being followed. This can:

▶   Facilitate continuity in the event of staff changeovers

▶   Provide accurate information for sharing with parents

▶   Provide clear records where there are concerns about child abuse (see Chapter 9)

▶   Show the outcomes of play planning and provision

▶   Form part of the assessment of the adult's work with the child.

In the case of a learner who is presenting a portfolio of observations for assessment, it is usual to number and date them in sequence. This helps when preparing an overview of the portfolio contents and indicates which criteria have been met within the work.

Method and Media Used (3)

The method chosen should be appropriate to the information being sought in the observation. Observation methods are detailed in Chapter 6. The media used will vary depending on the particular observation being carried out. The most commonly used medium will be pen and paper, particularly in the early stages of developing observation skills. Other media would be audio tape, which can be useful, e.g. when recording children's language, or video tape, e.g. where there is a specific problem with a child's behaviour (see Chapter 6).

Time Started/Finished (4)

This should be indicated precisely. In some cases, e.g. a narrative, the observation will last for a number of minutes only, a time sample may take place over half a day, while a checklist or event sample may be carried out over a number of days.

Number of Children Present (5)/Number of Adults Present (6)

This is important for several reasons. If the ratio of children to adults is high, it may affect the observer's ability to remain uninvolved, either because a child is interacting with the observer or because the observer may have to set the observation aside and become involved with the children. It may also help to put some of the child's actions/reactions into context.

Permission Obtained From (7)

It is essential that permission is sought either directly from the child's parent/carer or indirectly through the workplace supervisor. In the interests of confidentiality, the person's role rather than name should be used, e.g. The Child's Mother or The Nursery Supervisor, rather than Ms Smith or Mr O'Reilly.

The Setting (8)

This refers to the type of centre in which the observation is to be carried out, e.g. a primary school, playgroup, nursery, etc. For example, a description of the setting could read:

The observation took place in a community playgroup which is open for 3 hours per day, 4 days per week, and caters for 12 children of both sexes, whose ages range from 3 years to 4 years 6 months.

The Immediate Context (9)

This is a description of exactly where in the setting the observation took place. It defines the context in which the child is observed and should contain information on what she is doing, who she is with and, if necessary, what has just occurred. For example:

The child J is playing in the kitchen corner with two other girls, F and C. J has invited the other two over to play with her and has just announced that she will be the mammy and the others are the children. The three girls are sitting at a table with some cups, saucers and plates. There is a large cardboard box on the floor beside them, which J has referred to as the dishwasher.

Child Observed (10)

When a learner is completing an observation, the child's actual name should not be used for reasons of confidentiality (see Chapter 6). Either an initial or the code TC (Target Child) is acceptable.

Brief Description of the Child Observed (11)

This should include details of the child's sex, age in years and months and any other factual information which will be relevant to the observation. This could include details of the child's health, family details (if known) such as place in family or number of siblings, how long she has been in the centre and staff concerns, if any. For example:

J is female, aged 3 years and 4 months. She has been attending the centre for 5 mornings a week since she was 2 years old. She is in good health generally and rarely misses a day. She lives locally with her mother, father and her younger brother who attends the toddler section of the centre twice a week. She drops in to see him from time to time. Both her parents are in full-time employment and she spends the afternoons along with her brother in the house of a local childminder who collects her at around 1.00 p.m. It is planned that she will start primary school in September of next year.

The Observation Aim and Rationale (12)

This should explain what it is that you hope to learn from carrying out the observation and why. It should clearly relate to the child being observed and to the specific situation the child is in at that particular time. For example:

My aim is to assess the language development of the child J while she is involved in a role play in the kitchen corner. I am doing this because J seems to spend a lot of time in role-play situations at the moment. Role play offers many opportunities for language and I hope to assess both her verbal and non-verbal communication as well as noting how she uses language to socialise.

The Observation (13)

The main body of the observation should be focused on the child. Write down everything that you see and hear the child do according to the observation method chosen. You will need to mention what the carer is doing only if it directly affects the child and what is happening during the observation. Essentially, you are recording in detail the actions, interactions and language of the child.

The time the observation lasts will depend on the child, the aim and the observation method chosen as well as on unforeseen circumstances. If starting off with the narrative method, 5 minutes is probably enough initially, but this should increase to 10 or 15 minutes and upwards as the technique becomes more familiar; often the child will dictate the time as an activity may finish naturally. For an example of a narrative observation, see Appendix 3. For other observation methods, see Chapter 6.

The Evaluation (14)

This is where you analyse what you have observed. Essentially you are asking three key questions:

▶ What was I looking for?

▶ What did I find?

▶ What does it mean?

It is useful to start by briefly summarising your aim, i.e. what you were looking for – this will help to focus the evaluation. You then need to ask what you found during the observation. This involves careful re-reading of the observation with the aim in mind. For example, if you had aimed to observe the child's physical development, then you would look for examples of where this is demonstrated, including both gross motor and fine manipulative skills.

The next stage is to ask what all this means in terms of the child's present stage of development. The usual way to make sense of what you have observed is to compare it with what is considered appropriate for the age using a developmental checklist or guide. It is essential that you use acknowledged sources which are clearly referenced and not what you think is normal. Most textbooks which deal with holistic child development contain such information, giving a detailed guide to expected developmental milestones at each stage, helping you to make valid assessments and demonstrating that there is a wide range of behaviour, learning, skills and development within the norm.

Depending on what source is used, the information may be organised in different ways, but essentially will cover one or more of the areas of development:

Physical
Intellectual
Language   } P I L E S
Emotional
Social.

▶ **Physical development** includes gross motor skills such as walking, running, climbing and riding a bike as well as fine motor skills like using bricks, completing puzzles, threading beads or using a pencil or crayon – the skills which involve co-ordination of eye and hand movements.

▶ **Intellectual or cognitive development** covers the development of the child's thinking and includes sensory development, concept formation, problem-solving, memory and concentration and the development of creativity and imagination.

▶ **Language development** includes a child's non-verbal and verbal communication, expressive language, understanding of spoken language, vocabulary acquisition and understanding of the rules of language.

▶ **Emotional development** includes the expression of feelings, development of self-esteem, self-confidence, autonomy and responsibility.

▶ **Social development** covers the forming of relationships, social play, interactions with others, both adults and children, and the development of social skills such as eating, dressing, undressing and toileting.

▶ **Children's behaviour** is usually included within the last two areas.

Detailed information on a child's development in each of these areas gives us an all-round picture of the child's development at a given point in time. There is, however, a danger that in using guides of this type we may build up an expectation about the child and therefore perceive the observation as a kind of test which the child must pass or fail.

No child demonstrates all the skills and behaviours on cue. It is important to note the pattern and sequence of development. It is also important to remember that development is holistic. One area of development may be well on target while another may be slightly delayed. This is quite common in young children. For example, during the period when a child first begins to express language clearly, another area of development may be put on hold, so to speak, while the child's whole being concentrates on developing language.

Reference to child development theory is important here. Look for examples of where your observation appears to either agree with or contradict a theory that you have studied. For example, you have observed that a child of 18 months has put an object in and out of the same container several times. Your reading of child development tells you that children learn through repeating actions. Your evaluation here could refer to Jean Piaget, whose cognitive development theory was based on the notion of the child as an active learner who needs first-hand experiences of objects to inform him of what they can do and what he can do with them. You have seen evidence of this in the child's repetitive actions.

You could also examine aspects of whatever play the child is engaged in. Your discussion could include consideration of why a particular activity is provided for the child, whether it is suitable for the child's stage of development, the type of play and stage of play the child is engaged in. This can provide the observer with a clear insight into the child's interests and abilities. It shows the child's play progression, where support from the adult needs to be provided and to what extent the available equipment and materials are meeting the child's learning needs. This can form the basis of future planning for the child.

Personal Learning Gained (15)

In this section the focus is on what the observer has learned by carrying out the observation. This can cover learning about:

▶ The age group of the child observed

▶ Child development in general and the application of theory in practice

▶ The play provision available to the children

▶ The difficulties and distractions encountered in carrying out an observation

▶ The advantages or limitations of the observation method used.

In fact, it can cover just about any kind of learning which has taken place, but should not repeat information that was previously known about the child.

Recommendations (16)

This section offers an opportunity for the observer to make recommendations or suggestions about how the child's development could be supported. This could include areas such as the provision of specific play materials or equipment to enrich play or to enhance learning in a particular area, opportunities for specific experiences such as outings or outdoor play, or the application of a particular behaviour management strategy.

References and Bibliography (17)

See Appendix 2.

Signatures (18)

The work should always be signed and dated by the observer. In the case of a learner presenting a portfolio of observations, the work should also be signed and dated by a workplace supervisor or parent – usually by whoever permission has been sought from. This authenticates the work and verifies that it has been carried out as stated by the observer. After it has been assessed, it is also signed by the tutor. The time that elapses between carrying out the observation and signing it should generally be no more than a couple of weeks, otherwise the facts about the child will be outdated.

Interpretations and Judgements

Interpreting Information

When observing, there is always a likelihood that you will interpret what you see rather than simply record it. The most obvious example of this is the way in which we interpret the feelings of another. Your observation record should contain only facts and not opinions. For example, when recording the details of a child who is leafing through a book, you might find yourself writing something like 'He seems happy as he turns the pages.' This is your interpretation of what you see. It would be more appropriate to simply state 'He is smiling as he turns the pages.' Other common examples of this are:

'He is delighted to see his mother walking in.'
'He is getting hungry now – it is almost dinner time.'
'He is upset because she won't sit beside him.'

In all of these examples, the recorder has made some assumption about how the child is feeling and why. If an observation is to contain an accurate record of what the observer has seen and heard during the observation period, then statements like these are clearly out of place since they have not been either seen or heard, but assumed by the writer.

Making Judgements

Judgements can be influenced by your own childhood experiences and memories of how you felt in particular situations. For example, seeing a child standing alone may bring back memories of a lonely time in your childhood and lead you to assume that the child is lonely or forlorn, thus causing an emotional reaction in you which is likely to influence the outcome of your observation.

It is also possible that your work will contain some value judgements based on preconceived ideas you may have about a child's background. This could include family type, social class or culture. For example, because you know that a child lives in a small apartment with no garden, you might assume that he gets little physical exercise and use this as an explanation for his lack of competence in vigorous outdoor play. An observation of an African child might contain the assumption that her language development is delayed because of the fact that her first language is not English. Judgements are also easily made on the basis of comments you have heard made about the child by fellow workers, for example:

'He can be very aggressive at times.'
'She's a real little attention seeker.'
'I know for a fact that he never gets to bed on time.'
'I heard Laura say that she's a TV addict – it's no wonder her attention span is so bad.'

Comments like these can influence the observer without his realising it. An observation may appear to confirm what you thought you already knew about the child simply because you were influenced by the opinions of others and were selective in what you recorded.

Objectivity

Even the most experienced observers have difficulty remaining objective at all times. The fact is that as you get to know a child better, you will have certain expectations with regard to his abilities and behaviours and will sometimes deny the evidence of your own eyes. Your expectation that a child will perform a task in a particular way will probably be based on your knowledge that he has done it this way many times before. The danger is that you will carry this expectation through into your observation, and instead of recording what you actually see happening you record what you think is happening, i.e. what you have seen happen on previous occasions.

Factors Which Can Influence Objectivity

▶ **Previous knowledge of the child** – you may feel that you know this child so well that you have nothing new to learn here or that you can predict how the child will behave based on previous experiences.

▶ **Emotional responses to the child** – how you feel about him. This can be either positive or negative and is an area that you need to explore regularly and frequently, either with work colleagues or in your class group, so that you can identify and deal with possible bias on your part either toward or against a child.

▶ **The aim or purpose of the observation** – are you looking for something and determined to find it? When learning to become a child observer, many people perceive the observation as a sort of test which the child has to pass in order to make it appear that the observation has succeeded. It is important to become aware of this and remain open – simply record what you see and hear, not what you expect to see and hear.

▶ **Previous experiences** – experiences you may have had, either of this child or of an earlier observation with the same aim but carried out on a different child.

A Child Study

A **child study** is a series of observations carried out on the same child over a period of time, examining the different areas of his development. Several observation methods may be incorporated into the study, since the child will be observed at different times in a variety of situations. The study is used to:

▶ Create an integrated developmental picture of a child at a particular point in time.

▶ Identify the child's abilities and strengths for the purpose of promoting and supporting him to develop to his full potential. This is informed by an analysis of the observations and an understanding and application of child development theory.

A.   A Child Study Proposal

Table 7.1: Suggested Guidelines for Carrying Out a Child Study

Introduction	This should include an aim and rationale specific to the child you have chosen for your study.
Profile of the child	Description of the child (see page 133) to include additional appropriate details and comments about the following – family, health, education, diet, routine and any other information you consider relevant.
Timeframe	Usually over a week or so.
Location	In the early years service, at home or a combination.
Observation methods	Which methods you will use to observe which areas of development and the reason for your choice. You should use a range of observation methods.
Developmental theory	What developmental theories you will use to help you understand the child's stage of development, e.g. Piaget's thinking on egocentrism or Bowlby's theory of attachment and separation.

B.   Observations

You should carry out a number of observations using different methods and covering all the PILES/areas of development. Each observation should be presented as an individual piece of work, briefly evaluated and signed.

C.   Overall Evaluation

Based on your observations and summarising your evaluations, give an outline of each area of development; make reference to any child development theory which is relevant, referring in particular to the theories which you identified in your introduction. This picture should help you to pinpoint the child's strengths:

▶   What does he do well?

▶   What developments are particularly noticeable?

Remember that development will be uneven, so there will always be areas in which strengths are more obvious. For example, a child who is particularly interested in playing with construction toys may, during that period, show limited interest in other play materials. His strength, however, is in his interest in construction and he is developing skills of manipulation, dexterity, matching and classifying, learning about shape and size and the relationships between objects. Observations should help the adult plan to provide further opportunities for the child to use his strengths and to build on them. The child already referred to could, for example, be encouraged to use his interest in construction in other areas like the sand tray. The adult could encourage him to talk about what he is doing and in this way use his strength/interest to help develop his language.

D.   Critical Evaluation of the Study Itself

Here you should demonstrate your awareness of any issues which may arise. You might comment on some or all of the following.

▶   Sensitivity to the child, the family and your awareness of environmental influences on the child.

▶   Issues which you had to consider, such as objectivity, confidentiality, timing or appropriateness of the methods.

▶   Your own personal learning, the usefulness of the study or what you might have done differently.

E.   References and Bibliography

These include all references used throughout the entire study, including each separate observation (see Appendix 2).

Presenting a Portfolio of Observations

A portfolio of observations should reflect a range of children's ages, activities, areas of development and observation methods. This information is shown on a matrix chart (Figure 7.2), which reveals at a glance what criteria have been met.

The portfolio may also contain an index, which gives an overview of the contents.

Figure 7.2: Example of Observations Matrix

Age range	Area of Development				
	Physical	Cognitive	Language	Emotional	Social
0–1 year	obs. 3				
1–3 years		obs. 5	obs. 2		
3–6 years				obs. 1	obs. 4

Figure 7.3: Example of Observation Index

Observation Number	Area of Development	Age Range	Method
1	Emotional Development	3–6	Narrative
2	Language Development	1–3	Checklist
3	Physical Development	0–1	Checklist
4	Social Development	3–6	Trail/Flowchart
5	Cognitive Development	1–3	Narrative

SUMMARY

▶ Observation forms the basis of effective planning for each individual child. It is an integral part of the cycle of observing, evaluating, planning, implementing and observing.

▶ Accurate and objective description is the key to effective observation. Accuracy comes with practice and with regularly reviewing what has been written. Objectivity can be influenced by several factors and it is essential to become aware of what can potentially influence one's objectivity.

▶ Interpretations should be based on the known facts and not on assumptions about the child. Judgements should be avoided.

LEGAL ISSUES

This section covers the main aspects of the legal framework relevant to the child and the family. Chapter 8 briefly outlines how Government works and how laws are made. It then covers aspects of Irish law relating to marriage, marriage breakdown and partnerships that are not based on marriage. Chapter 9 is about the issues and procedures involved in child protection under the Child Care Act 1991 and set down in *Children First: National Guidelines for the Protection and Welfare of Children.* Particular focus is given to the role of the professional early years worker in the protection of all children under her care.

The Child Care Act 1991
Key Points of the Act

▶ The child's welfare is of paramount importance; safeguarding and promoting this welfare is a priority.

▶ The HSE has a duty to ensure that support services for children 'in need' are provided; unnecessary intrusion into family life should be minimised.

▶ Delays in court proceedings and provisions of services must be avoided.

▶ Service providers must listen to and work in partnership with children, parents, those who have parental responsibilities and any relevant others.

▶ Needs arising from race, culture and language must be taken account of in the delivery of services.

The Act is divided into 10 parts:

Part I – Preliminary

The main point in this section is that the Act defines a child as a person up to 18 years of age.

Part II – Promotion of Welfare of Children

This section covers areas such as voluntary care, adoption, provision for homeless children and the establishment of a Child Care Advisory Committee in each Health Service area. The promotion of the welfare of children and families, having regard to the principle that the welfare of the child is of paramount importance, underpins this whole section and indeed the entire Act.

Part III – Protection of Children in Emergencies

This covers the powers of Gardaí to remove to safety children who are in serious danger and the making of emergency care orders.

Part IV – Care Proceedings

This covers interim care orders, care orders and supervision orders.

Part V – Jurisdiction and Procedure

The court is enabled to a appoint solicitor and guardian *ad litem* for the child; it provides for privacy and informality and again the welfare of the child as the first and paramount consideration in any proceedings is stressed.

Part VI – Children in the Care of Health Services

Covers regulations regarding the placement of children in foster care, residential and/or with relatives; access; reviews and aftercare.

Part VII – Supervision of Pre-school Services

Deals with regulations for pre-schools, playgroups, crèches, day nurseries and other services for pre-school children.

Part VIII – Children's Residential Centres

Registration of residential centres and regulations regarding staffing, accommodation and facilities, etc.

Part IX – Administration

Outlines the functions of the Minister and of chief executive officers in the health services.

Part X – Miscellaneous and Supplementary

The main point here is in relation to the sale of solvents to children. Provision is made for fines and/or imprisonment.

8

THE LEGAL FRAMEWORK FOR FAMILIES AND CHILDREN

AREAS COVERED

▶ The Constitution (Bunreacht na hÉireann)
▶ The Government
▶ How Laws Are Made
▶ Irish Family Law

Introduction

When working with families and their children it is important for early years workers to have at least a rudimentary knowledge of the basic laws which govern family life in the society in which they are operating. Because the early years worker meets parents on a daily basis and is in a position of trust, she may be approached for general advice when one or other parent has a concern. This chapter gives an overview of how Ireland is governed and how laws are enacted. It outlines some of the laws relating to families and children; laws relating to marriage, marriage breakdown, partnerships not based on marriage and domestic violence. The position of and effects on children will also be covered.

The Constitution (Bunreacht na hÉireann)

The Constitution is a document which:

▸ Lays down the fundamental rules and principles for the Government of Ireland.

▸ Imposes obligations on those in power and has a higher legal status and authority than other laws (acts of administration or laws can be examined by judicial review on constitutional grounds).

▸ Guarantees basic fundamental rights, both personal and political.

The present Constitution was adopted by referendum in 1937. Any proposed change or amendment to the Constitution must be passed by both houses of the Oireachtas and then submitted to the people by way of referendum. Among the most recent changes are the restriction in 2004 of the automatic right to citizenship for all those born in Ireland and the ratification of the Lisbon Treaty in 2009.

Articles 41 and 42 of the Constitution outline the basic principles underlying Irish law in relation to the family.

The Family in the Irish Constitution

ARTICLES 41 AND 42 – THE FAMILY

41.1.1   The State recognises the Family as the natural primary and fundamental unit group of Society, and as a moral institution possessing inalienable and imprescriptible rights, antecedent and superior to all positive law.

41.1.2   The State, therefore, guarantees to protect the Family in its constitution and authority, as the necessary basis of social order and as indispensable to the welfare of the Nation and the State.

41.2.1   In particular, the State recognises that by her life within the home, woman gives to the State a support without which the common good cannot be achieved.

41.2.2   The State shall, therefore, endeavour to ensure that mothers shall not be obliged by economic necessity to engage in labour to the neglect of their duties in the home.

41.3.1   The State pledges itself to guard with special care the institution of Marriage, on which the Family is founded, and to protect it against attack.

42.1.1   The State acknowledges that the primary and natural educator of the child is the Family and guarantees to respect the inalienable right and duty of parents to provide, according to their means, for the religious and moral, intellectual, physical and social education of their children.

(*Bunreacht na hÉireann*, 1937)

ACTIVITY

Aim: To explore the ideas of family structure and organisation which are promoted by the Irish Constitution.

Read the Articles of the Constitution above in full. In small groups, discuss the following questions:

▶   What do you think is meant by Article 41.1.1?

▶   What is the role of women in the family as envisioned by the Constitution?

▶   Why is it in the interest of the State to guard marriage against attack?

▶   Are there any issues in Irish society today which you feel are undermining family and family life?

The Government

Ireland is a constitutional representational democracy governed by two houses of the **Oireachtas**. The Oireachtas is the national parliament and is made up of the **President**, the **Dáil** and the **Seanad**.

The **President** is the ceremonial Head of State who is elected by all citizens of the State and serves a 7-year term. The President can serve two terms if re-elected.

The **Dáil**, led by the **Taoiseach**, is comprised of 166 TDs (Teachtaí Dála) who are elected through a system of proportional representation (PR). The maximum term of office is 5 years but TDs can be re-elected any number of times. The main areas of work of the Dáil are legislation and finance; different departments have responsibility for different areas and the day-to-day work is carried out by the Minister, department secretaries and a team of civil servants. Although Governments and Ministers change, the civil servants are permanent employees of the State.

The **Seanad**, known as the second house of the Oireachtas, is made up of 60 persons, 49 of whom are elected from different areas of expertise and interest and 11 of whom are nominated by the Taoiseach. The Seanad elections are held within 90 days of a general election, so the term of office is related to the duration of the Dáil.

The main functions of the Seanad are to:

▶   Keep a check on the work of the Dáil

▶   Represent particular areas of interest, such as education and agriculture

▶   Provide additional expertise for input to policy formation and legislation.

TASK

Find out:

▸   Which Government departments are involved in children's affairs?

▸   Who are the TDs representing your area?

▸   Are there any Ministers from your area and what are their responsibilities?

▸   Are there any Senators from your area and what is their field of expertise or interest?

Local Government

Since it not possible to govern everything centrally, local authorities are empowered to provide, regulate and supervise local services such as housing, sanitation, roads and halting sites. Local government can also involve itself in legislation and each authority will have its own by-laws; the area that we are most aware of is probably the planning by-laws. Local government is administered by city and county councils.

ACTIVITY

Aim: To distinguish between local and central services.

▸   Brainstorm: List all the services provided in your area, e.g. schools, roads, libraries.

▸   Rearrange the list into those that are provided by central government and those that are provided by the local authorities.

How Laws Are Made

Laws are basically rules laid down for the regulation and controlling of the individual and society. The Irish Government makes Irish laws, but these in turn are sometimes prescribed by European and/or international law, e.g. the laws relating to employment equality.

New legislation or a change to an existing law may be instigated in either the Dáil or the Seanad. The process often begins with the Minister issuing a **Green Paper** (essentially a consultation paper) suggesting a policy development or putting forward alternative policies on a particular issue, with a view to generating a debate. Submissions from interested parties are invited and are considered in the formulation of the policy. In time a White Paper may be issued which will (ideally) take into account all the views received. A **White Paper** is a policy development document. There is no connection necessarily between Green and White Papers on the one hand and bills and acts on the other, although in particular instances they may be connected.

If the Minister decides to pursue a policy as formulated in a White Paper and legislative change is required, a bill has to be prepared. A **bill** is a proposal for legislation which must be passed by both houses of the Oireachtas. The essential point is that a bill remains a bill, i.e. a proposal for legislative change, until the President signs it into law, after which it becomes an **act**. Alternatively, the President can refer it to the High Court to examine its constitutionality.

Laws are upheld or enforced through the judiciary or court system.

Irish Family Law

The laws and conditions which are outlined below refer to civil law unless otherwise stated. Religious denominations each have their own separate rules and regulations in regard to marriage and marriage breakdown, but are still subject to civil law. The EU has a limited role in family law matters and that role is mainly concerned that decisions made in one member state can be implemented in another. International conventions have also been agreed dealing with conflicts of laws across all countries – not just the EU – and these also apply within Ireland.

Marriage

Until 1972, the minimum age for marriage in Ireland was 14 years for boys and 12 years for girls. This was based on canon law, which is Roman Catholic Church law. Although the age was raised in 1972, there was much concern that very young people were ill-prepared for marriage and were more at risk of their marriage breaking down.

Under the **Family Law Act 1995**, in order for a marriage to be valid both parties must be 18 years old, and 3 months' written notice of the intention to marry must have been given to the registrar where the marriage is due to take place. Most religious denominations have premises registered for the administration of civil marriages. In addition to the legal requirements outlined above, other conditions must be fulfilled in order for a marriage to be deemed valid. These are as follows:

▶   Each party must be free to marry.

▶   Each must be of sound mind and aware of what the marriage contract means.

▶   Neither party must be forced to marry against his or her will.

▶   One person must be female and one male.

▶   The parties must not be more closely related than first cousins.

▶   Regulations regarding residency and recognition of foreign divorces must be adhered to.

Marriage Breakdown: Background

The marriage rate has been dropping in Europe in recent times and Ireland reflects this trend. In 1980 approximately 22,000 couples got married in Ireland; in 1995 it had gone down to 15,500 but rose to over 22,000 in 2008. There has since been a slight decrease. In countries where divorce was available, a rise in the divorce rate coincided with this drop in marriage rates. Divorce has been available in Ireland since 1997, but the Irish Labour Force Surveys (ILFS) and demographic results from the Census of Population suggest that the incidence of marriage breakdown has been increasing dramatically in recent years. In 1986, 37,200 adults were separated. By 2006, five times this number – just over 200,000 – had experienced a broken marriage. Divorce rates appear to be declining since 2008.

If a marriage does not work out there are now three options available in Ireland to a couple choosing to end their civil contract and to split up:

▶   Nullity

▶   Separation

▶   Divorce (since 1997).

Nullity

An annulment is a declaration that the marriage never actually existed. Even now that divorce is available some people may prefer to try to establish that their marriage was null and void in the first place.

There are six grounds for establishing nullity and they are related to the regulations governing marriage. The six grounds are as follows.

1.   There was an already existing valid marriage.
2.   One or both were underage at the time of the marriage.
3.   The formalities were not adhered to, e.g. 3 months' notice was not given.
4.   Full consent was absent – they were forced or tricked into the marriage.
5.   They were too closely related.
6.   They were both the same sex, that is, two men or two women.

Marriages may also be annulled if facts emerge at a later date which would have had an influence over either party's decision at the time of the marriage, e.g. if a past psychiatric history was concealed. However, there are no hard and fast rules in many cases and it is up to the courts to judge each individual case.

Separation

Separation may be by order of a court (a judicial separation) or by agreement between the couple without recourse to any law. Many couples who separate in Ireland do so by common agreement, which involves no court hearings. Many would have consulted a solicitor in drawing up their mutual agreement.

Either a mutual agreement or a judicial separation merely means that the husband and wife no longer have to live together. They are not free to marry another person and they are free to be reconciled. Other matters can also be considered by the courts, including who will live in the family home and the maintenance of children.

The grounds for a **judicial separation** are:

▸   Adultery

▸   Unreasonable behaviour

▸   One year's continuous desertion

▸   One year's separation with consent or 3 years without consent

▸   No normal sexual relationship for at least a year

▸   Indisposition.

In some cases a combination of these grounds may exist.

Divorce

Divorce gives legal recognition to the fact that a marriage has irretrievably broken down and no longer exists in anything but name. It gives the right to remarry if one or both parties so wish.

In Ireland, **all four** of the following conditions must be fulfilled in order to obtain a divorce:

1.   The spouses have lived apart for at least 4 of the preceding 5 years.

2.   There is no reasonable prospect of reconciliation.

3.   Both spouses and any dependent children have been properly provided for.

4.   Either spouse lived in Ireland when the proceedings began (or lived here for at least a year before that date).

The table on page 152 indicates the trends in marital breakdown since 1998.

Children and Divorce

If a couple divorces, the court will always make orders relating to the children. Matters such as **custody**, **access** and **guardianship** (see pages 154–5) of children will invariably have been dealt with in some manner by the couple, given that they must be living apart for at least 4 years before a divorce can be granted. When the couple divorces the court will not normally disturb whatever agreements have been made if they properly provide for and protect the welfare of the children. If a dispute exists about the custody of the children or access by either parent, then the court will decide on such questions, and in such cases the welfare of the children will be the primary consideration. The court may request reports to be made about any issues which affect the children's welfare. Legal aid is available to couples who cannot afford to pay legal fees.

Table 8.1: Number of Orders Granted by Year

Year	Nullity Orders	Judicial Separations	Divorce
2002	41	968	2,591
2004	25	1,258	3,347
2006	25	1,099	3,467
2008	48	1,225	3,630
2009	20	1,100	3,341

Source: Irish Courts Service Report (2009).

Marriage Breakdown: Consequences for Children

Marital breakdown has serious consequences for children. It is generally recognised that it is not the separation or the divorce which causes problems for the children, but rather the problems and friction that preceded it, combined with how the parents deal with the split afterwards. How children react to and cope with the disruption to family life depends on how their needs have been met prior to and during the upheaval. It also depends on the nature of the marital split, i.e. whether it was reasonable and amicable or whether violent rows and animosity preceded it. Research indicates that all children are affected by the separation of their parents and some children are severely damaged by the experience. Children may experience some or all of the following, depending on their personality, the nature of the split and their age and stage of development:

▶ Grief

▶ Anger

▶ Resentment

▶ Denial

▶ Sadness and loss

▶ Insecurity

▶ Relief.

Children may exhibit emotional distress and experience behavioural difficulties prior to and after the breakdown. The effects may be long lasting, resulting in poor performance at school and work. Children may also have difficulties in their future relationships as adults. On the practical side, the 'absent' parent (i.e. the parent who no longer lives with the children on a daily basis) is more likely to lose contact and the family is likely to be poorer as a result of the breakdown.

When parents are helped to manage their problems, conflicts and separation in a positive way, it is more likely that the children will be better able to cope with the situation. Some recent studies suggest that it is less harmful for children to live with two parents who are not getting on than for those two parents to separate; however, other studies suggest just as strongly that it very much depends on the nature of the family relationships. For further information on family and family life, see Chapter 10.

Minimising the Negative Effects of Divorce and Separation

The Government is committed to providing support for couples and their families who are separating and the following measures are in place.

▶ The Family Support Agency was set up in 2003 to promote and support families and to prevent family breakdown.

▶ In recent years the Government has greatly increased funding for groups involved in marriage counselling.

▶ Legal aid has been increased, both in terms of expansion of the numbers of centres and of eligibility bands.

▶ A free Family Mediation Service is available to separating couples to help them sort out their affairs agreeably so that the trauma and disruption to the children can be kept to a minimum. The Family Mediation Service has been expanded and made more accessible, particularly to those who live in rural areas.

Unmarried Parents

When a child's parents are not married to each other the child has rights pertaining to both parents, including rights to maintenance and inheritance. These rights are laid out in the **Guardianship of Infants Act 1964**, which was the first piece of modern legislation to address the needs of children born outside of marriage or in the event of marriage breakdown. The **Status of Children Act 1987** equalised in law the status of children born in or out of wedlock. The important points of the 1987 Act were:

▶ To abolish the concept of illegitimacy

▶ To give unmarried fathers legal rights to be appointed guardians or to seek access and/or custody

▶ To provide for the establishment of paternity through presumption, declaration or blood test

▶ To update and extend the law in relation to maintenance payments.

The **Children Act 1997** further amended and expanded the law with regard to guardianship, custody, access and maintenance.

Guardianship

A guardian is a person who has legal rights and duties in respect of a child. The guardian is entitled to have a say in all decisions relating to the child's upbringing, such as:

▶ Where and with whom the child lives

▶ Choice of school

▶ Consent to medical treatment

▶ Consent for a passport application

▶ Religious upbringing

▶ Consent to adoption

▶ Responsibility to ensure the provision of adequate care.

A mother is always and automatically a guardian. Under the Children Act 1997, an unmarried father can become guardian of his child without going to court providing the mother and father sign a sworn agreement. Otherwise, the father must apply to the local district court to be appointed a guardian and this might involve proof of paternity (that is, proving that he is the father). Where a marriage breaks down, both parents may retain joint guardianship or the court may appoint just one parent or an independent guardian. (**Note:** Not to be confused with guardian *ad litem*, see Chapter 9.)

Establishing Paternity

▶ If a man's name is on the child's birth certificate, then paternity is presumed.

▶ If there is a court order for maintenance, access, custody or guardianship which names the father, then that is accepted as proof.

▶ If there is a dispute, then a paternity test can be done; a court order can be obtained in respect of this if it is not undertaken voluntarily.

▶ A positive paternity test does not automatically confer any rights in respect of that paternity, i.e. the man will still have to apply through the courts for access, etc.;

also, there is still a requirement for his consent to enter his name on the birth certificate.

Custody

The person or persons who have custody of a child have charge and care of the child on a day-to-day basis. The mother of a child who is born outside marriage has sole custody of the child and the father must apply to the courts for formal custody. The 1997 Act allows for joint custody orders to be made.

Access

Where one parent has full custody of the child, the other parent can apply for access to visit/see the child regularly or at specified times. The 1997 Act allows that other persons such as grandparents may also apply to the courts for access.

Maintenance

Maintenance refers to the payments made by one person to another towards the children's cost of living. Unmarried parents do not have a responsibility to maintain each other. Maintenance can be voluntary or by order of the court. Orders made by the courts will take into consideration the earnings of the person against whom the order is being made. Paying maintenance does not give any rights of access or guardianship.

Except where parents are in agreement, all decisions about guardianship, custody and access are made by the court with the first and primary consideration being given to the child's interests and welfare. While the mother's views will be considered in making a decision about any of the above, the court may grant an order in favour of the father without the mother's agreement.

Where unmarried parents are having difficulty in agreeing on shared parenting issues such as times of access or the amount of maintenance, the Family Mediation Service may be an alternative to going to court (which is expensive and tends to be adversarial). There are many positives to be gained from going to mediation:

▶   It encourages and supports co-operation between the parents.

▶   It allows parents to be in charge of their own decisions.

▶   It promotes partnership and positive communication.

The positive outcome for children whose parents have availed of mediation services and who have subsequently been less acrimonious in their dealings with one another has been shown in various research studies.

ACTIVITY

Aim: To explore the role of the early years professional in a changing social/legal environment.

Read the case study of the reconstructed family in Chapter 10, page 200.
Imagine that Sam is attending a pre-school service where you work.

What impact might Sam's family situation have on:

▶ Your work with Sam?

▶ Your contact with his parents/stepparents?

▶ The administrative work which would be involved for the early childhood worker?

Checklist: Have you considered the following?

▶ Sam's feelings and possible confusions

▶ The possibility that he may be spending nights/weekends with a different parent

▶ Sam's need to feel that his family situation is acceptable

▶ Issues of guardianship/access/custody

▶ The parents' need for support and counselling

▶ Contact numbers in case of emergency

▶ Consent forms

▶ Who can collect Sam

▶ Reporting progress and meetings to all concerned parties.

Draw up an outline plan of activities that you would use to work with Sam in relation to his family situation.

Registration of Births

By law, the birth of a child must be registered within 3 months of the birth and a surname must be chosen for the child.

When a woman is married there is a presumption in law that her husband is the father of the child and the birth will be registered in both parents' names automatically. If the parents are not married to one another, both parents can go together to the registrar's office to place the father's name in the Register of Births. Alternatively, one parent can bring a statutory declaration with them which names the father of the child.

If the child has been registered in the mother's name alone, it is possible to re-register at any date in order to place the father's name on the birth certificate. If the woman is married, her husband must sign a declaration that he is not the father before another man's name can be entered on the certificate.

The entering of the father's name on the birth certificate does not confer guardianship, access or custodial rights.

Where parents subsequently marry, the child automatically becomes a child of the marriage and there is no requirement to re-register if the father's name is already entered into the register. Additionally, on marrying the mother the father automatically becomes a joint guardian of his child.

If the mother subsequently marries another man, any orders made in favour of the father will remain in force. If the couple want the husband to adopt the child, then the father's consent will be required if he has been appointed guardian/custodian.

Domestic Violence

Domestic violence refers to violence in the home perpetrated by adults on their partners, parents and/or children. The most common forms of abuse are emotional, physical and sexual assault and it occurs across all social classes. The incidence of domestic violence is difficult to gauge as it is grossly under-reported. Women are slow to report incidents, often because of fear of reprisals but also because there is often no escape, and the attitude until recently was for the authorities to encourage the partners to resolve their own difficulties. Men may be slow to report for the same reasons, but also because of fear of ridicule. Domestic violence may also be under-reported because people find it difficult to admit that there is violence in their relationship.

In contrast to previous research results, some recent studies suggest that men are as likely as women to experience violence at the hands of their partners. However, there seems to be evidence to support the thinking that women experience more severe forms of violent domestic abuse than men. AMEN (a confidential helpline for men set up in 1997) has monitored studies of domestic violence and asserts that every study that attends to both sexes shows that a significant number of men experience domestic violence. In a study published in 2005, the following findings were notable.

▸ 15% of women and 6% of men suffer severe domestic abuse.

▸ 29% of women and 26% of men experience domestic abuse in some form.

▸ 13% of both men and women suffer physical abuse.

▸ 29% of women but only 5% of men report to the Gardaí.

(National Crime Council/ESRI Report, 2005)

In Ireland:

▶ **One in five women** have experienced domestic violence by a partner or ex-partner.

▶ Since 1996, **166 women have been murdered** in the Republic of Ireland. In 51% of the resolved cases, the woman was killed by her partner or ex-partner.

▶ In 2009, there were over **15,000 incidents** of domestic violence disclosed to the Women's Aid National Helpline. This included over 8,000 incidents of emotional abuse, 3,355 incidents of physical abuse and over 1,600 incidents of financial abuse. In the same year, 862 incidents of sexual abuse were disclosed to helpline support workers, including 335 incidents of rape.

▶ **One in eight women** surveyed in a Dublin maternity hospital had experienced domestic violence during pregnancy.

▶ **One in four perpetrators** of sexual violence against adult women are partners or ex-partners, yet there has been only one conviction under marital rape legislation since its introduction 19 years ago.

▶ In a recent one-day survey, nearly 700 women and children were receiving support from domestic violence services.

Interestingly, an examination of crime figures in relation to domestic violence shows that the numbers of barring orders and protection orders have decreased in the last decade, while figures in relation to safety orders show an increase. These figures may be conservative because of under-reporting as explained above.

Impact of Domestic Violence on Children
Each child will react differently, whether emotionally, behaviourally and/or physically. The following are some general reactions.

▶ Fearfulness and nervousness

▶ Low self-esteem

▶ Anger

▶ Helplessness and guilt

▶ Stress

▶ Insecurity

▶ Inability to concentrate

▶ Frequent illnesses and injuries

▶ Secrecy and shame

▶ Depression

▶ Imitation of violent and abusive behaviour.

In the long term there may be negative consequences for the person's ability to cope with life and to form healthy adult relationships. Research in this area is scant, as the focus to date has largely been on the adult victims of domestic abuse.

Strategies for Change

Any attempt to reduce the incidence of domestic violence must address gender issues and power imbalance in society. On a practical level there needs to be a safe place where victims can escape to with their children, and they also need to be able to obtain counselling and support. There is also a need for an integrated and combined effort on the part of all the services and agencies involved.

Cosc (the National Office for the Prevention of Domestic, Sexual and Gender-based Violence) was established in June 2007 with the key responsibility of ensuring the delivery of a well co-ordinated 'whole of Government' response to domestic, sexual and gender-based violence. Cosc's work covers issues relating to domestic and sexual violence against women and men, including older people in the community. One of Cosc's primary tasks has been the development of a National Strategy on Domestic, Sexual and Gender-based Violence. The strategy was approved by the Government in 2010 and Cosc will now focus on ensuring its implementation.

Agencies involved include the following.

▶ **Department of Justice, Equality and Law Reform/Gardaí**: A Woman and Child Unit has been established in Harcourt Street Garda Station, Dublin to deal specifically with violence against women and children. Special training for Garda personnel is now also provided.

▶ **Department of the Environment, Heritage and Local Government**: There is some provision of emergency accommodation but not nearly enough to meet the need. This results in families staying in refuges and hostels much longer than is necessary.

▶ **Department of Social Protection**: Financial assistance and social services are available; separate and emergency payments can be arranged fairly promptly.

▶ **Department of Health and Children**: Accident and emergency department personnel and GPs are more aware of the implications of domestic violence.

The Domestic Violence Act 1996 has gone some way to providing increased protection for adults and children who experience violence. The main provisions of the Act are as follows.

▶ The law has been extended to cover any adult with whom the person shares residence, not just the spouse.

▸ Power has been given to the Department of Health and Children to apply for protection on behalf of a person.

▸ If a person breaks the law, they can now be arrested without the need for a warrant.

Under the 1996 Act, four types of court order could be obtained to protect a spouse, partner, dependent child or persons in other domestic relationships.

A **safety order** prevents the person from using or threatening to use violence against the applicant, or molesting or frightening her. If they live in the same house, the respondent (the defendant in law) does not have to leave. It is effective for 5 years.

A **protection order** has the same effect as a safety order. It is an interim order which is effective until a decision on another order can be made.

The **interim barring order** and **barring order** require the respondent to leave home. The Domestic Violence (Amendment) Act 2002 directs that the respondent be notified of the order and the reasons as soon as possible, and when made *ex parte* (without the respondent being present in the court) the order must be confirmed or rescinded within 8 days.

Application by Health Authorities

The Domestic Violence Act empowers the Health Authorities to apply for an order to protect a person of any age if they believe that person to be in danger and unable to pursue an application for a barring or safety order themselves, perhaps because of fear.

SUMMARY

▸ The Constitution lays down the fundamental rules and principles by which Ireland is governed.

▸ The Government provides central services and makes laws. Local Government enacts by-laws and provides local services.

▸ Marriage breakdown has serious consequences for all children and the marriage laws reflect this, both in the marriage regulations themselves and in the divorce regulations.

▸ Whether parents are married or unmarried, the law is designed to protect the best interests of the child and to ensure that all children are treated equally.

▸ Domestic violence is a serious problem in our society and the legislation recognises that violence is inflicted by others apart from spouses and that men as well as women can experience it.

9

CHILD PROTECTION

AREAS COVERED

▶ The Child Care Act 1991

▶ Historical Perspective

▶ Incidence of Abuse

▶ Definitions of Child Abuse

▶ Signs and Indicators of Abuse

▶ Predisposing Factors

▶ The Role of the Early Childhood Worker Where Abuse Is Suspected

▶ Services for Abused Children

Introduction

Increasing concern about child protection is rooted in profound changes in Irish society. In the past, abuse and neglect of some children were often accepted as hard facts of life. More recently, the idea that children have a fundamental right to protection, whether there is obvious risk of abuse or not, has grown and is now reflected in the Child Care Act 1991 and in *Children First: The National Guidelines for the Protection and Welfare of Children 1999* (hereafter referred to as 'the National Guidelines'). Strengthening the rights of children generally has become a central issue involving numerous groups and institutions. A proposal to amend the Constitution in order to strenghten children's rights has yet to be acted upon.

This chapter aims to inform and highlight issues in relation to children's rights and child protection. The primary aim, however, is to familiarise the learner with law, policy and procedure in line with the National Guidelines. The guidelines are based on current best practice and procedures as implemented by the statutory and voluntary sectors.

The Child Care Act 1991

The Child Care Act 1991 has affirmed children's rights and needs and the concept of 'the best interests of the child'. The enshrinement in the Act of the principle that parental responsibilities are at least as important as parental rights points to a significant shift in focus in terms of child protection.

The Act has now been implemented in full and it is generally accepted that the basic needs of children should be met. In medical terms this acceptance of the need to protect as well as cure has long been accepted; out of this acceptance has grown protective programmes such as ante-natal care programmes and vaccination programmes. Great efforts are made on a daily basis to protect children from all sorts of dangers. No one waits until a child has been burned by fire or run down by a car to teach him about fires or road safety.

Historical Perspective

In the past children were considered to be the property of their parents, particularly the father, so parents could decide in what manner they would treat their children. Change began towards the end of the nineteenth century. In 1874, a scandal culminated in the establishment of the New York Society for the Prevention of Cruelty to Children. (The NSPCC in Britain and the ISPCC in Ireland are direct descendants.) Mary Ellen was an adopted child who was severely ill treated, abused and neglected. Neighbours were concerned but there was little that could be done because the parents 'owned' her, that is, until an enlightened lawyer decided to take a case against the parents under the laws relating to the ill-treatment of animals; he won the case.

During the early part of the twentieth century in Ireland, most child protection work was carried out by ISPCC officers and most residential care facilities for children were run by religious orders.

While tragedies and enquiries pushed policy-makers into action, other influences were probably also at play. Civil rights and human rights were brought to people's attention across America, Britain, Europe and Ireland in the late 1960s/early 1970s. The feminist movement and women took some of the darker issues from behind closed doors. Certainly the growing ability and freedom of women to speak out about physical and sexual violence within marriage had a direct bearing on the exposure of child abuse in all its forms.

The Child Care Act 1991, which replaced the 1908 Children's Act, was the first piece of child protection legislation enacted by the Irish State.

The child protection provisions of the Child Care Act 1991 were implemented by the end of 1995, but difficulties remain today – nearly 20 years later – in relation to scarcity of resources and how they are deployed.

Historical milestones relevant to protection

1992 The X Case: The State continues to protect the unborn child regardless of the circumstances of the teenager who has become pregnant as a result of rape or incest.

1993 The Kilkenny Incest Case: Its subsequent investigation gave impetus to significant improvements in child protection services.

1994 The Kelly Fitzgerald case brought to light the shortcomings in communications between social work departments.

1993–96 Madonna House, Goldenbridge Orphanage and Trudder House were the forerunners in bringing to light extensive abuse, collusion and cover-ups of child abuse in childcare institutions.

1994–present Cases of abuse of children by members of the Roman Catholic clergy and religious orders with yet more collusion and cover-ups.

1998 *McColgan v. North Western Health Board* set a precedent because a survivor of abuse successfully sued the Health Authority for neglect of its duty to protect her.

1998 Protection for Persons Reporting Abuse Act.

1999 Publication of *Children First: The National Guidelines for the Protection and Welfare of Children*.

2000 A White Paper on mandatory reporting was published.

2002 Residential Institutions Redress Act: The Redress Board was established under this legislation and up to December 2008, 14,768 applications for redress were received.

2002 The Garda Central Vetting Unit was established for the purpose of vetting certain prospective employees. It only deals with requests from organisations that are registered with the unit.

2002 Establishment of the Ombudsman for Children on a statutory basis. Its main responsibilities are to promote the rights and welfare of children and to investigate complaints made by children or on behalf of children against public bodies, schools and public hospitals.

2005 The Ferns Report dealing with the nature and handling of clerical child sexual abuse reports in the diocese of Ferns. Numerous recommendations were made which are currently being examined.

2006 Criminal Law (Sexual Offences) Act – the charge of statutory rape is no longer valid; it criminalises under-age (under 17) consensual sex.

2006 Report of extensive abuse in a childcare establishment which caters for separated children seeking asylum.

2007 Proposal to hold a referendum to change the Constitution, with a view to strengthening children's rights.

2007 The establishment of the Health Information and Quality Authority (HIQA), within which the Social Services Inspectorate operates. The work of the Inspectorate has been focused on children in care, primarily on inspection of residential care.

2008 The National Review of Compliance with *Children First: The National Guidelines*. Many recommendations are made to improve the overall effectiveness of the guidelines.

2009 The Ryan Report – the report of the commission that investigated the abuse of children in institutions in Ireland. Many recommendations were made with regard to the safeguarding of children in the care of various institutions.

2009 The Murphy Report – a report on the investigation into the handling by Church and State authorities of allegations and suspicions of child abuse against clerics in the Catholic Archdiocese of Dublin.

2010 Child Death Review Group – following the unnatural death of two teenagers in care and the subsequent revelation that numerous other children had died, this group was set up to investigate the circumstances surrounding children who died in care or who had just left the care of the social services.

Incidence of Abuse

The question of whether child abuse is more prevalent now than in the past is a difficult one to answer. Definitions of abuse have changed over time and there are variations in definitions between different countries today. Definitions in turn have an effect on recordkeeping and therefore on statistics and how they might be interpreted. If the present-day definition that beating children in school amounts to child abuse, then according to this definition it was rampant in Ireland prior to the change which outlawed corporal punishment in schools in 1982. However, records of child abuse in schools would show that it hardly existed at all.

Additionally, there was little openness surrounding the whole topic of abuse so that even those who were being abused, according to the legal definitions of the time, had little chance of being heard or of having the courage to speak out.

Organisations and resources have now been established to deal with the whole area of abuse and to facilitate people who want to get help for themselves or for others. The National Guidelines set out clearly and in detail what action is required when abuse is suspected or uncovered. Childline was set up by the ISPCC with the specific purpose of providing a freephone service to children who wished to talk about their situations. The media, while being sensationalist at times, have also played their part in the broadcasting and publication of material in relation to child abuse.

There is no doubt that today, more cases of abuse are being reported and dealt with by the courts; more people who are being abused, or at risk of being abused, are receiving help. Child abuse statistics show that the number of cases which have been reported to the authorities increase annually.

Definitions of Child Abuse

Different types of abuse are defined separately below, but in reality they are less easy to separate. Where a child is being physically abused within a family, that child is also being emotionally abused. Likewise, a child who is experiencing sexual abuse is being emotionally and physically abused. The following definitions are those set out in the National Guidelines.

▶ **Physical abuse** is any form of non-accidental injury or injury which results from wilful or neglectful failure to protect a child. Examples include shaking, hitting, punching, use of excessive force, poisoning, suffocating, allowing or creating substantial risk of significant harm to the child and Munchausen's Syndrome by Proxy.

▶ **Emotional abuse** is normally to be found in the relationship between a caregiver and a child rather than in a specific event or pattern of events. It occurs when a child's needs for affection, approval, consistency and security are not met. Examples would include persistent criticism, sarcasm, hostility, conditional parenting, unresponsiveness, inconsistency, unrealistic expectations, under- and over-protection or rejection of the child.

▶ **Neglect** is normally defined in terms of an omission, where a child suffers significant harm or impairment of development by being deprived of food, clothing, warmth, hygiene, intellectual stimulation, supervision and safety, attachment to and affection from adults or medical care.

▶ **Sexual abuse** occurs when a child is used by another person for his or her gratification or sexual arousal, or for that of others, e.g. masturbation or exposure in the presence of a child, inappropriate touching, intercourse or sexual exploitation as in the taking of photographs for sexual gratification purposes.

Figure 9.1: Bruising on Soft Tissue Areas

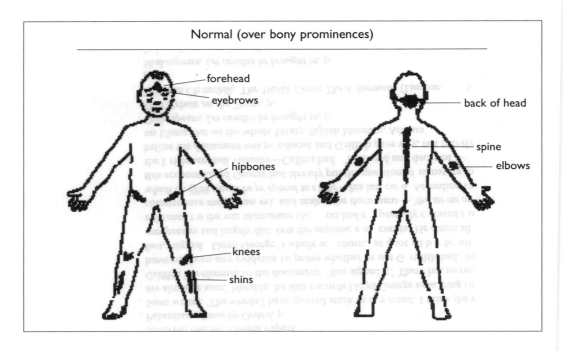

Normal (over bony prominences)

forehead
eyebrows
back of head
spine
hipbones
elbows
knees
shins

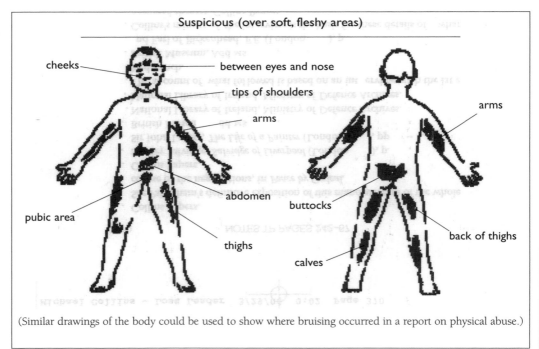

Suspicious (over soft, fleshy areas)

cheeks
between eyes and nose
tips of shoulders
arms
arms
abdomen
buttocks
pubic area
back of thighs
thighs
calves

(Similar drawings of the body could be used to show where bruising occurred in a report on physical abuse.)

Signs and Indicators of Abuse

Indicators of Physical Abuse

Physical

▸ Bruising in areas where bruises are not readily sustained, i.e. soft tissue areas (see Figure 9.1)

▸ Explanations for injuries where the explanation is not consistent with the injury

▸ Facial bruising

▸ Hand or finger marks/pressure bruises

▸ Bite marks

▸ Burns (especially cigarette), scalds

▸ Unexplained and frequent fractures

▸ Frequent and severe lacerations and abrasions

▸ Failure to thrive.

Behavioural

▸ Fearful and shying away from physical contact

▸ Frozen watchfulness

▸ Withdrawn or aggressive behaviour

▸ Sudden changes in behaviour.

Indicators of Emotional Abuse

Behavioural

▸ Attention-seeking behaviour

▸ Withdrawn or aggressive behaviour

▸ Telling frequent lies

▸ Inability to have fun

▸ Low self-esteem

▸ Tantrums – beyond normal developmental age for same

▸ Speech disorders, particularly stammering

▸ Indiscriminately affectionate.

Indicators of Child Neglect

Physical

▸ Poor hygiene

▸ Inadequate, dirty, torn or inappropriate clothing

▸ Untreated medical problems

▸ Poor nourishment/failure to thrive

▸ Emaciation

▸ Being left at home alone.

Behavioural

▸ Tiredness/listlessness

▸ Low self-esteem

▸ Inability to concentrate or be involved

▸ Always hungry.

Indicators of Sexual Abuse

Physical

▸ Bruises and scratches to genital area

▸ Soreness when walking, sitting, going to the toilet

▸ Pain or itching

▸ Sexually transmitted diseases

▸ Torn and stained underclothes

▸ Bedwetting, sleep disturbances

▸ Loss of appetite.

Behavioural

▸ Hints of sexual activity through words, drawings or play

▸ Sexually precocious behaviour

▸ Use of sexually explicit language

▸ Preoccupation with sexual matters

▸ Informed knowledge of adult sexual behaviour

▸ Low self-esteem

▸ Withdrawn or isolated from other children.

(These indicators are not exhaustive.)

It is important not to jump to conclusions: a burn may be caused by a genuine accident;
a sudden change in behaviour could be because an elderly relative who requires a lot of

care has moved in with the family. Mongolian blue spots which resemble a series of bruises appear naturally on the back and buttocks of some black babies. Circular bruising may be the result of 'cupping', a Chinese medical treatment.

Predisposing Factors

Some factors have been found consistently (predictive indicators) in family characteristics and/or circumstances where abuse has occurred. However, the same factors can also be found in families where there is no abuse, so predictive indicators of child abuse must be used with **extreme caution**. Statistics of child abuse show that child abuse occurs in all social classes and they also show that the people most likely to abuse children are parents, partners of parents who are not the child's natural parent, relatives and neighbours, in that order.

Parental Factors Associated with Child Abuse

Parents Who Were Abused Themselves
A combination of factors are at work here, for example:

▸ Cultural – 'It didn't do me any harm so it won't do my children any harm'.

▸ Past experience – love and violence are confused because of the parent's own experiences of being abused by parents/carers.

▸ Poor role models for the parents – parents do not know other ways of disciplining and controlling their children because this is how their parents did it.

▸ Low self-esteem – parents may be emotionally damaged and inadequate.

▸ Parents may be unable to control themselves.

▸ Parents may be unable to respond with warmth and affection.

▸ Parents may demand affection from their children in order to fulfil their own needs.

Very Young Parents
▸ Emotionally immature parents may not be able to cope with the physical and emotional demands of a young baby.

▸ There may be conflict between their own needs and the needs of their child.

▸ There may be a lack of support or negative reactions from their own parents.

▸ There may be an inability to recognise the needs of a baby/young child because of youth and inexperience.

▸ There may be resentment of a baby where there is a new and growing relationship between parents.

- The reality of caring for a baby does not fit in with the 'dream' that is reinforced by society, e.g. that babies bring happiness, smiles, fulfilment and that parents are never tired, frustrated or worn out with anxiety and worry.

Parents Who Expect Too Much of Their Children

- Approval and love are conditional on good behaviour and positive achievements.
- Skills and behaviour are expected from a child that are way beyond the child's age and stage of development.
- A child who fails to match up to expectations is seen by parents as bold, lazy or resistant.

Parents Who Abuse Substances

- Alcohol is often associated with violence; the adult may be predisposed to violent actions and reactions.
- Abuse of other substances is more often associated with neglect where money is spent on substances/drugs rather than on basic necessities such as food, clothing and heating. Abuse of substances may also lead to a general lack of responsiveness (inertia) on the part of the adult to the children and their needs.

Parents Who Are Under Stress

- Parents may be overwhelmed by any problem such as debt, grief, trauma or fear; the demands of a child may elicit an unreasonable response.
- Parents may blame the child partially or wholly for the stress.
- Parents may simply 'forget' to feed, clothe or show affection to the child, such is the level of their stress.

The reason for a person's stress may not be obvious to an outsider. It is important to remember that what is extremely stressful for one person may only constitute a minor problem for another. **We must never judge the actions or reactions of another according to our own abilities to deal with stressful situations.**

Parents Who Suffer from Psychiatric Illness/Mental Health Problems

- Mood swings and unpredictable and bizarre behaviour patterns can be very distressful and traumatic for children.
- Depression in a parent can lead to a total neglect of children and a total inability to respond to a child's needs.

▶ Post-natal depression can disrupt the bonding process and the mother's response to her baby in the early weeks and months.

Child Factors Associated with Child Abuse

Children in the Age Range 1–4 Years

▶ It is during this period that children are at their most demanding in terms of the individual attention which they need. The novelty of a new baby has worn off, and besides, a baby who has literally found its feet is much more demanding than one who has no option but to lie in the cot. At this period, the child is also beginning to assert his independence and individuality.

Children Who Are Perceived as Being 'Difficult'

▶ Disrupion to the early bonding and attachment process between mother and infant; where the bonds of attachment have been weakened, the care of the child may be perceived as being very difficult.

▶ Children who are difficult to feed.

▶ Children who are difficult to comfort; a baby who cries a lot.

▶ Children who are born prematurely may have a combination of all of the above. Such situations may lead to overwhelming stress for the parent. Additionally, when children are difficult to feed or comfort, parents may feel a sense of failure.

Children Who Are 'Different'

▶ A child who does not live up to the parents' expectations.

▶ A child who is not the sex that the parents had hoped for.

▶ A child who has a disability.

A child may be perceived by parents to be different without this being obvious to others; in these situations it is the perception that is significant rather than the reality. Basically these are situations where the parent has rejected the child.

The above factors may contribute to our understanding of child abuse and abusive situations, but many people who lack resources and cope with highly stressful situations and/or extremely demanding children would never resort to abuse. On the other hand, abuse can and does occur in families and to individuals who would seem on the surface to have no difficulties at all.

The Role of the Early Childhood Worker Where Abuse Is Suspected

▶ Keep meticulous records at all times; these records must be dated and signed.

▶ Record only facts and direct observations; hearsay and hunches will not be admitted as evidence in a court of law.

▶ Discuss concerns with senior staff/experienced colleagues/designated child protection officer.

▶ Interview the parents/guardians regarding those concerns unless there is reason to believe that this would place the child at further risk. The supervisor or manager may prefer to do this, either with or without the member of staff being present. It is important for early childhood workers to be aware that the source of the allegation will be revealed to the parents/guardians. If the case comes to court the person who discovered the abuse will have to give evidence. It is almost impossible for the authorities to investigate, pursue and prove cases of abuse when those who have the evidence are not willing to be identified.

▶ Refer to the local childcare manager/social work team.

If there is direct evidence of abuse or if a child or someone else discloses facts of abuse to the early childhood worker:

▶ Don't panic; remain calm.

▶ Reassure the child/person that he was right to tell.

▶ Give the child the time and opportunity to say what he has to say. He may not do this all at once.

▶ Avoid shock/horror responses.

▶ Explain to the child what action will be taken – keep it simple.

▶ Report the matter to the person in charge.

▶ The person in charge should report the matter to the local social work team.

Remember:

▶ Leave verification and examinations to those who are professionally trained in the area.

When physical injury or sexual abuse has occurred, the child will be subjected to at least one physical examination, whether you have tried to look for evidence or not. It is good professional practice to keep intrusion, questioning and stressful situations to a minimum.

▶ Do not offer false reassurance.

'I will make sure that everything will be all right now.' 'I will never let anyone hurt you again.' (These are examples of promises that nobody can ever guarantee.)

▶ Do not promise to keep secrets.

In this way you will not find yourself in a situation of being unable to obtain help for a person unless you break your promise. You can reassure him that you will not do anything without his knowing or without discussing it with him first.

▶ Avoid 'guilt-creating'/blaming responses.

Questioning why the person did not act in a particular way, e.g. run away, shout or tell sooner. Making suggestions as to how he could have acted is of little use after something has happened and only serves to help the person feel that somehow he was partially to blame. Survivors are too ready to blame themselves anyway without your help.

▶ Avoid telling the person how to feel.

Horrified responses are often difficult to suppress, but such responses are telling the other person what you think he should have felt – 'Oh, how horrible.' 'You must feel terrible.' 'What a monster!'

A child may feel confused, hurt, betrayed and indeed terrible, but you should enable him to express his feelings rather than putting words into his mouth.

▶ Record as soon as possible, and in the child's exact words if you can, what has been said.

Your expertise lies in the area of being able to communicate with and comfort the child. You can provide an environment which will support the child at such a difficult time. You will be able to explain or interpret what is going on in a way that the child can understand because you will be familiar with his level of functioning, his understanding and his vocabulary.

Duties and Roles in Relation to Child Protection

Role of the Early Childhood Worker

▶ To provide care and stimulation to each child according to each child's needs.

▶ To monitor the overall progress of each child.

▶ To maintain regular, accurate, impartial, dated and signed records of each child's progress. Observations are particularly useful in this area.

▶ To maintain a close but professional relationship with parents/carers.

▶ To be aware of signs and symptoms of abuse in all its forms.

▶ To keep the best interests of the child in mind at all times.

▶ In times of doubt, to be prepared to err on the side of caution.

Role of the Manager/Director of the Early Years Setting

▶ To ensure that professional standards are maintained.

▶ To ensure that records of all notes, logs and correspondence are dated, signed and maintained.

▶ To be aware of procedures to be followed in the case of suspected abuse.

▶ To liaise with the Health Authorities and any other relevant personnel. If a report is being made, he should use the Standard Reporting Form (see Appendix 5).

▶ To provide support and in-service training for staff.

▶ To be prepared to take action in the case of suspected abuse.

▶ To provide direct support and counselling for any staff member involved in an ongoing case.

Role of the Designated Child Protection Person/Officer

▶ Advise colleagues, managers and supervisors within organisations/workplaces about individual cases as appropriate.

▶ Advise on best practice and ensure that the organisation's child protection policy and procedures are followed.

▶ Organise and/or facilitate training and workshops on the guidelines for child protection.

▶ Report suspicions and allegations of child abuse to the Health Service Executive where there is a concern.

▶ Create and maintain links with the Health Service Executive and other relevant agencies and resource groups.

▶ Facilitate follow-up action.

▶ Maintain proper records on all cases referred to them in a secure and confidential manner.

▶ Keep up to date on current developments regarding provision, practice, legal obligations and policy.

▶ Ensure that child protection policy and procedures are reviewed annually.

▶ Ensure that the organisation's policies and procedures are brought to the attention of employees and volunteers.

(The 'designated person' is the title given to a person appointed within an organisation to deal with child protection issues that are brought to light. In a school, for example, this could be one of the teachers.)

Role of the Social Worker

▶ To investigate reports of child abuse

▶ To assess the risk involved and what action, if any, is required to be taken

▶ To keep relevant authorities informed of developments in the case

▶ To liaise with all relevant personnel, i.e. Gardaí, medical and referring personnel

▶ To maintain supportive and ongoing contact with parents

▶ To form a relationship with the child and to maintain supportive contact

▶ To provide reports for case conferences and court hearings.

Role of the Gardaí

▶ To investigate whether a crime has been committed.

▶ To institute criminal proceedings against alleged abusers.

▶ To provide back-up support for social workers, doctors, etc. if their investigations are being hampered or resisted.

▶ To remove a child/children from immediate harm under Section 12 of the Act if the need arises.

▶ To participate in strategy meetings, case conferences and reviews.

Role of the Childcare Manager

▶ To take ultimate responsibility for the care and protection of all children in his area.

▶ To convene and chair the child protection case conference at which decisions about particular children are made.

▶ To negotiate a child protection plan involving all key people, including parents/carers.

▶ To ensure that decisions are followed through and that child protection reviews take place.

▶ To establish and maintain the Child Protection Notification System.

CASE STUDY

Family	Name	Age
Mother:	Jennifer Reynolds	26 years
Father:	Joshua Okono	28 years
Children:	Leah Reynolds	6 years
	Zara Reynolds	2 years 6 months
	Paul Reynolds	7 months

Income: Joshua is employed as a chef in a local restaurant. He has a work permit which will run out in six weeks' time.

Jennifer is qualified as a nurse but works full time at home.

Child Benefit in respect of all three children.

Accomodation: Terraced three-bedroom local authority house which Jennifer has lived in since her second child was born.

Jennifer is separated from the father of her two eldest children; she and Joshua have been together for almost two years. They plan to marry when Jennifer's divorce comes through.

Leah is in senior infants in primary school and according to her teacher, Ms Conron, she is a very bright child and is a pleasure to have in class.

Zara has been attending the childcare centre for over a year. When she started she was a relatively quiet child but friendly and joined in all activities. She has been making progress in all areas of development. She is a great 'talker' and has a vocabulary way beyond what you might expect from a 2-and-a-half-year-old.

Paul was born prematurely and he has been generally unwell since birth; he has been hospitalised for short periods on numerous occasions. He only sleeps for short periods and is difficult to feed; because of this he has failed to thrive. Jennifer is distraught with worry over Paul and is exhausted. The health visitor, Mrs Hegarty, is a friend of Jennifer's and is very supportive but there is little that she can do to relieve the day-to-day pressures. An application for home help in the short term has been made but has not yet been processed. In fact, with one child in school and another in pre-school it is unlikely that the application will be successful.

Over the last few weeks staff have noticed a significant change in Zara's behaviour. She spends a lot of time sitting hugging her knees, rocking and sucking her thumb. She has complained of stomach aches and a sore bottom. Jennifer is always so rushed and pressurised that there has not been time to discuss the changes in detail yet. However, today Zara arrived into the centre with a long deep scratch down the entire length of one cheek. Her mother offered no explanation and Zara would not say how it had happened either. When the child was being collected the room supervisor asked her mother into the office. As soon as the door was closed, Jennifer burst into tears. She admitted she had 'snapped' the previous afternoon when she found Zara trying to put Paul into a waste basket; she struck her with the back of her hand and she was wearing a ring at the time – hence the deep cut. It bled for a good while but she was ashamed to go to the doctor ... she knows them all too, which makes it harder for her, she says.

She added, 'I swore I would never hit one of my children; my parents were always hitting us, especially my father.' You took the opportunity to ask about the stomach pains and sore bottom and Jennifer immediately explained that the child has always suffered from constipation but that it has worsened in the last few months. Zara has been seen by Dr Pettigrew, the GP, who has assured the mother that it is nothing to be worried about … it will sort itself out. The mother ended the interview by saying, 'I'm at my wits' end, I just cannot go on.'

▶   Identify the main issues relevant to child protection/abuse in this situation.

▶   Identify Zara's needs in this situation, paying particular attention to the needs which you consider are not being met.

▶   What is the first step you would take in this situation?

An Outline of Action in the Case of Suspected Child Abuse

(Before reading the following, please study Figure 9.2.) The early childhood worker will be directly involved up to the decision to inform the HSE and may be involved in discussions, case conferences and a court hearing if one takes place.

A student who is on placement should discuss her concerns with her supervisor and her tutor. She will probably not be involved beyond this.

Fig. 9.2: Child Protection Assessment/Investigation Process

PHASE 1

(i)   Allegation or suspicion of child abuse

(ii)   Discussion with designated child protection officer

(iii)   Referral to Social Work Department

(iv)   Social worker consults records and makes initial enquiries

(v)   Social worker consults with team leader/senior social worker

PHASE 2

(i)   Notification to childcare manager. Options may then include:

• Notification to Gardaí

• Strategy meeting with key people

• Assessment of risk by social services team

PHASE 3

(i)   Child protection case conference

(ii)   Negotiation of child protection plan involving all key people, including parents if appropriate

(iii)   Treatment/intervention if required

(iv)   Child protection review

The Law – Orders, Terms and Roles

Orders and Terms

Emergency Care Order

An emergency care order is an order which authorises the placement of a child in the care of the HSE in cases where there is reasonable cause to believe that a child will suffer significant harm if not removed immediately from his place of residence. An order may also be made if the child is likely to be removed from the present situation placing him at risk, e.g. if a child is in hospital and might be at serious risk if returned home.

The Gardaí may remove a child to safety without a warrant where they consider the child's health or welfare to be at risk.

Interim Order

An interim order maintains a child in the care of the HSE until an application for a care order has been processed and a decision made.

Supervision Order

A supervision order authorises the local HSE to have a child's health and welfare checked out and supervised where there is reasonable grounds for believing that the child is at risk.

Care Order

A care order places a child under the care of the local HSE. The HSE takes over the rights and responsibilities of the parents and has legal responsibility to look after the health and welfare of the child.

The Child Protection Notification System (CPNS)

This is managed and maintained by the childcare manager. A child's name may be submitted for notification following a preliminary assessment where abuse is suspected or where it has actually happened. It should be constantly updated. There should be 24-hour access to the system; the local HSE should have agreed on who may have access to the system and also set up procedures for identifying these people.

The Child Protection Conference

The child protection conference brings together any professionals who have been involved and who have relevant information to share. It may include all or some of the above in addition to specialists, legal representatives and, increasingly, the family itself. The aim of the conference is to make decisions and draw up a child protection plan.

SCENARIO

Sean, aged 4 years, and his sister Maria, aged 2 years, attend an early childhood service. It is Friday at around 6.15 p.m. You and another member of staff are in the centre with these two children, waiting for them to be collected. Their parents, prominent people in the community, arrive to collect their children and both are visibly drunk.

Write down in about 200 words a sequence to this scenario outlining what might happen.

In your sequence, consider the following:

▶   **What might be the children's reactions?**

▶   **What might be the parents' reactions?**

▶   **What might you be feeling?**

▶   **What would be the correct procedure to follow in this situation?**

The Guardian Ad Litem

The guardian *ad litem* is appointed by the court to look after the best interests of the child in difficult cases. The guardian *ad litem* consults with the child, the child's family and any other organisations that know the child and the family case files are also reviewed. These consultations are crucial to ensure that the child's best interests are presented independently to the court and that the child's wishes, where appropriate, are made known to the judge.

Principles for Best Practice in Child Protection

The following principles should inform best practice in child protection:

▶   The welfare of the child is of paramount importance.

▶   A balance must be struck between protecting children and respecting the rights and needs of parents/carers and families, but the child's welfare must come first.

▶   Children have a right to be taken seriously.

▶   Children should be consulted and involved in relation to all matters and decisions that affect them, taking into account their age and stage of development.

▶   Early intervention and support should be made available to children and families in order to minimise risk.

> ▶   Parents and carers have a right to respect and to be consulted about matters which affect their families.

> ▶   Actions taken to protect a child should not be intrusive and should minimise distress.

> ▶   Intervention should not deal with the child in isolation. The child has to be seen in a family context.

> ▶   The criminal dimension which may be involved must be acknowledged.

> ▶   Children should only be separated from their parents and family when all other possibilities have been exhausted. Reunion with families from whom children have been separated should always be a consideration.

> ▶   Effective prevention, detection and treatment of child abuse require a co-ordinated multidisciplinary approach.

> ▶   Any intervention should take account of diversity in families and lifestyles.

> ▶   Training for effective child protection should be mandatory in all establishments which care for children.

> ▶   Roles and responsibilities should be clearly defined and understood within organisations and services for children.

> (Adapted from the National Guidelines)

Supporting the Early Childhood Worker

Only about a third of cases which are reported result in court cases and care proceedings. For the most part, children who are at risk continue to attend their local schools and early years services. On the surface, it may seem that very few changes occur as a result of making a report, but the worker must continue to work with the child and family. If professionalism and impartiality are maintained at all times and the 'best interests of the child' are always kept in mind, then it will be possible to re-establish working relationships with the parent, which may have suffered because of the abuse allegations being made by the early years worker.

For the person working directly with children and parents, the stress and anxiety which are provoked in situations where abuse occurs cannot and should not be underestimated. If this person does not take action a child may suffer further abuse, and if he does take action he should receive adequate support from colleagues, management and other professionals.

Allegations of Abuse Against Early Childhood Workers

When allegations of abuse are made against staff it can be a very traumatic time for all those involved. Nevertheless, it is equally important that the procedures which are in place for dealing with allegations of abuse by any adult are also adhered to in relation to allegations against staff. If the allegations are serious then the worker will be suspended pending investigation. In the case of an allegation against a staff member there is even more need for support for the staff of the setting. The reasons for such support include the following.

▶ When abuse involves an outsider there will probably be one or maybe two children involved; if abuse occurs within the setting there may be several children involved.

▶ The staff member involved may be well known or may even be a friend.

▶ Guilty feelings and/or feelings of anger may be very strong.

Because of the increased awareness of child abuse generally, people, especially men, who work with young children are often fearful that they will be wrongly accused and this will damage them irreparably even if the allegations are not true. If workers adhere strictly to principles of good practice then this is unlikely to happen and the worker, if accused, will have the confidence that he has done nothing wrong.

Poor professional practices such as shouting at children, ridiculing them or imposing extreme 'time outs' should be dealt with through supervision, and the member of staff should be helped through extra training and support to enable him to develop appropriate practices. Bad practice should never be condoned for any reason.

ACTIVITY

Aim: To identify ways in which the early childhood worker can help to empower children.

Form small groups.
▶ Review the role of the adult/carer in promoting all-round healthy, social and emotional development.
▶ Plan a range of activities for children of different ages, which would help them to master some of the skills listed on page 182. Different groups could focus on different age groups and feed back to the whole group.

Example of activity: 'What if' games — 'What if you fell and hurt your knee?' This type of activity will help children to learn problem-solving skills and to cope with the unexpected.

When working with children, do not focus on abusive or dangerous situations since children will learn more easily from situations that are familiar to them.

Checklist

In the activities above, include some that cover the fact that children need to know how:

▶ To be safe	▶ To protect their own bodies
▶ To say 'no'	▶ To get help
▶ To tell	▶ To be believed
▶ Not to keep secrets	▶ To refuse touches
▶ To cope with strangers	▶ To break rules.

Empowering the Child

The encouragement and promotion of healthy social and emotional development is vital for the well-being of all children, whatever their circumstances. Promoting confidence and independence and a sense of self-worth in children may help them to tell about some abusive situation or to avoid it altogether. Although it is essential that children learn some skills of self-protection, it is important to keep in mind that this in no way exonerates the adult from the responsibility of protecting them. Children cannot be expected to protect themselves and there is no conclusive research showing that children who have avoided abuse did so because they had any particular skills. Being skilled in any, or all, of the areas mentioned below gives children a greater feeling of control and perhaps assertiveness; research seems to indicate that in the area of sexual abuse it is often, although by no means always, the timid, unsure child who is targeted.

The ability of children to cope in different situations is greatly enhanced if they have been helped to:

▶ Increase their self-awareness

▶ Build up self-esteem

▶ Develop an ability to express themselves (language skills)

▶ Take control where it is age and stage appropriate

▶ Cope with the unexpected

▶ Identify their champions/people who will stand up for them

▶ Develop problem-solving skills.

Services for Abused Children

The main services provided fall into the following broad categories:

▶   Prevention

▶   Support

▶   Investigation

▶   Therapy.

Prevention and Support

The role of the adult in early childhood services in support and prevention has already been outlined and must be emphasised. The legal or statutory responsibility of supporting children and families who are at risk and in the prevention of abuse lies with the Health Services Executive and childcare managers.

Under the Child Care Act 1991, the Health Services Executive has a duty to:

▶   Provide for children in need

▶   Prevent ill-treatment and neglect

▶   Promote the welfare of all children.

These services are outlined in more detail in Chapter 11. The following services are particularly relevant in the area of child protection – domiciliary support (support for families within their home), accommodation, day care and family centres.

Investigation

The statutory/legal duty to investigate cases of reported abuse lies with the social work team and the procedure has been outlined earlier in the chapter. In addition to the work of the social worker, other specialists in the area of psychology and paediatrics may be involved in establishing the nature and extent of the abuse, both physically and mentally. Specialist units in the children's hospitals – Crumlin, Temple Street and Tallaght (all in Dublin) – deal with the investigation and treatment of child sexual abuse.

Therapy

Depending on the nature and the extent of the abuse there are many specialists who can help children and families to overcome the trauma of abuse. Social workers and psychologists will provide support and counselling. Qualified play therapists may help children deal with their difficulties through play. A psychiatrist may be involved if there are severe psychiatric difficulties. A family therapist may work with the whole family to help restore healthy family relationships. As indicated earlier, for the vast majority of pre-school children the best therapy will be to remain in the early childhood service which is familiar to the child and the family – indeed, in some areas there may not be any other options. When this happens it is important that the early childhood worker liaises closely with any specialist therapist. It is equally important that the worker recognises the effects of stress and trauma on children and is able to provide the appropriate support, care, attention, stimulation and environment.

Every child is an individual with a distinct personality and therefore reactions to abuse will vary from child to child. Children may become aggressive and anti-social (fight) or they may become withdrawn, timid and sad (flight). Certainly the child's sense of himself as a worthy human being is damaged, as is his ability to form relationships, because abuse has meant that his trust in adults has been betrayed both by the adults who abused him as well as by all the adults around who did nothing to protect him.

In general, children who are troubled are difficult rather than easy to work with; the anger of one or the unresponsiveness of another may try the patience of the most professional of workers. Children who are severely damaged may need specialist therapeutic help, but this will not be of great benefit unless the child also has contact with caring, consistent adults on a daily basis.

The overriding need of troubled children is the need for their self-image and self-respect to be restored. This may take a long time.

Although the ultimate statutory responsibility lies with the HSE, voluntary agencies also play a big part in the area of child protection throughout Ireland. Barnardos Child and Family Services and the Irish Society for the Prevention of Cruelty to Children (ISPCC) are the two main national organisations who work in the area of child support and protection (see Chapter 11).

The *Children First: National Guidelines* were first published in 1999 and there is no doubt that adherence to the guidelines has contributed greatly to the care and protection of the nation's children. However, problems continue to arise due to the fact that the

TASK

Aim: To become familiar with child support and protection services in your area. Services and facilities vary greatly from area to area.

▸   What are the child support and protection services provided by your local (a) Health Service Executive and (b) voluntary agencies?

▸   Do you have child protection policies and procedures in your place of work? Are they written?

▸   What is the name of the senior social worker responsible for child protection services in your area?

guidelines are just that – guidelines – and have never been placed on a statutory footing. As a result, consistent, uniform and reliable implementation of the guidelines has not happened throughout the State. *The National Review of Compliance with Guidelines*, published in 2008, and *The Report of the Ombudsman on the Guidelines*, published in mid-2010, highlight these and many other serious issues, such as the lack of full 24-hour access to the Child Protection Notification System or the fact that resources in terms of social workers – who are essential to investigations – stand at about one-third of what is required. Recent revelations of abuse of children in foster care, children missing from care and the number of unnatural deaths of children in care or of those just out of care also serve to highlight serious shortcomings in resources and practice.

Legislation in relation to mandatory reporting of child abuse and a referendum on children's rights are also issues that need to be addressed.

SUMMARY

▸   The definition and understanding of child abuse and protection have changed over time and it is only since the 1970s that laws, procedures and policies for dealing with child abuse have been developed.

▸   Research indicates that some factors in a child's life or family predispose abuse, but these must be used with **extreme caution**; it is most important never to make assumptions or jump to conclusions.

▸   Good professional practice includes being aware of signs of abuse, drawing up policies and procedures and following these in all cases of suspected abuse, whether allegations are against unknown adults, family members or staff.

▸   All early childhood workers should be familiar with *The National Guidelines for the Protection and Welfare of Children*.

▸   The early childhood worker must be aware of the needs of all children and strive to empower them generally. When children have been abused the worker must take their additional needs into account, especially their damaged self-esteem and the fact that their trust in adults has been betrayed.

▸   Ultimate responsibility for child welfare, child protection and investigation lies with the Health Service Executive but voluntary agencies also provide important services in the area. It is important to be familiar with the local services.

References

Barnardos, 2000, *Guidelines for the Protection of Children in Early Years Services*, An Comhchoiste Réamhscolaíochta Teo, Barnardos, NCRC, Childminding Ireland, IPPA, NCNA.

Department of Health and Children, 1999, *Children First: The National Guidelines for the Protection and Welfare of Children*, Dublin: Stationery Office (also available online at www.omc.gov.ie).

Department of Health and Children, 2002, *Our Duty to Care: The Principles of Good Practice for the Protection of Children and Young People*, Dublin: Stationery Office (also available online at www.omc.gov.ie).

ISPCC, *Preventing Child Abuse Information Leaflet*, available online at www.ispcc.ie/media/publications.

Office of the Minister for Children and Youth Affairs, 2008, *National Review of Compliance with Children First: National Guidelines for the Protection and Welfare of Children*, Dublin: Stationery Office (also available online at www.omc.gov.ie/documents).

Ombudsman for Children's Office, 2010, *A Report Based on the Investigation into the Implementation of Children First: National Guidelines for the Protection and Welfare of Children*, Dublin: OCO (also available online at www.oco.ie).

SECTION FIVE

SOCIAL ISSUES

This section covers relevant aspects of the social framework for families and children in Ireland. Chapter 10 focuses on sociological concepts relevant to early childhood care and education, placing them within the context of the modern Irish family. Chapter 11 gives an overview of the Irish social services – housing, health, income maintenance, family support and education services.

10

SOCIOLOGY: KEY CONCEPTS FOR EARLY CHILDHOOD WORKERS

AREAS COVERED

▶   Socialisation
▶   Culture
▶   Social Roles
▶   The Family
▶   The Changing Face of the Irish Family

Introduction

The word 'sociology' was coined by Auguste Comte (1798–1857). Sociology is the scientific study of society, the causes and consequences of social change and the principles of social order and stability. It takes a look at the obvious from a not-so-obvious angle.

This chapter defines sociological concepts relevant to social development in early childhood. It describes varying forms and structures of families and partnerships, with particular reference to the modern Irish family. The focus taken is quite narrow and largely ignores historical, theoretical, economic and other influences.

Socialisation

Socialisation is the process by which human beings learn to live according to the values, rules and expectations of the society in which they live. The process involves learning through experience and through relationships. During the process children learn how to behave in different situations and they grow into adults who can function in a variety of social roles in that particular society.

Socialisation is divided into two stages: primary and secondary. **Primary socialisation** refers to the first stage, when the child learns basic patterns of acceptable behaviour, language and social skills. These are learned from those people who are closest to the child, i.e. parents, close family and main carers. These are referred to as the primary agents of socialisation. Early childhood experts consider that at this stage the child should have a small number of carers to relate to, and it is also important that these carers are working in partnership with each other so that the child receives consistent messages about appropriate ways to behave. The Child Care Act 1991 takes account of this important and intense stage of socialisation and has provided guidelines for staff–child ratios in early years settings (see Chapter 2).

Secondary socialisation takes place when children begin to have contact with the wider community, e.g. neighbours, friends, schools, clubs and churches. At this stage children begin to adapt to the wider world and learn to relate to a variety of people in a variety of different ways. Peers or friends have a huge influence on children from quite an early age, and they exert pressure on each other to conform and be part of the group. The media, particularly television and the internet, are increasingly influential secondary agents of socialisation in the modern developed world.

Figure 10.1: Primary and Secondary Socialisation

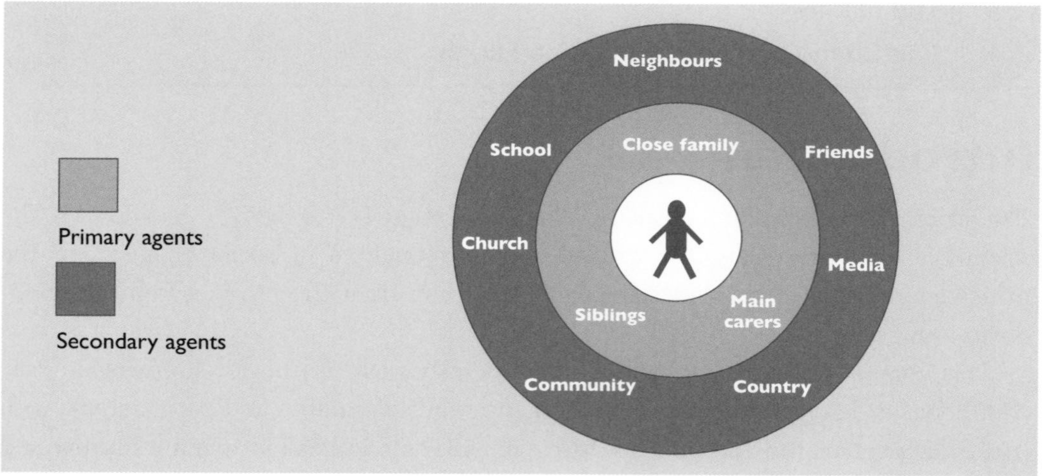

Culture

A **society** is a group of people who share the same culture, e.g. Irish people. Societies usually organise themselves in response to their environment. For example, the weather, economics and natural resources are factors which influence society. People in other cultures do things in a way that may seem weird and strange to us; equally, the way that we do things may seem weird and strange to others. Neither are weird or strange – just different. However, despite differences there are some major components in common – language, symbols, values, norms, beliefs and material culture.

Culture is the set of beliefs, values and norms that shapes the way individuals behave in a society. Aspects of culture change over time. Irish people share the same culture. Culture is complex and there are some differences in the way life is conducted. These differences might, for instance, reflect regional or social class variations.

Beliefs are a general set of opinions about how things should be. *In our society, we believe that children should be protected and cared for until they reach adulthood.*

Values are ideas that derive from beliefs and are about what is thought to be just, correct and proper. *Human life is given a high value and therefore it is considered a serious wrongdoing to take another person's life, but in times of war and conflict, a person may be rewarded for killing people.*

Norms are patterns of behaviour that are agreed and expected; they are common to everyone in a particular society and are sometimes enshrined in the laws of the country. *It is the norm in Ireland to shake hands when introduced to someone and everyone will feel comfortable with this; in some Islamic societies, however, shaking hands with a person of the opposite sex is considered highly improper and rules about greetings are different.*

Customs refer to patterns of behaviour that are common practice. These are sometimes called 'folkways' and are less crucial to social life than norms. *It is a custom in rural Ireland (albeit dying out in modern Ireland) when someone dies to have a wake where people can come to the deceased's home to pay their respects.*

The influence of travel and popular media has given rise to a convergence of cultures in the modern world and distinct, identifiable cultures and cultural traits may now be found only in more remote or marginalised societies.

ACTIVITY

Aim: To help distinguish between the different sociological terms described above.

Brainstorm the following:

▸ Decide on a society or nationality on which to focus (if Irish, then it will be easier to identify 'Irish' components).

▸ List all symbols, beliefs, values, norms and customs that you think are characteristic and specific to that culture.

Let me explain.

We aren't robbing the stuff because we want it, or just for the buzz. No. We're a mini-company. Three of us are in Transition year, in school. The brother who actually owns the wheelchair isn't. He's in Sixth year. We used to call him Superman, but he asked us to stop after Christopher Reeve died; it was upsetting his ma whenever she answered the landline. 'Is Superman there?' So, fair enough: we stopped.

Anyway, as part of our Transition year programme, me and Ms Nigeria and not-Superman's brother had to form a mini-company, to help us learn about the real world and commerce and that. And we didn't want to do the usual stuff, like making sock hangers and Rice Krispie cakes. So, we sat at a desk and watched closely by our delightful teacher, Ms They-Don't-Know-I-Was-Locked-Last-Night, we came up with the idea, and the name.

Black Hoodie Solutions.

from Doyle, Roddy, 2007, 'Black Hoodie', in *Deportees*, London: Jonathan Cape, pp. 130–53.

▸   What roles, values and beliefs are evident in the above story?

The Family

What Is a Family?

The definition of the 'family' used by the UN and broadly reflected by many sociological definitions is as follows: 'Any combination of two or more persons who are bound together by ties of mutual consent, birth and/or adoption or placement and who, together, assume responsibility for, inter alia, the care and maintenance of group members through procreation or adoption, the socialisation of children and the social control of members.'

This description includes families based on married and unmarried partnerships. The family remains one of the most important institutions in our society and it is recognised that there is a great diversity in family structures and forms in modern Irish society. However, the constitutional definition of families in Ireland includes only those based on marriage. The work of a number of national voluntary organisations focuses on the need for constitutional change in order to afford equal rights to all families – One Family, the national membership organisation of one-parent families; Treoir, The National Information Centre for parents who are not married to each other; and Marriage Equality, which lobbies for recognition of and equal rights for families with same-sex parents.

Recent census figures reveal that households with no children are the fastest-growing type of household in Ireland; European figures show that two-thirds of all households are those without children. Over three-quarters of families in Ireland contain two or fewer children, according to recent censuses.

Functions of the Family

In pre-industrial societies, family functions evolved in response to needs – their own and that of the community in which the family lived. These functions were primarily concerned with survival (production – making goods – and reproduction – making children!) and each family's contribution was essential to that survival.

The main functions of the pre-industrial family were as follows.

▶   **Socialisation:** Children required a group of dedicated carers to socialise them into society. The family were also the educators of the children.

▶   **Economic support:** While some people, usually women, were preoccupied with childbearing and childrearing, other committed members of the family were required to provide the basic necessities like food and accommodation. Family members were more dependent on each other economically when there was no social welfare system and the State did not provide support.

▶   **Regulation of sexual behaviour:** Almost all societies had some rules and regulations in this area. Unregulated sexual behaviour tended to cause lots of conflict. Contraception and family planning were not an option and it was necessary to provide a stable situation prior to the birth of children. In some societies the regulation of sexual activity was essential to the maintenance of family wealth and was tied into laws governing property and inheritance. Many churches reinforced such regulations on moral grounds.

▶   **Reproduction:** Societies needed to maintain their populations and families were seen, for the most part, to be the best place to rear children, whatever the family structure.

▶   **Emotional support:** Very little is known about the amount and origin of emotional support for family members in pre-industrial times. It is presumed that the mother was close to her children while they were young. In extended family situations she also probably supported her children when they had children if she survived long enough.

The Family Today

In modern times many of the traditional functions of the family have been transferred to other social systems. The family has changed from being primarily a unit of production and reproduction to being a unit of consumption of goods and services.

While most children probably spend their first few years being cared for by close family, this period of primary socialisation can be very short. Crèches, nurseries and pre-schools can provide full day care from the age of 3 months, and later on schools provide education.

The social services system can provide all the basics necessary for survival – housing, food and clothing. In extreme cases, the State can take over the parenting role by taking children into care. The Gardaí can provide protection.

Sexual behaviour no longer needs to be regulated in the same way because contraception has given people greater ability to separate reproduction from sexual activity. Relationships and the quality of the emotional bonds have taken centre stage to some extent. The relatively modern Westernised notion of romantic love which tends to drive relationships in Irish society defines and sets standards for the emotional relationship. If the emotional bond breaks down then the partnership often breaks down, regardless of the needs of the children or the economic circumstances of the family members.

Although the family unit continues to be an important and valuable factor in our society, there are some negative aspects to family life which cannot be ignored.

▶   **Violence:** Violence within families is probably as old as families themselves. In Ireland violence in the home has gained increasing recognition since the 1970s and refuges and services have grown accordingly (see Chapter 8).

▶   **Sexual abuse:** Most sexual abuse of children occurs within families and this aspect has only been highlighted in Ireland since about the 1980s. Sexual abuse seems to be generally perpetrated by male relatives and the full extent of this is not known (see Chapter 9).

▶   **The unequal position of women:** Women had less economic independence in the past; now they have more opportunities for economic independence but their unequal position within the family continues because they tend to have more responsibility for childcare. Recent studies suggest women continue to do the larger share of housework.

▶   **The economic burden of children:** In pre-industrial societies children were an asset. They provided labour so that the family production unit could produce more and in this way accumulate wealth. Today children consume the family wealth because of the length of their dependence and their protracted education.

ACTIVITY

Aim: To explore changes in family structures and definitions during the last half of the twentieth century.

In 1949, the family was defined as follows: 'A family is a social group characterised by common residence, economic co-operation and reproduction. It includes adults of both sexes, at least two of whom maintain a socially approved sexual relationship and one or more children owned or adopted by the sexually co-habiting adults.'

▸   List points that you think are still valid in Irish society today.

▸   List points that you think are no longer valid today.

Types of Families

Figure 10.2: Types of Family

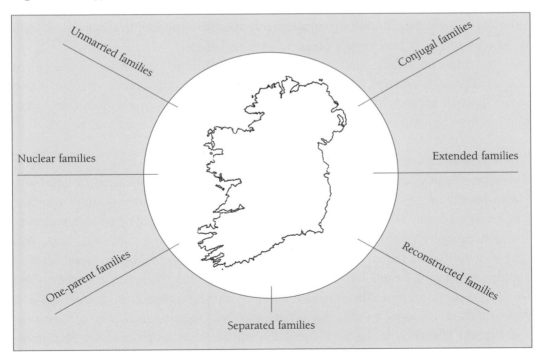

In most societies, different family structures and marriage patterns have grown in response to economic or population structures. Polygamy (where a man or a woman can have more than one spouse) gives rise to different types of extended family structures. In a society such as Ireland, whose laws only allow monogamy (which means one person in partnership with another), it is a crime to engage in other forms of marriage. A family organised around a married couple and their children is known as a conjugal family.

A large group of people who are living together and who are not closely related may be just friends, but if they are dependent on each other in their social and economic organisation then they are referred to as a commune.

There are three main types of family organisation in the modern Western world, all of which are based on monogamy. These are:

(a)   The nuclear family
(b)   The extended family
(c)   The reconstructed family.

The Nuclear Family

The nuclear family consists of parents and their children living in a unit that is separate from the wider family. Within this arrangement, partners and children depend on each other for support and are mostly independent of relatives.

The nuclear family also includes the one-parent family, which consists of one parent and a child/children living together. One-parent families occur because the parent has never lived in a partnership or because of death, separation or divorce. One-parent families have become more common in many Western, industrialised societies.

The Extended Family

This type of family consists of the nuclear unit plus other relatives living with, or in very close proximity to, each other. Other relatives may mean grandparents, aunts or uncles. The extended family is more common where living together in large groups is necessary for economic survival, as in agricultural societies or where family industries exist. This type of family also predominates where there is extreme poverty, as the members may supply mutual support and aid to each other in the form of clothing, cooking utensils and sleeping accommodation. The extended family is also important among Travellers and Asian families. The notion that many generations lived together in mutual contentment and support in Ireland in the past is probably mistaken, as people died younger, many people never married and those who did so married at an older age than at present.

The Reconstructed Family

A reconstructed family or stepfamily is one where two people who have had children within a previous relationship marry or co-habit and each bring their children to live together and have more children together. Divorce and separation are on the increase and research in Britain and the USA indicates that the majority of divorced men and women form another partnership within 5 years. This practice is known as **serial monogamy**. Reconstructed families may pose many problems in defining who our relatives are, as the following case illustration shows.

ACTIVITY

Aim: To introduce the family tree as a tool for representing family structure.

A Family Tree

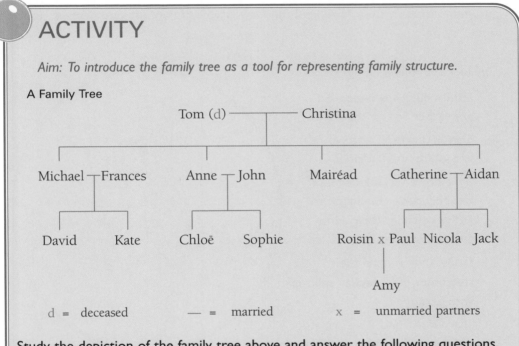

d = deceased   — = married   x = unmarried partners

Study the depiction of the family tree above and answer the following questions.

▶ How many grandchildren does Christina have?

▶ If they all live separately, how many nuclear family units are there?

▶ What is the relationship between Mairéad and Amy?

▶ If the grandmother, Christina, lives with her daughter Anne, how many people would be living in that extended household?

▶ Draw your own family tree.

▶ Draw a family tree for a family where the grandfather had three wives (as is possible outside Europe/in parts of Africa, Asia).

CASE STUDY

Sarah was divorced from her first husband, Youenn, when their three children were quite young; Shareen was 6 years, Ali was 4 years and Áine was 2 years. Two years later Sarah formed a relationship with Andy and he moved in to live with her and the children; with him was his daughter Leanne (11 years) from his previous marriage to Emma. They did not get married until 3 years later when Sarah was pregnant with Sam. Sam was only 3 years old when Sarah and Andy split up. Shareen, Ali and Áine maintain contact with their father, Youenn, who has a new partner called Alice, and they have two children, Marcus, 5 years, and Anna, 3 years.

Consider the following questions.

- ▶ When did Andy become a stepfather to the children?
- ▶ Can he become a stepfather without being married?
- ▶ Do Andy's parents become the children's grandparents and his siblings their aunts and uncles?
- ▶ Does Andy remain their stepfather after he has split up with Sarah?
- ▶ Shareen, Ali and Áine are step-siblings to Sam, Marcus and Anna — are Marcus and Anna related to Sam?
- ▶ What is the relationship between Leanne and Sam?
- ▶ Draw a family tree depicting the above reconstructed family.

The Changing Face of the Irish Family

The gender revolution, the sexual revolution, economics and education are just some of the factors that have transformed the face of family life in Ireland over the past 50 years. Four of the significant changes are as follows.

1. A sharp decline in the number of children in each family.

Two generations ago, families were much larger – five or six children was commonplace. Today, the standard family size is two or three children – larger families are the exception.

Table 10.1: Marriage and Birth Rates in Ireland, 1950–2009

Year	Marriages		Births	
	No.	Rates	No.	Rates
1950	16,018	5.4	63,565	21.4
1960	15,465	5.5	60,730	21.5
1970	20,778	7.1	64,092	21.8
1980	21,792	6.4	74,064	21.8
1990	17,838	5.1	53,044	15.1
2000	19,168	5.1	54,239	14.3
2005	20,723	5.0	61.040	14.8
2008	22,443	5.0	75,332	17.2
2009	21,541	4.8	74,728	18.7

Source: Central Statistics Office (www.cso.ie).

Table 10.2: Births Outside Marriage, 1960–2009

	1960	1979	1989	1999	2001	2006	2007	2008	2009
Total no. of live births	60,735	72,539	52,018	53,354	57,882	65,425	70,620	75,065	74,278
Total no. of births outside marriage	968	3,337	6,671	16,461	18,049	21,379	23,170	24,844	24,532
Births outside marriage as a total of all births	1.6%	4.6%	12.8%	30.9%	31.2%	32.7%	32.8%	33%	33%

Source: Central Statistics Office (www.cso.ie).

2. A sharp increase in the number of children born outside of marriage.

In 1960, never-married parents would have been virtually non-existent. These women and their children would have been largely invisible, as most of those children would have been placed for adoption, with a smaller number subsumed into the mother's family of origin. The introduction of the Unmarried Mother's Allowance in 1973 provided a means of supporting children outside of marriage. However, the greatest increase in the incidence of births to unmarried mothers has taken place since 1990, suggesting that economics alone is not the sole reason for the increase. Other factors may include changes in social mores and values and a decrease in adherence to religious regulations.

Today, one-third of all births are to mothers who are not married. Although there has been a tenfold increase in the number of births to unmarried mothers in the last 50 years, the profile of the unmarried mother has greatly changed. Around 10% of unmarried mothers are co-habiting, so a large cohort of unmarried mothers are not going to become lone parents. Another characteristic of unmarried mothers which they share with married mothers is that the age at which they have their first child is increasing, i.e. older first-time mothers. However, studies show that the older first-time unmarried mothers tend to be in a stable relationship and co-habiting. Younger unmarried mothers are overwhelmingly entering a phase of lone parenthood and there is an extremely strong relationship between low educational attainment and the likelihood of becoming a never-married lone mother; this in turn has implications for life chances for them and their children.

There has been a huge increase in the number of lone parents generally. For our purposes here, lone parents are defined as parents who are divorced, separated, widowed, never married or those who have partners in long-stay institutions such as hospital or prison. One of the most striking features when one examines the patterns of lone parenthood is that even as recently as 20 years ago, most lone parents were widows

Figure 10.3: One-parent Families

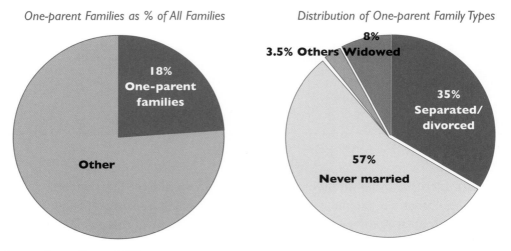

Source: Census figures 2002.

(64% in 1989). Just 11% were reported as being separated, and interestingly, a further 17% were classified as married, with only 7% describing themselves as unmarried. In an almost complete reversal, lone parents who never married account for 57% of all lone parents today, while widows account for a mere 8% (see Figure 10.3).

There is also a stark contrast between the profile of fathers and mothers who are lone parents. Most lone fathers (73%) are over 30 years old and have emerged from a marriage through death, divorce or separation. Mothers tend to be younger and only 40% have come to lone parenthood through marriage.

Figure 10.4a: Male Lone Parents

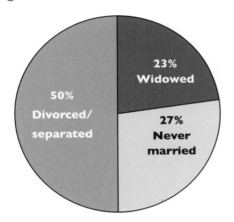

Figure 10.4b: Female Lone Parents

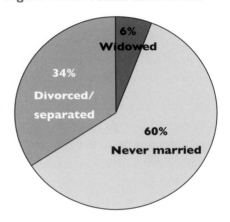

Source: Central Statistics Office (www.cso.ie).

3. Co-habitation.

Information in relation to co-habiting couples was gathered for the first time in the 1996 census and there is less information on co-habiting than on married couples. In the 10 years from 1996, numbers co-habiting grew from 33,300 to 121,800, so it is now a significant feature of the picture of the family in Ireland and also throws some light on the decrease in the rate of marriage.

There is a trend, especially among younger people of all social classes, to co-habit as a prelude to or as an alternative to marriage. In 2006, at age 25, twice the number of people were co-habiting as were married. Around 60% of co-habiting couples do not have children, but the incidence decreases with age; that is, the older the co-habiting couple is, the more likely they are to have children.

In the case of same-sex couples, marriage is not a legal option for them, so they only have the option of co-habiting. Again, data has only been available since 1996 and numbers have risen steeply, from 150 in 1996 to 2,090 in 2006. The figures in both years may well be understated for numerous reasons, not least because of the prejudice and discrimination that exist in relation to same-sex couples. Same-sex couples are overwhelmingly from a well-educated, upper middle-class section of Irish society.

Table 10.3: **Changing Family Structures, 1986–2006**

Number and percentage of family units by type							
Year	Married	%	Co-habiting	%	One-parent	%	Total
1986	634,767	85.8	N/A*	N/A	104,713	14.2	739,480
1996	646,421	80.0	31,298	3.9	129,116	16.0	806,835
2002	692,985	74.9	77,616	8.4	153,863	16.7	924,464
2006	742,177	70.4	121,763	11.6	189,240	18.0	1,053,120

* Figures for co-habitation were not available from the census that year.

Source: Central Statistics Office – Housing and Households (www.cso.ie).

4. A rise in the incidence of marital breakdown.

The number of one-parent families resulting from separation and/or divorce has been increasing steadily and currently accounts for just over a third (35%) of all lone parents. The number of recorded marriages which had broken down in 2006 was 198,592, up from 133,800 in 2002 – an increase of 48%. However, since divorce was introduced in Ireland in 1996, a number of people whose marriage has broken down will have remarried or established another partnership, thus moving in and out of lone parenthood.

Since the Constitution was written there have been many social and legal changes which have had profound effects on family life in Ireland. Most of these have taken place from 1970 onwards. The impact of EU membership on our social and economic policies has been significant. The increase in the economic independence of women, the decrease of the stigma of out-of-wedlock births, the influence of the media, travel (emigration and immigration) and the altered position of the Catholic Church are just some of the factors that have contributed to the changes in composition structures and patterns of family life in Ireland. Some of these changes are mirrored in other countries, particularly in Europe, and some are unique. For a more in-depth study, see *Family Figures: Family Types and Family Dynamics in Ireland 1986–2006* (full reference below).

SUMMARY

▸ Society passes on its culture, values, beliefs, norms and customs through the socialisation process.

▸ Children learn how to expect others to behave and how to behave themselves in society by learning social roles.

▸ The family is the primary socialising agent and therefore is a very important element in practically all societies.

▸ The structures and functions of the family have changed greatly since the industrial revolution.

▸ Many of the traditional functions of the family are now undertaken by the State.

▸ Since the foundation of the Irish State and particularly since joining the European Union, there have been major changes in social and economic policies which have affected the family.

▸ Family composition, structures and patterns have changed considerably in the last 20 years.

References

Bunreacht na hÉireann, 1937, Dublin: Stationery Office (www.taoiseach.gov.ie/constitutionofireland).

Census of Population, 2006, *Principal Demographic Results*, Dublin: CSO Government Publications (www.cso.ie).

Doyle, Roddy, 2007, 'Black Hoodie' in *Deportees*, London: Jonathan Cape.

Lunn, P., T. Fahey and C. Hannan, 2009, *Family Figures: Family Types and Family Dynamics in Ireland 1986–2006*, Dublin: Economic and Social Research Institute (also available online at www.esri.ie).

11

SOCIAL SERVICES

AREAS COVERED

▶   Overview of Social Services in Ireland

▶   Housing

▶   Health Services

▶   Income Maintenance

▶   Family Support and Child Welfare Services

▶   Education

▶   Voluntary Services

Introduction

The main areas of social service provision are housing, health, income maintenance, personal social services and education. In Ireland they have developed in a piecemeal and haphazard fashion but they do affect, and are used by, almost the entire population at some time in their lives. Almost one half of Government spending is on social services. Everyone benefits from the system at some level – education is free and compulsory and all families are entitled to claim Child Benefit. Hospital and healthcare services are available at varying costs to all. However, the greater the stresses on the person/family/group, the more they are going to need to use the social services that are available to them.

This chapter outlines services provision in each sector – except early childhood education, which is covered in Chapter 1. A brief history of the development of the service in Ireland and an examination of social problems related to the service will be included.

Overview of Social Services in Ireland

Social services are shaped by social policy, which in turn is shaped by economics, demographics and politics. A report to the National Economic and Social Forum in the mid 1970s defined social policy as 'those actions of Government which deliberately or accidentally affect the distribution of resources, status, opportunities and life chances among social groups and categories of people within the country and thus help to shape the general character and equity of its social relations.'

Furthermore, NESC has outlined the aims of social policy in Ireland:

▶   The reduction of inequalities of income and wealth

▶   The elimination of inequalities of opportunity

▶   The provision of employment

▶   The provision of access to services for all

▶   The development of services for disadvantaged groups

▶   The development of responsible citizenship.

In general, one of the principal aims of social policy is to alleviate poverty.

What Is Poverty?

The National Anti-Poverty Strategy (NAPS), published by the Government in 1997, adopted the following definition of poverty:

> People are living in poverty if their income and resources (material, cultural and social) are so inadequate as to preclude them from having a standard of living that is regarded as acceptable by Irish society generally. As a result of inadequate income and resources people may be excluded and marginalised from participating in activities that are considered the norm for other people in society.

This definition has been reiterated in the 2007 *National Action Plan for Social Inclusion 2007–2016.*

How many people are poor and on what basis are they classified as poor? There are two types of poverty: relative and consistent.

Relative poverty, or at risk of poverty, is hard to define; it means that some people are poor compared to others, or are poor in terms of what is acceptable as a basic standard of living in the country in which they live. The most common approach is to adopt a poverty line, and those whose income is below this line are considered to be living in poverty. In Ireland, 60% of the median income (median income is the income of the middle person in the country's income distribution) has been adopted as the primary poverty line.

In 2010, the minimum weekly disposable income (after taxes and including all benefits) that one adult needs to receive to be out of poverty was set (using CSO survey and ESRI figures) at €224.75. For each additional adult in the household, this minimum income figure is increased by €148.33 (66% of the poverty line figure), and for each child in the household the minimum income figure is increased by €74.17 (33% of the poverty line). It is interesting to note that most basic social welfare payments fall below the poverty line threshold. (Other issues relating to poverty and inequality are covered in Chapter 13.)

Consistent poverty is relative poverty combined with long-term lack of basic items. In 2007, the Government revised the deprivation indicators of consistent poverty to focus to a greater degree on items reflecting social inclusion and participation in society.

The indicators of deprivations are if one is consistently lacking two or more of the 11 items on the list below.

1.   Two pairs of strong shoes
2.   A warm, waterproof overcoat
3.   Buy new, not secondhand, clothes
4.   Eat meals with meat, chicken, fish (or vegetarian equivalent) every second day
5.   Have a roast joint or its equivalent once a week
6.   Had to go without heating during the last year through lack of money
7.   Keep the home adequately warm
8.   Buy presents for family or friends at least once a year
9.   Replace any worn-out furniture
10.   Have family or friends for a drink or meal once a month
11.   Have a morning, afternoon or evening out in the last fortnight, for entertainment

Due to the recesssion and decreases in income, it is expected that definitions of poverty lines will change over the next 4 years.

The provision of health and social care in Ireland is through a combination of statutory, voluntary and private services. Informal services provided by families, friends and social networks also play an important part.

Statutory Services

These services are provided by the State and are prescribed by State law. The State is responsible for funding such services, although that does not necessarily mean that they are free to everyone; some are public and some are private. This is referred to as a two-tiered system.

Statutory services are provided in the following areas.

1.   Housing – Department of the Environment, Heritage and Local Government
2.   Health – Department of Health and Children
3.   Income Maintenance (Social Welfare) – Department of Social Protection
4.   Personal Social Services – Department of Health and Children
5.   Education – Department of Education and Skills

Voluntary Services

These services are provided by voluntary bodies, charities and volunteers. A service is described as voluntary when it has been set up by people who identify a need and who organise the resources to meet that need without being required to do so by law. Voluntary agencies or groups may receive Government grants but that usually falls far short of their full financial requirements, so a lot of fundraising and voluntary work are often involved.

Voluntary organisations can have a number of different functions and sometimes all these functions are fulfilled by a single organisation.

▶   Providing information, e.g. Threshold (housing and accomodation)

▶   Supporting individuals or families through services and/or counselling, e.g. Barnardos (Child and Family Services), rape crisis centres

▶   Campaigning for change in State provision or in laws, e.g. Children's Rights Alliance

▶   Providing money/material for people in need, e.g. St Vincent de Paul.

It is incorrect to assume that all those working for voluntary organisations are volunteers and unpaid. Most established voluntary organisations have permanent employees and are subject to standard labour laws and rates of pay.

Private Services

These services are primarily set up to make a profit while meeting an identified need. A large number of pre-school services in Ireland are private services, as are the majority of caring institutions for the elderly.

TASK

Aim: To become acquainted with the voluntary services in your local area.

Find out the following.

▸   What are the voluntary agencies in your area?

▸   What kind of service do they provide?

▸   What is their target population?

▸   Where do they get funding (Government grants/fundraising)?

▸   How many staff are salaried and how many are volunteers?

▸   What level of training do staff and volunteers receive?

▸   Which of these services are specific to children?

Housing

The recognised sectors in Irish housing are:

1. Owner occupied
2. Local authority or public housing
3. Private rented
4. Social and affordable housing.

Table 11.1: Sectors in Irish Housing, 1946–2006

Sector	1946	1961	1981	2002	2006
Owner occupied (%)	52.7	59.8	76.1	77.4	73.1
Local authority (%)	16.5	18.4	15.5	6.9	7.2
Private rented (%)	26.1	17.2	13.3	11	9.9
Other (social housing) (%)	4.7	4.6	2.4	1	3.5
Total housing stock	662,654	676,402	726,363	1,288,000	1,462,296

Source: Census of Population, various years.

While the main aim of Irish Government policy in relation to housing has been that every family should have access to adequate housing, one of the central features of its policy has been the encouragement of owner occupation through various measures – tax relief on mortgages, grants and subsidies. Quite apart from the encouragement of home ownership, the Government is also concerned with the maintenance of standards, environmental issues and with the provision of housing to persons who cannot afford to buy their own. Three sectors have existed in the Irish system throughout the history of the Irish State. In recent years social or voluntary housing has also become a feature of the housing scene, albeit a minor one. The Department of Environment, Heritage and Local Government is responsible for regulations governing the provision of housing in the State. Those who own their own houses are more secure, both financially (each mortgage payment is an investment) and in the sense that they have more choice about where they live.

Discrimination may flourish in the private rented sector because the owner has complete control in terms of choice of tenant to whom he rents. Tenant rights are very few and difficult to enforce. Under the Housing (Miscellaneous Provisions) Act 1992, regulations were introduced in relation to rent books, standards for rented dwellings and registration of rented houses. Subsidies for tenants in this sector include the Rent Allowance Scheme and tax relief for some people.

The Residential Tenancies Act 2004 contains significant reforms of the private rental sector. These reforms include provision for an improved security of tenure; new termination procedures where notice periods are linked to length of tenancy; the establishment of a statutory Private Residential Tenancies Board (PRTB) which will include a dispute resolution/mediation service; new tenancy registration requirements, and higher penalties for offences. The Act also extends local authority powers to address anti-social behaviour.

Local authority (public) housing accounts for an ever decreasing section of Irish housing stock, although the trend was reversed slightly between 2006 and 2008. This is in part due to the fact that local authorities are completing comparatively fewer housing units than are being completed in the private sector and partly because some of the existing public stock is being sold off to existing tenants. Housing statistics show that there was a considerable number (44,783) of local authority houses purchased by tenants in 2002, but in 2006 this fell to 23,547, probably because of the unprecedented rise in the price of houses.

Table 11.2: **House Completions by Sector**

	Local authority	Voluntary/ co-operative	Private	Total
2005	4,201	1,350	75,398	80,957
2006	3,967	1,240	88,211	93,419
2007	4,986	1,685	71,356	78,027
2008	4,905	1,896	44,923	51,724

Source: CSO, various years.

The escalation of house prices until 2007 has had the effect of making home ownership less and less attainable for many and the numbers of people applying for public/social housing has risen accordingly. It is interesting to note that when the economic downturn occurred, while the number of private house completions plummeted, those in the local authority section remained fairly steady and those in the voluntary/co-operative section actually increased.

Public housing provision aims to meet the needs of those who:

▸   Are living in unfit or overcrowded conditions

▸   Do not have sufficient finances to buy their own house

▸   Have special needs, e.g. elderly people or those who have a disability

▸   Have become homeless.

A number of measures have been introduced to diversify and extend the approaches to the provision of public housing.

SUMMARY OF NEW SCHEMES INTRODUCED OR EXTENDED

Rental Accommodation Scheme — Local authorities will be responsible for accommodation for those who are in receipt of a Supplementary Welfare Allowance.

Action Plan for Social and Affordable Housing — A 5-year action plan to develop an integrated and systematic approach.

Public Private Partnerships — To encourage the development of housing developments which incorporate private, public and social housing units.

Social Rented Accommodation — Local authority houses are allocated on a scheme of letting priorities and rent is related to ability to pay (differential rents).

Improvement works in lieu of rehousing — A local authority may take responsibility for renovating or extending privately owned houses in order to provide adequate accommodation.

Local Authority Extension Schemes — Aim to improve accommodation in existing local authority houses.

Tenant Purchase Schemes — Tenants of at least 1 year may apply to purchase the house outright or to part-purchase – shared ownership.

Voluntary and Co-operative Housing — **Capital assistance** and **capital loans and subsidies** will be made available to voluntary bodies providing accommodation to meet specialist need. Grants of up to 100% can be provided.

Affordable Housing Schemes — Affordable housing is provided for under the Shared Ownership and Sustaining Progress Initiative. This means that newly built houses are made available at discounted prices. In addition, the Planning and Development Acts 2000–2004 require that 20% of zoned land for development is to be reserved to meet social and affordable housing needs. Other measures include the Mortgage Allowance Scheme and local authority, home improvement and house purchase loans.

Mortgage allowance scheme

Provision of low-cost sites

Local authority loans for house purchase and improvements

Disabled Person's Grant

Essential Repairs Grants

A less desirable characteristic of public housing provision in the past has been the tendency to build large estates or flat complexes where people were isolated, often without proper amenities and services. The key objective of current housing policy is to build sustainable communities and to meet individual accommodation needs in a manner that facilitates and empowers personal choice and autonomy. Sustainable communities are places where people want to live and work, now and in the future. They meet the diverse needs of existing and future residents, are sensitive to their environment and contribute to a high quality of life. They are safe and inclusive, well-planned, built and run, offer equality of opportunity and good services for all. This aim is grounded in the view of housing and its positive potential in contributing to overall social and economic well-being.

Delivering Homes, Sustaining Communities, a policy document published in February 2007, presents a vision for the future for housing. It is a companion to the *National Development Plan 2007–2013: Transforming Ireland – A Better Quality of Life for All*, which provides the resources for required investment, and the *National Action Plan for Social Inclusion*, which focuses on social inclusion issues in particular. The broad approach to housing set out in the *Housing Policy Framework – Building Sustainable Communities* has been endorsed and elaborated by the social partners in *Towards 2016. Towards 2016 –* the 10-year strategic framework for economic and social development – reflects significant commitments in the housing area. As well as endorsing the policy approach set out in the *Housing Policy Framework*, the agreement reflects a desire to transform Irish housing services over the coming decade by improving the quality of housing as well as expanding the provision of housing supports.

The Housing (Miscellaneous Provisions) Act 2009 establishes the legislative framework for a more strategic approach by local authorities for the delivery and management of housing services.

Voluntary housing accounts for a very small proportion of houses in Ireland today. Initially, such housing was provided by businesses to encourage and provide for workers who migrated to the city, e.g. Guinness was one of the first. Voluntary housing today is aimed at vulnerable groups who might not be able to get housing on their own. Ireland has one of the least developed voluntary housing movements in the EU. The Irish Council for Social Housing was formed in 1982 and represents over 300 affiliated housing associations and voluntary groups involved in providing housing or accommodation for vulnerable groups. The best known of these organisations are Focus Ireland, the Simon Community and St Vincent de Paul, to name but a few. Local authorities remain the main providers of housing for those in need who cannot afford it on their own.

Homelessness

The legal definition of homelessness comes from the Housing Act 1998. A person is considered homeless if, in the opinion of the local authority:

▶   They have no accommodation they can reasonably occupy or remain in occupation of

▶   They are living in temporary accommodation because they have nowhere else to go

▶   They cannot afford to get their own accommodation.

This definition includes those who are living with family, but in overcrowded conditions, those living with friends or in bed and breakfasts.

The Act, while not placing a statutory duty on local authorities to accommodate homeless people, did empower them to provide a range of suitable options in conjunction with other agencies. The Department of the Environment, Heritage and Local Government issued guidelines to this effect.

The Child Care Act 1991 addressed the needs of homeless youths for the first time in legislation.

Homelessness has been highlighted by a number of voluntary agencies over the past few decades, most notably Focus Ireland and the Simon Community. As part of the Government strategy on homelessness, the Homeless Agency was established in 2001 and is now responsible for the management and co-ordination of services in the Dublin area, where the number of homeless people was increasing at an unprecedented rate because of increases in marriage breakdown, immigration and soaring house prices.

The following groups are at the greatest risk of becoming homeless:

▶   Long-term unemployed people

▶   One-parent families

▶   People who are discharged from long-stay institutions

▶   Children out of long-term care

▶   Youths who run away from or are rejected by their families.

Measuring the extent of homelessness is difficult because it depends on the definition of homeless by different agencies, as well as by individuals themselves, and also because people who are homeless move about or are hidden (i.e. staying with friends or family). As part of the Government strategy to constantly assess the housing need, local authorities must assess the numbers of homeless people in their area every 3 years. Tables 11.3, 11.4 and 11.5 give a snapshot of the national housing needs as assessed by all the local authorities at present. Despite successive commitments to address housing needs, there was a considerable increase in the numbers requiring housing. The majority of people requiring housing are in the younger age groups, and of course this ties in with the statistics on families and children who are in need. Another significant statistic arising out of the assessment is that 715 young people who had been in care were homeless in 2008. Counts of the number of people actually sleeping rough vary widely. The official statistic of the Department of the Environment, Heritage and Local

Government recorded a total of 113 sleeping rough in all of Ireland in 2008 (with Dublin Council recording no rough sleepers at all!), while *Counted In*, a survey of homelessness in the Dublin area, alone recorded 110 rough sleepers in March of the same year.

Table 11.3: Housing Needs Assesments for Various Years

1991	1993	1996	1999	2002	2005	2008	Change in net need from 2005 to 2008	Change in net need from 1991 to 2008
20,343	28,200	27,427	39,176	48,413	42,946	56,249	31.0%	177%

Source: Council for Social Housing.

Table 11.4: Breakdown of Ages of Housing Applicant, March 2008

Up to 17 years	18–25 years	26–30 years	31–40 years	41–50 years	51–60 years	61–70 years	71+ years	Total
16	12,178	9,900	15,799	9,438	5,449	2,361	1,108	56,249

Source: Council for Social Housing.

Table 11.5: Families with Children

	Single with children	Married with children	Total
2005	16,795	5,540	22,335
2008	25,550	7,655	33,205
Increase	52%	38%	48%

Source: Council for Social Housing.

The implications of being homeless are many, including:

▶ Discrimination

▶ Risk of exploitation

▶ Difficulty in acquiring social welfare, a medical card, etc. without a fixed address

▶ The near impossibility of getting a job

▶ Deterioration of physical and mental health.

Effects of Homelessness on Children

It is difficult to consider the effects of homelessness and poor housing on children in isolation, as the problems are usually compounded by other adverse circumstances, e.g. poverty and marital breakdown. Many families who become homeless are accommodated by the Health Service Executive in bed and breakfasts because of the lack of suitable housing.

Poor housing, inadequate household amenities and overcrowded conditions are associated with:

▸ Poor social and emotional adjustment and lower educational attainments.

▸ A higher incidence of physical illnesses because of damp, infestation, lack of hygiene facilities and accidents. The family may be confined to one room where space is at a premium and it may be difficult for the children to get to sleep.

▸ Stress – adults who are trying to rear children in such adverse conditions may become worn out from the everyday effort to survive and may not have the physical, mental or emotional energy to cater adequately for the children's overall needs.

▸ Overly strict parenting – overcrowding, lack of privacy, lack of space and the sheer pressure on parents to keep the children quiet and out of other people's way can lead to parents having to be very strict. There are often rules about noise and running in corridors, all of which culminate in an extremely restrictive experience for the child. This in turn leads to understimulation, pent-up energy and frustration. Children who have to live in such conditions may be more aggressive and impulsive and have a greater difficulty concentrating.

▸ Security – the family may be moving around from hostel to hostel or between bed and breakfast accomodation, and typically this can go on for some time before the family's housing needs are met. Their familiar environment and routines will have totally changed. Schooling may be disrupted and the family isolated from neighbours and friends. Parents will not be able to prepare children for changes because the parents themselves will not know what is going to happen.

▸ Powerlessness – if parents feel powerless in this situation, children will feel even more so.

Development in every area at all stages can be severely affected. In such situations the provision of good childcare services can be a lifeline.

Health Services

The Department of Health and Children is responsible for health service provision in Ireland and these services are delivered through the Health Service Executive (HSE). Total investment provision for the health sector is over €15 billion. (This includes personal social services delivered by the National Children's Office.)

Ireland has a two-tiered health service – a private service for those who can afford to pay the fees or who can afford to pay for health insurance each year, and a public service which is available to everyone and provided free for those whose income falls below a certain threshold. The public service is inadequate to meet the demands at present and waiting lists are invariably long. The environments in which private services are offered are generally more comfortable, less stressful and offer more privacy than the public service environment.

The four administrative areas of the Health Service Executive are:

1. **Dublin/North East:** Cavan, Monaghan, Louth, Meath and Community Care Areas 6, 7 and 8 in North Dublin.
2. **Dublin/Mid Leinster:** Kildare, Laois, Longford, Offaly, Westmeath, Wicklow and Community Care Areas 1, 2, 3, 4 and 5 in South Dublin.
3. **Western:** Clare, Limerick, Galway, Mayo, Sligo, Donegal, Leitrim, Roscommon and North Tipperary.
4. **Southern:** Carlow, Kilkenny, South Tipperary, Wexford, Waterford, Cork and Kerry.

The HSE delivers services under three interdependent programmes:

1. Primary, Community and Continuing Care (PCCC).

This area is responsible for the provision of all health and personal social services, including primary care, mental health, disability services, community hospital and continuing care services. These services are organised through four administrative areas and are delivered through 32 Local Health Offices which will have direct lines to their national office.

2. The National Hospitals Office (NHO).

This area is responsible for managing and co-ordinating the delivery of acute hospital services in all 53 statutory and non-statutory hospitals and emergency care centres. It is also responsible for approving specialised treatment to patients in other countries. To facilitate closer co-operation and integration with PCCC at local level, the hospital networks will be aligned to the four administrative areas.

3. Population Health.

This area is responsible for promoting and protecting the health of the entire population and target groups with particular emphasis on health inequalities. Population Health is responsible for immunisations, infection control and environmental health. It will be organised through local health offices and the hospital networks.

The National Anti-Poverty Strategy (NAPS) includes specific targets for the reduction of inequalities in and the improvement of equal access to health services for all

Figure 11.1: Health Service Executive Areas

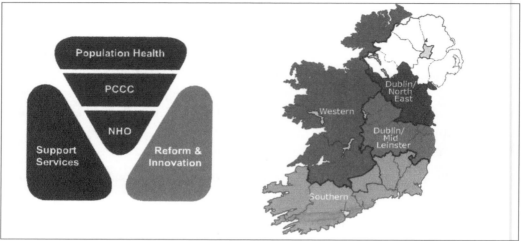

Source: Health Service Executive (www.hse.ie).

Eligibility for Health Services

The main legislation governing eligibility is the Health Act 1970. Anyone who is normally resident in the country (i.e. one who is living here and intends to continue to live here for a minimum of 1 year) is eligible for health and personal social services. For persons entitled to services under EU regulations, the requirement to be 'ordinarily resident' does not apply. Eligibility is not the same as entitlement.

Briefly, since the Health Act 1970, under the general medical services, eligible persons can access health and social services under two main schemes.

Eligibility for a medical card is assessed by way of a means test, and if eligible it covers healthcare for the cardholder, his spouse and any children under the age of 16 years. The means test specifies the weekly income limits to qualifying for either the medical or 'doctor-only' card; there may be allowances made over and above the income limit for certain expenses incurred in respect of childcare costs, rent/mortgage payments, travel costs to work or special diet.

Medical card holders are entitled to:

▶   General practitioner services

▶   Prescribed drugs and medicines (with some exceptions)*

▶   All inpatient public hospital services in public wards

- All outpatient public hospital services
- All consultant services within public hospital services
- Dental, ophthalmic and aural services and appliances
- A maternity and infant care service
- A maternity cash grant.

* A charge per prescription item has been introduced for medical card holders. Over 1.25 million people held medical cards in 2009 and almost another 100,000 held doctor-only cards.

People who exceed the income limit for a medical card may be eligible to apply for a 'doctor-only' card (introduced in 2005), which entitles them to free GP services only.

Non-card holders are entitled to some subsidised services:

- All inpatient public services in public wards (including consultant's fees) subject to set public hospital charges.
- Outpatient public hospital services, subject to a set charge excluding dental, aural and ophthalmic services.
- Free maternity and infant care services.
- A refund on prescribed drugs when over a specified amount is spent in any given quarter. These amounts are revised from time to time.
- Free drugs and medicines under the Long-Term Illness Scheme.

Details of public hospital charges, the Drugs Refund Scheme and medical card guidelines are revised regularly and up-to-date details are available from the Health Service Executive.

A number of other schemes govern eligibility for access to services for certain groups of the population. These include the Long-Term Illness Scheme, Infectious Diseases Regulations, Maternity and Infant Care Scheme, School Medical Service, Nursing Home Subvention Scheme, Public Dental Service, preventive services such as immunisation schemes and early detection services such as breast cancer screening.

Long-Term Illness Scheme

People who have any of the following long-term conditions can obtain drugs, medicines, medical and surgical aids in relation to that condition free of charge, regardless of their income: mental handicap, mental illness (for children under 16 years only), phenylketonuria, cystic fibrosis, spina bifida, hydrocephalus, diabetes mellitus, diabetes insipidus, haemophilia, cerebral palsy, epilepsy, multiple sclerosis, muscular dystrophy, parkinsonism and acute leukaemia, and conditions associated with Thalidomide.

Drugs Payment Scheme

Under this scheme no individual or family, regardless of income, pays more than a certain amount (in 2011 this was €120 per family or individual) per calendar month towards the cost of approved, prescribed medicines.

The National Treatment Purchase Fund (NTPF)

This was set up in Ireland as a result of the National Health Strategy 2001, which laid down that no adult should wait longer than 6 months and no child longer than 3 months to begin treatment following referral from the outpatient department of a public hospital. Patients may be treated in private hospitals in Ireland or the UK, or indeed further afield if necessary. By 2010, 165,000 people had received treatment under the NTPF. The scheme:

▸ Aims to reduce waiting times for public patients who have been waiting the longest

▸ Will arrange and purchase treatment and/or procedures for public patients only with the patient's permission

▸ Covers all the costs of the treatment including travel and the expenses of an accompanying person.

Health Services for Children

The following services are available free to all regardless of income.

▸ A mother and infant care service which includes the services of a family doctor, inpatient and outpatient services in a maternity unit/hospital for the mother during pregnancy and for the mother and baby for up to 6 weeks after the birth.

▸ Medical tests and screening for metabolic disorders for all newborn babies.

▸ Developmental and supportive visits from a public health visitor after the birth of a baby.

▸ Developmental examination at 9 months at the local health centre.

▸ Free dental treatment for pregnant women.

▸ A health examination service for pre-school and primary school children.

▸ All necessary follow-up services for problems discovered during these examinations, including dental, optical and aural problems.

▸ A national screening service for scoliosis from Our Lady's Hospital, Crumlin, Dublin.

▸ Inpatient and outpatient hospital services for all children under 16 years who have mental handicap, mental illness, phenylketonuria, cystic fibrosis, spina bifida, hydrocephalus, haemophilia or cerebral palsy.

▶   Immunisation against a number of infectious diseases.

Table 11.6: Immunisation Schedule for Children Born after 1 July 2008

Age	Where	Vaccine
Birth	Hospital or clinic	BCG vaccination (a vaccine to protect against tuberculosis)
2 months	GP	6 in 1 (diphtheria, tetanus, whooping cough (pertussis), polio, HiB (haemophilus influenzae type B) and hepatitis B is provided in one single injection) plus a vaccine against pneumococcal disease in a separate injection
4 months	GP	6 in 1 (diphtheria, tetanus, whooping cough (pertussis), polio, HiB (haemophilus influenzae type B) and hepatitis B is provided in one single injection) plus a vaccine against meningococcal C in a separate injection
6 months	GP	6 in 1 (diphtheria, tetanus, whooping cough (pertussis), polio, HiB (haemophilus influenzae type B) and hepatitis B is provided in one single injection) plus vaccines against meningococcal C and pneumococcal disease
12 months	GP	MMR (measles, mumps and rubella) (pdf) vaccine, plus a vaccine against pneumococcal disease
13 months	GP	Vaccine against meningococcal C and HiB (haemophilus influenzae type B)
4–5 years	GP	4 in 1 (diphtheria, tetanus, whooping cough (pertussis) and polio), or school plus MMR (measles, mumps and rubella) (pdf) vaccine
11–14 years	School	Td (tetanus and low-dose diphtheria)

Source: Health Service Executive (www.hse.ie).

The Health Strategy 2001, *Quality and Fairness*, which has been published by the Department of Health and Children, sets out detailed plans for the development and improvement of the health services over 10 years until 2011. It sets out an action plan which includes target dates.

The strategy sets out four main goals:

1. Policies which promote health, reduce inequalities and ensure a better health service for all.
2. Fair access, which aims to ensure equality of access.

3.   Responsive and appropriate care delivery.
4.   High performance.

Also included in the strategy is a commitment to introduce clear statutory provisions on entitlement and to define the full range of health and personal social services.

The Health Information and Quality Authority (HIQA) was established in May 2007 as part of the Government's health reform programme. The functions of HIQA are as follows.

▸   Setting standards in health and social services

▸   Monitoring healthcare quality

▸   Social Services Inspectorate

▸   Health technology assessment

▸   Health information.

It spans the entire health and social services system, with the exception of mental health services.

The state of health services and delivery is still considered to be far from ideal, with reports that queues in accident and emergency departments continue to get longer and mental health services are considered to be particularly poor. Like other departments, funding for services provided by the Department of Health and Children was cut in the 2010 Budget and seems likely to be cut even further in future budgets. Therefore, some of the services and schemes outlined above will probably have to change.

Income Maintenance

In Ireland, 'income maintenance' is more commonly referred to as 'social welfare'. It is the system by which the State aims to provide a basic income for all individuals, families and their children at times when they are unable to earn an income from employment, e.g. due to illness, unemployment, disability or old age. The Department of Social Protection is responsible for the provision of social welfare and related services.

The Irish social welfare system embraces three types of income maintenance schemes:

1.   Social insurance
2.   Social assistance
3.   Universal allowances.

1. Social Insurance

Social insurance (contributory benefits) is based on Pay-Related Social Insurance (PRSI) contributions. Entitlement to social insurance benefits is conditional on the claimant having a certain number of contributions paid or credited in a specific period of time.

2. Social Assistance

Social assistance (non-contributory allowances or assistance). One of the basic requirements to qualify for payment under the social assistance schemes is that persons making a claim must satisfy a means test which shows that they have insufficient income to cover the basic necessities of life. The system of the means test here is different to that used for assessing eligibility for the medical card; it is highly complex and a Deciding Officer makes decisions about eligibility.

The Habitual Residence Condition is a condition that an individual must satisfy in order to qualify for certain social welfare payments. This condition requires that a person must be living within Ireland and the UK for 2 years or more and now lives in Ireland and intends to remain here.

EU/EEA citizens who are employed or self-employed in Ireland do not have to satisfy the Habitual Residence Condition in order to qualify for the following benefits (known as 'family benefits'):

▶   One-Parent Family Payment

▶   Orphan's Non-Contributory Pension

▶   Family Income Supplement

▶   Child Benefit.

The Social Welfare Appeals Office was set up in 1991 to deal with all appeals against decisions made by Deciding Officers.

The Supplementary Welfare Allowance is payable to those who do not qualify for assistance or benefits. Social Welfare Officers who are attached to health centres administer this allowance. There are also special grants and supplements available under this scheme, such as:

▶   Rent and Mortgage Interest Supplements

▶   Back to School Clothing and Footwear Allowance

▶   Supplements for special housing and dietary needs

▶   Exceptional Needs Payments

▶   Urgent Needs Payments.

The amount of payment, conditions and eligibility regarding social insurance, social assistance and supplementary welfare payments change regularly (typically after the annual budget), so it is advisable to get an up-to-date copy of the *Guide to Social Welfare Services* from the local office.

Figure 11.2: Income Supports

Employment Supports	Unemployability Supplement
Family Income Supplements	Medical Care Scheme
Farm Assist	Constant Attendance Allowance
Back to Work Allowance (Employees)	Death Benefits (Survivor's Benefits)
Back to Work Enterprise Allowance	
Part-Time Job Incentive Scheme	**Payments for Retired or Older People**
Back to Education Allowance	Retirement Pension
	Old Age (Contributory) Pension
Unemployment Supports	Old Age (Non-Contributory) Pension
Jobseekers Benefit	Pre-Retirement Allowance
Jobseekers Assistance	
	Extra Benefits
Child-related Payments	Bereavement Grant
Child Benefit	Widowed Parent's Grant
Maternity Benefit	Fuel Allowance
Adoptive Benefit	Smokeless Fuel Allowance
Health and Safety Benefit	Electricity Allowance
Orphan's Contributory Allowance	Natural Gas Allowance
Guardian's Payements	Bottled Gas Refill Allowance
	Free Television Licence
One-parent Families	Telephone Allowance
Widow's or Widower's (Contributory) Pension	
Widowed Parent Grant	**Supplementary Welfare Allowances**
One-Parent Family Payment	Supplementary Welfare Allowance
	Back to School Clothing and Footwear Allowance
Disability and Caring	
Disability Benefit	
Invalidity Pension	
Disability Allowance	
Blind Pension	
Carer's Benefit	
Carer's Allowance	
Injury Benefit	

TASK
Pick a random selection of the income supports listed in the above table and find out the conditions that need to be fulfilled in order to be eligible to claim each one.

3. Universal Allowances

Child Benefit is one example of a universal allowance in Ireland. It is paid in respect of all children regardless of income or PRSI contributions. This allowance is not taxed.

Other Services Provided Under the Department of Social Protection

▸ **Employment Support Services** facilitate, advise and assist unemployed people and lone parents to take advantage of the full range of options for employment, education, training and self-employment.

▸ **Voluntary and Community Services** administer a range of grant schemes and programmes supporting community development. They provide financial assistance toward the staffing and equipping of local resource centres and grants to locally based groups and voluntary organisations. They also provide funding for projects which tackle the problems of indebtedness and moneylending.

▸ **The Office of Social Inclusion** has overall responsibility for co-ordinating and driving the Government's social inclusion agenda, which includes the *National Action Plan for Social Inclusion 2007–2016* (NAPinclusion; see below) and the social inclusion elements of the National Social Partnership Agreement, *Towards 2016*, and the *National Development Plan 2007–2013*.

▸ **The Citizens Information Board** is the statutory body that supports the provision of information, advice and advocacy on a broad range of public and social services. It provides the Citizens Information website (www.citizensinformation.ie) and supports the voluntary network of Citizens Information Centres and the Citizens Information Phone Service. It also funds and supports the Money Advice and Budgeting Service (MABS). MABS has been in existence since 1992 and is made up of representatives from the Department of Social Protection, the St Vincent de Paul Society, credit unions and the Citizens Advice service, among others; the main aim is to assist and support people in money management and dealing with debt.

▸ **The Pensions Board and the Office of the Pension's Ombudsman.**

▸ **The Family Support Agency** was established in 2003 under the auspices of the Family Affairs Unit. It has the responsibility to:

  ▸ Undertake research and act as advisor to the Minister

  ▸ Provide a family mediation service

  ▸ Support Family and Community Resource Centre programmes, including counselling and bereavement services.

The National Action Plan for Social Inclusion (NAPinclusion), complemented by the social inclusion elements of the *National Development Plan 2007–2013: Transforming Ireland – A Better Quality of Life for All*, sets out how the social inclusion strategy will be achieved over the period 2007 to 2016. The overall goal of the plan is to eliminate consistent poverty by 2016 through action plans and delivery of services that will encompass all groups in society throughtout the life cycle. This will involve integration and co-operation between and across national and local authorities, development boards and other relevant agencies.

Family Support and Child Welfare Services

The Child Care Act 1991 empowers the Department of Health and Children to develop services in the following areas:

1.   Family support
2.   Alternative care (foster care, residential care and provision for homeless children)
3.   Adoption services
4.   Child protection services (see Chapter 9).

1. Family Support

Central to the Child Care Act 1991 is the idea that it is best for a child to grow up in his own family if at all possible. Family support, therefore, is about promoting the welfare and healthy development of all children, but particularly those who are living in adverse and stressful situations. Of course, family support cannot be divorced from support provided in all the other social service areas, namely housing, health, income and education.

Ferguson and Kenny (1995) identify three types of family support.

A. Developmental Family Support

Services build on the social supports and strengths which already exist in the family and community, e.g. community groups, personal development groups, recreational projects and parent education.

B. Compensatory Family Support

Services seek to compensate for the effects of living in situations of disadvantage and stress, e.g. through the provision of high-quality pre-school services and parent support groups.

C. Protective Family Support

Services seek to strengthen the ability of individuals within families to survive identified risks. Direct support to individuals and families is provided through the social work service; because of the heavy demand on limited resources, most of these services are problem focused, which means that priority is given to families who are most seriously at risk of complete breakdown or where a child is seriously at risk of neglect or abuse. Some examples of protective family support services are:

- Social Work Services
- Family Resource Centres
- Domiciliary Support Services
- Day Care Services
- Day Fostering
- Community Mothers Scheme/Homestart.

Social Work Services

Social workers are employed in all HSE Areas to provide supportive counselling and child protection services; they also intervene where child abuse is suspected. Apart from individual support they will recommend families to other supportive services and make referrals.

Family Resource Centres

In these centres, families can take advantage of many services under one roof, i.e. supportive counselling, parenting programmes, self-help groups, courses in self-development, early childhood education and after-school services as well as specialist services such as speech therapy, play therapy and child and family guidance services. Different centres may offer different services depending on the resources and needs of the local population.

Domiciliary Support Services

Domiciliary childcare worker, family support worker and home help services can be offered to families in their own home where day-to-day care of the home and the children is causing intolerable stress and strain for the family, e.g. perhaps where a parent is recovering from an illness. A **domiciliary childcare worker** will help the parents to develop parenting skills and will model ways of responding to children's needs.

The **family support worker** aims to enable families to increase their coping mechanisms and manage their affairs – organising, budgeting, routines, coping with stress, and so on.

The **home help** is employed to help with housework.

Day Care Services

This means children are looked after in a pre-school or after-school service.

Day Fostering

This means children will spend each day with a foster family but will return home in the evenings. This is another option for families who are seriously stressed and unable to cope. It gives the family a chance to tackle their problems and children are spared the trauma of complete separation.

Community Mothers Scheme/Homestart

The Community Mothers Scheme is aimed at new mothers and operates in the Eastern Regional Health Authority. Homestart is aimed at families with children under 5 years and operates in the Southern and Eastern areas. They are both examples of domiciliary support which is given by trained volunteers with the services being administered by Health Service personnel. Volunteers, with training and supervision, offer support, friendship and practical help to families with babies and very young children.

2. Alternative Care

Children come into care in three ways:

1. **Abandonment:** The child becomes the legal responsibility of the Department of Health and Children.

2. **Compulsory care:** The child is taken into care for his own protection and well-being by the authorities and legal responsibility is taken by the Department of Health and Children.

3. **Voluntary care:** Children may be placed in care with the parents' consent. Indeed, the parents may request it until they can sort out their difficulty. (For more details of child care and protection, see Chapter 9.)

Having been received into care, arrangements for the child's care is then organised through (a) foster care or (b) residential care.

Foster Care

This means that the child is placed with a family who then share home and family life with that child. Foster care can be short term when, for example, a lone parent is hospitalised and has no family back-up. With short-term foster care, maintaining contact with the child's natural family is usually important. When children come into long-term care and returning to their natural family is not possible in the foreseeable future, a long-term foster family will be sought for the child. Contact with his own family may or may not be possible. All foster parents are assessed by a social worker prior to placement. A social worker also provides support for the child and family for the duration of the placement. Foster care in Ireland is governed by the **Child Care Act 1991** and the **Child Care (Placement of Children in Foster Care) Regulations 1995**. In addition, the **National Standards for Foster Care, 2003** have a major role to play in ensuring that the foster care placements are adequately supported and that children in foster care are receiving the best possible care. Under the **Child Care (Amendment) Act 2007**, the foster parents or relatives who have been caring for a child for a continuous period of at least 5 years may apply to the court for an order which may, subject to conditions, give the foster parents or relatives broadly the same rights as parents have to make decisions about their children. In particular, they will be able to give consent for medical and psychiatric examinations, treatment and assessments and sign the forms for the issue of a passport. **The Irish Foster Care Association** is a voluntary organisation working with the HSE throughout Ireland to promote fostering as the best option for children who cannot live with their own family. The association offers advice, information and support for foster carers.

There are currently about 4,500 children in foster care in Ireland. The Department of Health and Children pays a weekly maintenance allowance for each foster child and extra allowances as required.

Foster care is generally considered to be the preferred option but sometimes there are no foster families available, and sometimes trained and expert childcare staff can be in a better position to cater for the special needs of a particular child.

Residential Care

In the past, residential homes were large, impersonal and institutional places; today residential care can be in a small group home run by the HSE, a children's residential centre registered under the 1991 Act, a school or other suitable place of residence. The Child Care (Placement of Children in Residential Care) Regulations 1995 state the requirements for the placing of children in residential care and the standards for residential centres that are registered with the HSE. The centres are subject to inspection by the **Social Services Inspectorate (SSI)** under HIQA.

The HSE can provide further assistance to young people up to the age of 21 who have been in care. This assistance may include arranging accommodation or contributing towards maintenance while the young person continues at school or college.

The Inspectorate reports also show that the vast majority of children taken into care are placed in foster care (about 80%). Two major concerns about the State care of children have been highlighted in recent times. One is the number of children who have died while in the care of the State or shortly after being discharged from care. In the years 2000 to 2010, latest figures reveal that 84 children died of unnatural causes

(10 unlawful killings, 21 suicides, 14 drug-related deaths and the remaining 39 were accidental deaths). While there is no doubt that, on the whole, children who are taken into care are experiencing serious difficulties in their lives, being placed in care does not provide adequate care and protection for a considerable number of them. The Social Services Inspectorate (SSI) identifies the lack of coherent plans as adding further stress and risk to the lives of children, especially older children and those leaving care.

Table. 11.7: Number of Children in Care, Various Years

Year	Total no.	Less separated children seeking asylum	New total
2001	5,517	1,009	4,508
2004	5,060	190	4,870
2006	5,461	214	5,247
2008	5,586	137	5,449

Source: Irish Social Services Inspectorate reports 2008.

Figure. 11.3: Children in Care, 2008

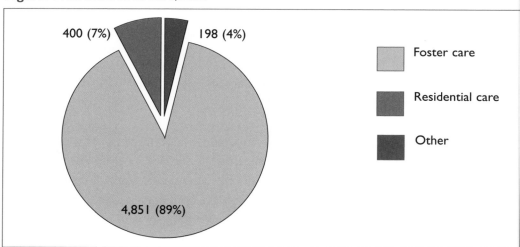

Source: Irish Social Services Directorate.

The other concern is in relation to separated children seeking asylum who are in the care of the State. The number of children seeking asylum who are in care has decreased dramatically since the Dublin Convention (see Chapter 13). However, there seems to be some confusion about the numbers – for instance, the SSI's 2008 annual report identifies 137 of these children in care, while a report from Barnardos for the same year identifies 291; this is a considerable difference. Even more worryingly, both concur that 454 of these children have gone missing in the years 2000 to 2010. A lack of consistency in how separated children are treated and cared for in Ireland has been highlighted by Barnardos, the Ombudsman for Children and indeed by the SSI itself, with different sections of the Child Care Act 1991 used by different professionals. Unlike other children in the care of the HSE, separated children are placed in privately contracted hostels that are unregistered and profit-making and subsequently not governed by the National Standards for Children's Residential Centres (2001) nor inspected by HIQA. The staff are not necessarily appropriately trained and there is no dedicated social worker assigned to each child. Yet as acknowledged by the HSE in 2010:

> Many of these children may have high levels of vulnerability and have experienced gross trauma. Many face problems and challenges on issues including separation and bereavement from family and friends, social isolation, language barriers, emotional and mental health problems, discrimination and racism. In addition, they have to live with the anxiety of possible removal from the country or uncertainty as to their future.

Overall, the numbers of children coming into care has increased year on year despite attempts to reduce child poverty and increase support services for families at risk. There is no doubt that overall services for children in care have improved dramatically, but much more is required.

3. Adoption Services

The Department of Health and Children makes provision for a full range of adoption services. This includes professional and counselling services to pregnant women, birth mothers, adoptive families and adoptees. Adoption services are also provided through voluntary adoption agencies in each area. The Adoption Authority of Ireland is the statutory body which ratifies all adoption placements.

When a child is adopted, this means that the birth mother/natural mother and/or father relinquishes all legal rights to her child and these rights are passed in full to the adoptive parents. This does not happen overnight but involves a lengthy assessment of the adoptive parents and in-depth counselling with the birth mother/parents. There is also a considerable time lapse (at least 3 to 6 months) between the placement of a child for adoption and the mother's signing of the final consent form. Maintaining links between the child, the birth mother and the adoptive parents is now also a feature of adoption work.

Foreign Adoptions

Under the Adoption Act 1991, there is a statutory responsibility to carry out assessments for couples/families planning to adopt abroad. The number of Irish children being adopted has been steadily decreasing, but the number of adoptions of children overseas has been increasing.

Table 11.8: Birth and Adoption Trends in Ireland, 1964–2008

Year	Total births	Non-marital births	% of total births of children born in Ireland	Number of adoptions of children born in Ireland	Adoptions as % of non-marital births
1964	64,072	1,292	2.02	1,003	77.6
1974	68,907	2,309	3.35	1,415	61.3
1984	64,062	5,116	7.99	1,195	23.4
1994	47,928	9,904	20.66	424	4.3
2004	61,684	19,935	32.32	273	1.4
2006	64,237	21,295	33.5	222	1.04
2008	75,065	24,844	33.09	200	0.80

Source: Abstracted from CSO statistics for various years.

Of the 273 adoption orders made in 2004, 185 were family adoptions – 177 of which were made in favour of the child's mother and her husband, 20 in respect of children from overseas and a further 22 orders were made in respect of children who had been placed in long-term foster care.

Table 11.9: Trends in Overseas Adoptions, 1991–2008

Year	Numbers of declarations granted	Numbers of adoptions effected overseas
1991	4	61
1996	117	72
2000	282	225
2004	461	486
2006	400	406
2008	494	490

Source: The Adoption Board.

Column 2 in Table 11.9 above refers to declarations of eligibility and suitability to adopt, which allows the person(s) interested in overseas adoption to proceed. (The anomaly occurs because column 2 may include applications from previous years.)

The vast majority of 'overseas' children adopted here are from Vietnam (46%), then Russia (29%).

Ireland signed the Hague Convention in 1993 and in 2009 finally ratified it and made it part of Irish law. This means that in the future, intercountry adoptions into Ireland will be between those countries that have ratified the Hague Convention or that have a bilateral agreement with Ireland. This establishes co-operation, cuts down on trafficking risks and serves the bests interests of the child.

Tracing birth parents is an area of adoptive work that is increasing steadily. The Adoption Authority will assist people who have been adopted, adoptive parents and natural family members of adopted people to access information. To this end the National Adoption Contact Register was launched in 2005. To date, 7,627 people have registered and 374 matches (parents to child) have been generated.

Education

The Education Act 1998 is the main legislation which currently drives the education system. Total provision in 2010 for the education sector was €8.1 billion.

Education is compulsory for all children between the ages of 6 and 16 years. In practice the majority of children start school between the ages of 4 and 5. Parents can choose to educate their children outside the school system but have to show that their children are receiving an appropriate education. Official and practical support for this is limited.

Formal education in Ireland is provided by the Department of Education and Skills at primary, secondary and third level. The system has two tiers: private schools must operate in accordance with the education laws and the State supports private schools in that it pays the salaries of teachers. However, there are considerable costs attached to education apart from tuition fees, e.g. books, uniforms and so-called 'voluntary contributions'. At primary and secondary level, supplementary welfare grants are available for those who are on long-term benefit or who can prove that the costs involved would cause undue hardship. At third level, a grant is available to individual students, but this is means tested.

There is a need to combat educational disadvantage at many levels, quite apart from financial support to individual families who are experiencing hardship. Recent research and figures show that:

▶ Approximately 1,000 pupils per year fail to make the transition between primary and secondary school.

▸ Children living in disadvantaged areas experience severe literacy problems that are three times the national average.

▸ 15% of young people leave school without a Leaving Certificate qualification and 3% have no qualification at all.

▸ The average class size at the end of 2009 was 24.2, which makes the Irish teacher–pupil ratio above average for the EU.

These figures suggest that there needs to be considerable input into the primary sector, but Ireland continues to invest more per pupil at the higher levels of education. The Government spends almost 50% more per head at third level than at primary level. (Details of early childhood education services provision are given in Chapter 1.)

Social Inclusion – Delivering Equality of Opportunity in Schools (DEIS)

Over the past decade, the following schemes have been put in place in an effort to combat disadvantage.

▸ **The Home School Community Liaison Scheme** aims to support students at risk of failing or of dropping out.

▸ **The School Completion Programme** targets individual young people of school-going age, both in and out of school, and arranges supports to address inequalities in education access, participation and outcomes.

▸ **The Support Teachers Project** targets children whose learning is affected by their behaviour, which may be disruptive, disturbed or withdrawn. Support Teachers focuses on social, emotional and personal development in working with children, allowing children to experience success in their school life through working on strengths, which may require the curriculum to be adapted to suit the child's level of need.

▸ **Giving Children an Even Break** provides additional teaching and financial allocations to participating schools in order to combat disadvantage. It means a reduction of class sizes in the participating schools and the input of additional resources.

▸ **Breaking the Cycle** discriminated positively in favour of schools in selected urban and rural areas that have high concentrations of children who are at risk of not reaching their potential in the education system because of their socio-economic backgrounds. Strategies include extra staff and additional funding and co-ordination.

▶ **Disadvantaged Area Scheme** – schools seeking disadvantaged status were assessed and prioritised as to need on the basis of socio-economic and educational indicators such as unemployment levels, housing, medical card holders and information on basic literacy and numeracy. In addition, in assessing the relative levels of disadvantage among applicant schools, account was taken of pupil–teacher ratios. Support involves an increased capitation grant and extra finance for materials and classroom equipment.

▶ **Literacy and Numeracy Schemes** facilitate extra teacher training to deliver programmes aimed to reduce literacy problems and promote mathematical skills, e.g. programmes such as First Step, Reading Recovery and Maths Recovery.

Education for Children with Additional Needs

Education for children with special needs may be provided in ordinary classes in mainstream schools, in special classes in mainstream schools or in special schools. In mainstream schools they may get help from learning support and resource teachers and from special needs assistants (SNAs). These supports for children with special educational needs are available in primary schools and post-primary schools. Some children attend special classes in mainstream schools. These classes generally have low pupil–teacher ratios. There are also over 107 special schools catering for particular types of disability and special needs.

Under the Education for Persons with Special Educational Needs Act 2004, each child assessed with a special educational need should have a personal education plan. However, as of 2010 this has not yet been implemented. **The National Council for Special Education, Special Educational Needs Organisers (SENOs), the Special Education Support Service (SESS)** and the **National Educational Psychological Service (NEPS)** are the principal organisations and structures that support and co-ordinate services for children with additional needs.

There are also some extra resources for the education of children from the Traveller community (see Chapter 13) and for children for whom English is not their first language.

Early school-leaver programmes such as the Schools Completion Programme, the Vocational Training Opportunities Scheme, Youthreach and post-Leaving Certificate courses are aimed at increasing the number of young people staying in second-level schools or helping people get access to second-chance or alternative education.

The recent recession has resulted in serious cutbacks in education generally, but particularly to some of these programmes.

Voluntary Services

The provision of services and support through voluntary agencies has always been very important in Ireland and there is a large number of voluntary organisations in operation. It is not possible to cover all those which provide services to families with young children. Some voluntary services have already been outlined. Two nationwide organisations that provide a range of services to families and children are described below.

Barnardos

In consultation with statutory and other agencies, Barnardos provides and develops selected services for disadvantaged children and their families. These services include:

▶   Family support services tailored to meet the needs of individual families.

▶   National Children's Resource Centre, which includes a library and reference section and offers the service to parents and professionals working with or on behalf of children.

▶   Origins information and tracing service aims to help people access personal information held by Government departments or by religious orders concerning their care in industrial schools and helps in tracing family members.

▶   Beacon Guardian ad Litem service advises the courts on the best interests of the child (for further information, see Chapter 9).

▶   Drop-in services such as parent and toddler groups and toy library service.

▶   Pre-school and after-school services.

▶   Counselling and support – includes a parenting support programme aimed at enhancing parenting skills.

▶   Adoption Advisory Service – includes advisory and support services for anyone who has been involved in an adoption process – adoptive parents, relinquishing parents, person who has been adopted and those thinking of adopting.

▶   Advisory service for people who are setting up early years services.

▶   Training services – in relation to early years services, Barnardos has been at the forefront in offering Highscope Training to early years workers.

▶   Solas – a children's bereavement service.

▶   Advocacy and lobbying – Barnardos campaigns unceasingly for changes necessary to bring about improvement in the lives of children and families.

▶   Vetting services for certain childcare organisations.

Four priority issues have been identified in their current 12-year plan up to 2016:

1. Child poverty

2. Child protection

3. Educational disadvantage

4. Alcohol abuse.

The Irish Society for the Prevention of Cruelty to Children (ISPCC)

The ISPCC offers child-centred services aimed at improving child–parent relationships and reducing levels of violence in families. It also runs several direct access services for children. These services include the following.

▸ **The National Childline Service** is a national freephone active listening service for children. Almost a quarter of a million calls were answered by Childline in 2005. In addition, in 2005 Childline launched an automated text service which can be used by children who are deaf or hard of hearing. Further, in 2005 Childline-Online went live, offering support and information to young people via the website www.childline.ie

▸ **4me mentoring** is aimed at 13–18-year-olds with a focus of supporting those at risk from misusing alcohol and drugs.

▸ **The 4me service** works to prevent early school leaving.

▸ **The Children's Rights Information Bureau** (CRIB) aims to strengthen and highlight the notion of children as full citizens.

▸ **Leanbh** seeks to work with children who are begging on the streets and to identify and work with their parents.

▸ **Child Focus–Childhood Support Worker Service** is a home-based service working with vulnerable children aged 0–12 years old. It also aims to support and educate parents.

▸ **The Schools Outreach Programme** gives talks and helps with school project work.

▸ **Children's Rights Promotion** provides information to children on their rights by publishing booklets and giving talks.

TASK

Each member of the group selects a different voluntary organisation or group and gathers information about that service under the following headings:
- ▶ Origins and size
- ▶ Funding
- ▶ Services offered
- ▶ Issues which concern the organisation

This could be used for a research project in various modules.

SUMMARY

- ▶ Services for families and children are provided through State, voluntary and private bodies.
- ▶ The system of service provision in Ireland is two-tiered – private and public.
- ▶ The main areas of social service provision are housing, health, income maintenance, family support services and education.
- ▶ Services may vary from area to area.

References

Ferguson, H. and P. Kenny, 1995, *On Behalf of the Child: Child Welfare, Child Protection and the Child Care Act (1991)*, Dublin: A&A Farmar.

SECTION SIX

EQUALITY AND DIVERSITY

This section is designed to promote awareness of the concepts of individuality, equality and difference. The chapters need to be read in sequence. Chapter 12 aims to enable the reader, through activities and exercises, to increase self-awareness, challenge assumptions which can lead to discriminatory practice and become familiar with the vocabulary used throughout Chapters 13 and 14. The activities and exercises in Chapter 12 can be carried out individually but greater benefit may be achieved if they are undertaken in a group context. However, a word of caution – some of these exercises are of a personal nature. Groups and their tutors should be aware at all times of the need for sensitivity and confidentiality. In no circumstances should people be expected to reveal information unless they are happy to do so.

Chapter 13 examines the effects of prejudice and discrimination on people's lives. It identifies the groups in Ireland most likely to suffer these effects and focuses particularly on social class, the Travelling community, race and racism and disability. The chapter looks at changes which have taken place and outlines the current legislative situation. Chapter 14 deals with the practical application of the principles of equality in early childhood work.

12

LOOKING AT OURSELVES

AREAS COVERED

▸ Individuals and Equality

▸ Definitions

Introduction

Each of us carries our own personal and cultural identity. This shapes our attitudes to ourselves, to others and to the world around us. People who are involved in work with children need to explore and understand how attitudes are shaped so that they will become aware of the impact that socialisation and experiences may have on children.

This chapter aims to facilitate the development of an understanding of individuality, equality and diversity, to raise awareness of the issues involved, to challenge assumptions that we may have about ourselves and others and to introduce the terminology most commonly used in this area.

The first part is organised into a series of self-exploratory activities because any exploration of the area of equality and diversity must begin with oneself. While most activities can be done by individuals, greater benefit in terms of knowledge and insight will be gained if the activities are done in a group setting, followed by group discussion. People should not be expected to reveal personal information unless they feel comfortable doing so when working in a group. All participants must observe rules of confidentiality.

Exercise 1: I Am a Unique Individual

Life may seem simpler when we classify and categorise, for example when we group people into 'toddlers', 'teenagers' or 'elderly'. In doing this, however, the uniqueness of the individual is lost.

Aim: To explore and describe the uniqueness of the individual. The list on page 243 is far from comprehensive but covers a variety of areas to show that our individuality is many faceted.

Using **List 12.1**:

▸ Spend some time on your own filling out details about yourself.

▸ In a small group:

— Identify what you have in common with one another

— Identify what makes each person different and unique.

Exercise 2

Aim: To explore personal identity and how we make assumptions about people on the basis of very little information.

Collect photos or pictures of people from a variety of minority/majority groups around the world (use the internet, magazines, etc.). Attach each photo to the top of a blank page and give one to each person in the group.

The person must write their first impression (fairly quickly) of the person in the picture at the bottom of the page and then fold it over and pass it to the next person. Without looking at what the previous person has written, person no. 2 should write their impression, fold it over, pass it on and continue until everyone has recorded a first impression of each picture.

Ask for volunteers to read out the statements and then pin them up where they can be seen.

In the large group, discuss the following.

▸ Did participants agree in their impressions?

▸ Where did the biggest differences occur?

▸ Why did differences or similarities occur?

▸ Do you think this is how people see themselves?

▸ How might your impressions affect the other person's life and choices?

(Adapted from the Council of Europe, 1995, *All Different All Equal,* education pack, Dublin: YARD.)

List 12.1

First name
Family name
Colour of hair
Height
Birthday
Sex
Number of people in family
Place in family
Religion
Nationality
Talents
Temperament
Likes
Dislikes
Health
Hobbies
What makes me sad?
What makes me happy?
What makes me angry?

This page may be photocopied.

Individuals and Equality

A basic idea underpinning the concept of equality is the recognition of the dignity of individuals and their right to respect as human beings. A genuine acceptance of this ideal means that individuals should be enabled to participate in society to the best of their ability; this in turn would bring about some equalisation of power, wealth and resources. The acceptance and celebration of differences should lead to an overall balance and harmony among individuals in society. **This is not to say that people are all the same or that they should be treated in the same way.** It is obvious that an adult is not the same as a child or that a person who uses a wheelchair is not the same as a person who is walking. It is just as important to realise that one adult is not the same as another adult or that one child is not the same as another child.

Activities for Work with Children

Aim: To help children to develop self-awareness and self-esteem.

Using the headings in List 12.1 (page 243), devise developmentally appropriate activities to help young children develop self-awareness.

These activities can involve the children in the use of a variety of different skills at all levels of ability, e.g. cutting out pictures and silhouettes, naming and using colours, drawing, looking things up, weighing, measuring, using family photos and using scraps to make collages and personal histories. Ask the child whether or not she would like to display her work.

Exercise 3

Aim: To raise awareness of similarities and differences as well as an appreciation of the complexity of identity.

Ask participants to quickly list their favourite:

▶ Food

▶ Drink

▶ Singer/band

▶ Sport

▶ Pastime

▶ Book

▶ Movie

▶ TV show

▶ Use the completed list to introduce yourself to the group, e.g. 'I am John Murphy and I like pasta and my favourite drink is ...' and so on.

▶ In the large group consider what the similarities and differences are between the group members.

▶ Identify as far as possible the country of origin of each item on the list, e.g. tea comes from India, potatoes originated from South America, pasta is associated with Italy. Sport may be difficult, but interesting!

▶ Use post-its to mark where everything originates from on a map of the world.

Reflect in writing what you have learned from this activity: this could be included in a Reflective Journal.

Exercise 4: Values and Roles

Aim: This activity explores how roles are filled in families and if there are any identifiable patterns.

The beliefs and values which shape our behaviour come from our parents, families, friends, community and the society in which we live. The family has a primary influence on what we learn about social roles and behaviour, both our own and those of others.

Read the tasks below and rank them in the order of importance you believe society places on them.

▶ In the large group, chart the information from the whole group (e.g. bar charts, graphs, etc.) showing which tasks have the least/most value and who carries out each task (child/adult/male/female).

▶ Discuss why some roles/tasks are more valued than others.

▶ Cooking   ▶ Setting the TV/DVD

▶ Cleaning   ▶ Remembering birthdays

▶ Shopping for food   ▶ Minding children

▶ Mowing the lawn   ▶ Household decoration — indoor

▶ Weeding the garden   ▶ Household decoration — outdoor

▶ Household repairs   ▶ Christmas shopping

▶ Paying the bills   ▶ Babysitting

▶ Looking after the car   ▶ Organising holidays and outings

▶ Looking after people when they   ▶ Taking out the rubbish
  are ill
                                         ▶ Earning the main income

(Additional tasks may be added to the list.)

Exercise 5: Celebrating Diversity

Diversity exists even in a seemingly homogenous group. Within any particular group, regardless of how much they may have in common, people will have different backgrounds and preferences.

Aim: This activity aims to provide an opportunity to explore diversity and to reflect on its implications.

▸ Prepare the answers to at least some questions from List 12.3 on page 248. (Remember, you do not have to reveal anything about yourself if you do not feel comfortable doing so.)

▸ Share with the whole group:
  — One thing that you think you have in common with the group
  — One thing that you think makes you different from the rest of the group.

▸ List the differences and the similarities on a chart.

▸ Discuss how the group might celebrate these differences.

▸ Plan and carry out appropriate activities for the children in your work placement to help them explore and celebrate diversity in their lives.

Definitions

This section will introduce and explore some of the main terms and concepts associated with equality and diversity.

Prejudice is defined as an attitude, judgement or feeling formed without any direct knowledge of the group or individual but based on preconceived ideas or stereotypes. Prejudice can be positive as well as negative and we all have some prejudices.

Stereotype is defined as a simplistic generalisation about or caricature of any individual or group. A stereotype is often derogatory, i.e. a put-down. It attributes characteristics to individuals on the basis of the group to which they are seen to belong and no allowance is made for individual differences.

Labelling means identifying an individual or group by reference to one characteristic or perceived characteristic of that person or group; the term 'classifying' can also be used.

Scapegoating occurs when someone (or group) wrongly blames another individual or group against whom they are prejudiced for their problems and difficulties. For example, when people came to Ireland from other EU countries to work, some Irish people blamed them for taking their jobs. In fact, Ireland was experiencing full employment at that time.

List 12.3

Name/nickname/pet name
Where you are from
Where your parents are from
Type of family (small, large, extended, lone parent, etc.)
A custom or tradition that is practised by your family. For example, how does your family celebrate birthdays, Christmas and other festivals?
Taste in clothes
Taste in music
Food preferences
What sort of partner are you attracted to?

This page may be photocopied.

Chain Racism

Stigma refers to a name or stereotype to which shame, disgrace or negative connotations are attached. Some terms in common usage are stigmatising because they highlight an undesirable characteristic and devalue the individual, e.g. poor, mentally ill, criminal, handicapped, etc.

Discrimination means policies, practices or behaviour which lead to the unfair treatment of individuals or groups because of their identity or their perceived identity.

> *Prejudice translated into action becomes discrimination.*

There are three main forms of discrimination.

1. **Direct discrimination:** Treating someone unfairly solely because of their perceived difference, e.g. 'Only two children at a time are allowed to enter this shop.'

2. **Indirect discrimination:** Setting down conditions for something, for example a job or service, that automatically disqualifies certain people without good reason, e.g. 'Applicants must have fluent English.'

   Discrimination **by association** happens when a person associated with another person is treated less favourably because of that association.

3. **Unequal burdens:** Failing to remove obstacles that disbar certain people, e.g. a lack of ramps or lifts in a building automatically disbars people who use wheelchairs.

Exercise 6

For each of the following statements, identify which is an example of the terms explained above. Make up some more statements to help you apply the terms in practice.

- 'You could not trust a woman to run a large business because she wouldn't be able to keep her head in a crisis.'
- 'All Irishmen are drunks.'
- 'Asthmatics must be careful to avoid undue stress.'
- 'Room 3a is where the special needs go for extra tuition.'
- 'All redheads are hot tempered.'
- 'Children must not play on the grass.'

Power is essential to discrimination. No other person can discriminate against you, or in your favour, unless that person has the power to do so. Think of the individuals and groups who have power in our society and those who lack power. It is not politicians, bankers or bishops who suffer from prejudice or discrimination. It is those who are poor, who are Travellers or who have a disability, i.e. those who lack power. During the latter half of the twentieth century many pressure and support groups emerged in an attempt by groups and individuals to take some control over their situations, to combat prejudice and discrimination through education and ultimately through equality legislation.

ACTIVITY

Language Matters

Divide into groups of three or four. Give each group a copy of the Language Matters worksheet on page 252. In the groups, discuss the names we use to describe people using these questions.

▸   Which names are in common usage?

▸   Which ones might the people being described prefer to be called?

▸   Why do people use different versions of names?

▸   Ask the group to add some more and also fill in the empty spaces with different examples.

▸   Which names are positive and which are negative?

Figure 12.2: Language Matters

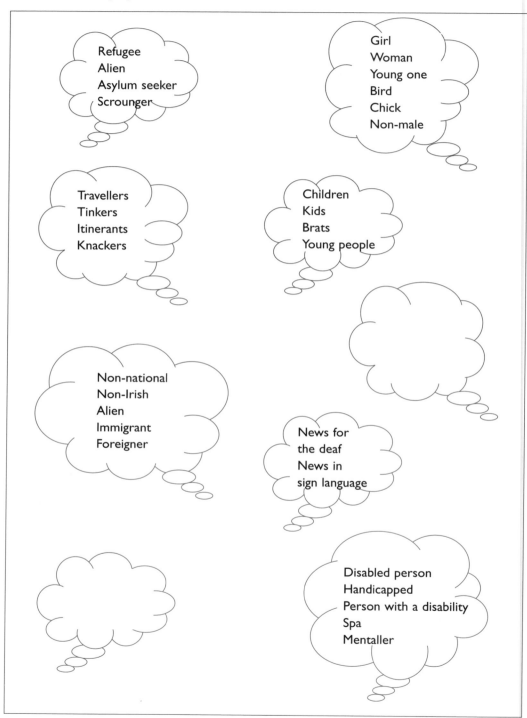

(Adapted from CSPE resource)

This page may be photocopied.

ACTIVITY

We all have prejudices to some degree – it is part of human nature. Being aware of these attitudes and prejudices and how they can affect us and others is an important step in developing a more just and equal society.

▶ Write about two instances of discrimination which you have personally experienced.

▶ Write about two instances when you have shown prejudice or discrimination toward another.

▶ The excerpt from 'Black Hoodie' on pages 192–4 is about prejudice and stereotypes. What are the main examples in the story?

These can be related to age, gender, education or any other issue.

SUMMARY

▶ Each individual is unique and it is important to appreciate, respect and celebrate diversity.

▶ Awareness of our own values and attitudes and how these are formed is an important part of the process of learning to recognise the dignity and worth of every human being.

▶ An understanding of the meaning and implications of prejudice, discrimination and associated terms is an equally important part of learning to challenge assumptions and raise awareness.

13

PREJUDICE AND DISCRIMINATION IN IRELAND

Introduction

This chapter explores the effects of prejudice and discrimination on people's lives, how attitudes and practices can be modified and changed and the effects and limitations of legislative change.

However, it is not possible to cover all aspects of prejudice and discrimination for all people, so a number of areas have been selected for inclusion in this chapter, namely:

▶ Social class – focusing on the effects of poverty on people's lives.

▶ Ethnic groups – focusing on race and racism, members of the Travelling community and immigrants in modern Ireland.

▶ Disability – focusing on disability.

This is not to indicate that the experiences of people who are discriminated against on the basis of age, gender, religion or for any other reason are not important. Although individual experiences will differ and issues may vary in detail, the effects of discrimination and the strategies for change will be broadly similar for people in all groups. Activities included in this chapter and in Chapters 12 and 14 can be adapted to facilitate the exploration of prejudice and discrimination in other areas.

Social Class

Social stratification describes how societies are divided into different strata or layers, where the people at each layer share similar levels of power, status and privilege.

Social class based on socio-economic status is the main form of social stratification in Ireland and Western industrialised societies today and is classified using an international classification code (see Appendix 6).

The social class of children is derived from the occupation of their parent(s). Until the 1981 census women had their social class ascribed to them according to the occupation of their father or their husband. Now a woman's social class is derived mainly from her own occupation.

The social class system is, in theory, **open** and one can move up or down the scale during the course of one's lifetime; this is called **social mobility**. A person might be born into a family where the father is a general labourer (social class 8/9); in theory that person could train, study, go to college and become a medical consultant (social class 1). However, the class into which we are born (**class of origin**) has a huge influence on how we live our lives and on where we end up (**class of destination**). It influences where we live, how we spend our leisure time, the papers we read, our educational prospects and our earning potential. The most significant aspect of the social class system is the inequality that exists between social classes in the distribution of wealth and income. It is estimated that 10% of the population own nearly half the wealth in the country; therefore, 90% of the population shares the other half – but not equally.

CASE STUDY 1: ZARA

Zara is 5 years old. She lives at home with her parents, her two brothers, a sister and baby niece. Her father was made redundant 2 years ago from a factory job and is still unemployed; her mother works part time, evenings and weekends in a city centre restaurant.

The family lives in a three-bedroom house in a large housing estate which has no playground for younger children; the parents are afraid to let their younger children play on the local green because of stray dogs, litter (including syringes) and gangs of older children. Zara shares her bedroom with her sister and niece, who is nearly 2. Zara likes to go to sleep with the TV on.

She has just started school and is delighted with herself; she has shiny new books and loads of friends. Sometimes it is very hard to get up for school if the baby has been crying during the night. There are 26 children in her class. Sometimes she can't hear the teacher very well. Sometimes it is very hard to sit quietly at her desk for hours on end when she is not used to it. Her dad likes to help with her homework but he is not very good at reading. Her dad says you must work hard and learn to read and write so that you can get on better in life.

CASE STUDY 2: JACK

Jack is 5 years old. He lives at home with his parents and two older brothers. His father is an engineer and his mother is a nurse who works part time.

The family lives in a large five-bedroom house in a new estate which has its own playground, but the house is in a cul-de-sac so Jack and his friends can play outside quite safely. At weekends his father and mother take the family out to adventure playgrounds, museums, farms, theatre and all sorts of exciting places. At holiday time, the whole family goes to the seaside. The family has a boat and he is learning to sail. He loves fishing too.

Jack shares his bedroom with his 8-year-old brother. His oldest brother has a room of his own. Jack doesn't mind sharing and he will be moving into his own bedroom when he is 6. He has loads of books and every night someone reads or tells him a story.

He is nearly able to read himself because he has just started 'big' school – a private school. He has attended a Montessori school for 2 years; he did not like the change at first but he is getting used to it. There are 15 other children in the class and his teacher is lovely. There is a huge gym hall in the school and he loves it when they go there. There are loads of toys, games and computers in the classroom. He is not allowed to spend as much time as he would like playing with his computer at home and he is not allowed to watch much TV either.

Jack's dad says you must work hard and then you can be anything you want when you grow up; Jack wants to be a solar engineer.

ACTIVITY

Aim: To highlight how social class can influence the life chances of a child from the early years.

Read the case outlines above of Zara and Jack. Discuss the following.

▶   How might their early years affect how well they do in school?
▶   How might their lives outside school affect their development?
▶   How might the different school environments affect how well they adjust and learn?
▶   What are the main causes of the differences between Zara's and Jack's lives?

Poverty and Discrimination

According to the *National Action Plan for Social Inclusion 2007–2016*:

> People are living in poverty if their income and resources (material, cultural and social) are so inadequate as to preclude them from having a standard of living which is regarded as acceptable by Irish society generally. As a result of inadequate income and other resources people may be excluded and marginalised from participating in activities which are considered the norm for other people in society.

This means that people are living in poverty if they do not have enough money to do the things that most people in Ireland take for granted, such as buying good food or heating your home. Poverty is more than not having the money for material things. It can also mean not having enough money for social activities or holidays. This can lead to people feeling cut off from the rest of society because they don't have the money to participate.

Table 13.1: Poverty Rates Over 10 Years

	Consistent poverty (%)	At risk of poverty (%)
1997	9.7	18.8
2001	5.2	21.9
2004	6.8	19.4
2008	4.2	14.4

Source: Living in Ireland Surveys (LIIS) up to 2001; EU Survey on Living and Income Conditions (EU–SILC) from 2004; Combat Poverty for 2008.

Poverty in Ireland is measured by the Central Statistics Office. Two measurements, *consistent poverty* and *at risk of poverty*, are used – see Chapter 11 for an explanation of these terms.

Consistent Poverty

Combat Poverty noted that according to the most recent statistics, 14.4% of the Irish population are at risk of poverty and 4.2% experience consistent poverty. However, some social groups have higher poverty rates than the rest of the population: lone-parent families, the unemployed and people with disabilities or long-term illnesses.

	At risk of poverty (%)	Consistent poverty (%)
Total population	14.4	4.2
Lone parents	36.4	17.8
Unemployed people	23.0	9.7
Ill or disabled people	25.5	13.2

Source: Combat Poverty Agency (2008).

Trying to make ends meet incurs high levels of stress and anxiety and so living in poverty has negative implications for physical and mental health and affects every area of life. Poverty has many dimensions. Studies in various Western countries indicate that:

▶   Poor families tend to live in 'poor' areas which lack, or have inadequate, basic services and amenities such as housing, health services, transport, schools, recreational facilities and parks.

▶   A baby born into a poor family may have received less pre-natal care, may have a lower birth weight and is less likely to be immunised or breast fed.

▶   A child of a poor family is least likely to have access to early childhood care and education (see Chapter 1).

▶   Children living in poverty are more likely to have learning difficulties and behavioural difficulties.

▶   Children living in poor families are more likely to drop out of school with no qualifications.

▶   A child from a poor family is least likely to have access to adequate housing and health care.

▶   Isolation, stigma and helplessness are widespread.

▶   Where everyone is poor and over-stressed there is less support to go around.

Because of all this, poor children and families are caught up in what is termed the 'cycle' of poverty: poor housing, ill-health, inadequate education and fewer opportunities means that the children are likely to repeat the pattern and become 'poor' parents in the economic sense.

Strategies for Alleviating Poverty

In the past, strategies for alleviating poverty were related to ideas about why people were poor in the first place. A popular theory was that people who were poor had only themselves to blame; they were inadequate, unworthy and useless. According to the *Human Development Report 1998*, the idea continues to persist today that the responsibility for being poor is often assigned to the poor themselves. But the 'cycle' of poverty has been recognised and there is some commitment to breaking this cycle. In Ireland, efforts to eliminate poverty have been haphazard. Examples include the following.

▸ The Department of Social Protection has taken initiatives by allowing people who have been unemployed to retain some benefits while finding their feet in employment and/or education.

▸ Social welfare benefits have been increased, the detrimental effects of being on long-term benefits have been recognised and efforts made to address them; community employment schemes have been initiated.

▸ Legislation has provided some protection for low-paid, part-time workers.

▸ The Child Care Act 1991 empowers the Minister specifically to provide support services for families and children at risk.

▸ Early Start, Breaking the Cycle, The Traveller Education Programme, Home School Liaison Scheme, Educational Disadvantage Committee and Delivering Equality of Opportunity in Schools are the main initiatives launched by the Department of Education and Skills.

▸ Local groups have attempted to address problems specific to their own areas, aiding and supporting employment and self-help initiatives. Area Partnerships involving the private, public and voluntary sectors have been particularly effective in this regard.

Government strategies relevant to children include commitments to:

▸ End child poverty

▸ Pay specific attention to vulnerable groups

▸ Achieve a rate of child income support to be set at around 35% of the minimum adult social welfare payment

▶   Improve the housing situation and to have sufficient and appropriate emergency accommodation available to those who become homeless

▶   Combat educational disadvantage.

These have been seriously set back by the suspension or withdrawal of Government funding and a rowing back on commitments made in earlier national agreements.

Table 13.2: Government Commitments

UN Convention ratified in 1992	Guarantees every child the right to an 'adequate' standard of living
National Anti-Poverty Strategy 2002–2007 National Action Plan against Poverty and Social Inclusion 2003–2005	Commitment to reduce, if possible eliminate, child poverty by 2007 and move towards greater equality for all children
National Children's Strategy 2000	To provide the financial supports necessary to eliminate child poverty
Programme for Government 2002	Ending child poverty is a core element of the Government's efforts
Sustaining Progress 2003–2005	Reiterates commitment of ending child poverty through 10 special initiatives
Health Strategy 2001	Expands medical card scheme to include a further 200,000 people/families on low income
Education Welfare Act 2000	Provides for the introduction of the Home School Liaison Scheme
Housing (Traveller Accommodation) Act 1998	Obliges local authorities to provide accommodation for Traveller families
Homelessness: An Integrated Strategy, 2000	Prioritises the elimination of the use of bed and breakfast accommodation, except in the very short term
National Play Policy 2000	Maximises the range of public play opportunities, especially for marginalised groups
National Action Plan Against Racism 2005–2008	Requires bodies who are implementing anti-poverty programmes to include anti-racism strategies and to accommodate diversity

Delivering Equality of Opportunity in Schools (DEIS) 2005	Aims to standardise the system for identifying and reviewing levels of disadvantage and to establish an integrated School Support Programme
ECCE Scheme (Free Pre-school Year) 2009	Aims to provide access to early education services for all pre-school children
National Childcare Investment Programme (NCIP) 2010	Aims to create up to 50,000 new childcare places to assist parents to access affordable, quality childcare
Community Childcare Subvention (CCS) 2010	Aims to enable community-based, not-for-profit childcare services to provide quality childcare services at reduced rates to disadvantaged parents. Recognises the value of quality pre-school experiences in helping to break the cycle of poverty

Ethnic Groups

A minority ethnic group is a group who shares a cultural heritage which is distinct from the majority society.

The Traveller Community

Travellers are a minority ethnic group. With a population of around 21,500, they have been the largest minority ethnic group in Ireland for many years (0.6% of the population according to the 2006 census). They have a long history (over 1,000 years or more), lifestyle, customs, traditions and a value system which makes them a group recognised by themselves and others as distinctive and unique. Unfortunately, they experience prejudice and discrimination that results in an ongoing struggle for survival and that frequently results in actual physical harassment.

Traveller Culture
Some distinguishing features of Travellers culture are:

▸ Nomadism, which basically means travelling or moving around.

▸ A distinct language known as 'shelta', 'cant' or 'gammon', although use of this language has declined.

▸ A high rate of inter-marriage; to be a Traveller you must have one parent who was/is a Traveller; you cannot become a Traveller by marrying one or by opting out of settled society and taking to the roads.

▶ Strong connections with extended families – in fact, the nuclear family as such makes little sense to Travellers because the extended family is such an intrinsic part of their lives and lifestyle.

While these are general features of Traveller culture, it is important to remember that each person and each family will have adopted customs and traditions to varying degrees, as is evident in any particular group in any society.

Travellers and Discrimination
Travellers experience discrimination and prejudice in the following areas:

▶ Economy
▶ Health
▶ Accommodation
▶ Education
▶ General lifestyle.

Traveller Economy
The 'Traveller economy' is the term used to describe work initiated by Travellers themselves. Up to 50 or so years ago, the Travellers were largely a rural people with an economy based on a wide range of activities that included tin-smithing (mending buckets, utensils, selling pots and pans), seasonal farming, recycling and flower-making. The advent of plastic, machines and industrialisation made these skills and occupations obsolete.

This forced many of the population to move to urban areas to try to change their traditional economic activities. Some Travellers are self-employed to an extent, dealing in scrap and recycling.

The key features of the Traveller economy are the following.

▶ **Mobility:** Nomadism always had a basic economic function, but it does not allow for the development of a trade which might require storage facilities or heavy equipment. Improved facilities in the design and building of more recent halting sites still does not accommodate this sort of economic activity.

▶ **Extended family:** This acts as a basic operative unit and the home base and work base are the same. Children are often involved in income generation from an early age, which may contribute to the perception that continuing in education is unimportant.

▶ **Flexibility:** When tin-smithing and repairing became largely obsolete, Travellers were able to adapt their skills to recycling scrap and car parts. It is interesting that in a time of growing interest in and recognition of the value of recycling among the settled (particularly the middle-class) community, this is an area that is used to denigrate and criticise the Travelling population.

▶ **Employment patterns:** Although Travellers engaged in seasonal farm work in the past, working under a boss, particularly a settled person who has little or no understanding or appreciation of their way of life, would not be easy for Travellers. According to the 2006 census, 73% of Traveller men are unemployed compared to 9.4% of the settled population. Many families therefore are dependent on social welfare for survival. However, many Travellers supplement their income through informal economic activity such as scrap dealing.

Despite these limitations, there has been some progress in the area of employment initiatives, such as whole-community initiatives where the settled community with the Travelling community join together to provide services and/or opportunities. It is a flexible system adapted to the needs of the community it serves, which at the moment seems to be mainly Travellers. One such example is where Traveller women have been trained to provide childcare services, which in turn has enabled other Traveller women to access training and education. This provides much needed employment and educational opportunity and, more importantly, has a profound effect of empowerment. Such initiatives require support on two levels – financial support from the Government and a willing participation by both communities.

Banks and building societies do not generally deal with Travellers, which as well as being discriminatory closes off a lot of financial options to them and leaves them with all the disadvantages and insecurities of a cash economy. Adult Travellers are fearful of approaching these institutions because of the amount of form filling that has to be done. Most Travellers who wish to borrow money have to go to a moneylender.

Traveller Health

The health and welfare of Travellers is a sad reflection on the intolerable living conditions of the majority of the Traveller population. The All-Ireland Traveller Health Study (2010) reveals that in comparison to the settled community:

▶ Stillborn children are twice as likely among Travellers.

▶ Infant mortality is over twice as likely among Travellers.

▶ Sudden infant death is nearly four times as likely to occur in the Traveller community.

▶ Traveller children are three times more likely to be hospitalised in the first year of life.

▶ Less than 4% of Travellers live to be over 65 years compared to 11% of the settled population. Men's life expectancy is 15 years less and women's is 12 years less than that of settled people. In the settled community women tend to live longer than men do, but in the Travelling community this is reversed.

▶ In all age groups Travellers have higher mortality rates.

▶ More Travellers than settled people die owing to the following:
— Accidents
— Metabolic disorders in the 0–14 year age group
— Respiratory ailments
— Congenital problems.

Health problems are exacerbated by:

▶ General distrust of the system and a lack of confidence in asserting their rights due, in part, to poor literacy among the adult population.

▶ Poor living conditions – one in four Travellers has no piped water or electricity.

▶ Discrimination – up to one-fifth of Travellers have difficulty finding a GP who will accept them as a patient.

▶ Health promotion – lack of education and training material that is relevant and meaningful contributes to a low uptake of health services on the part of Travellers.

Because they are a distinct cultural group with different needs and perceptions of healthcare, a different approach to service provision is required. The system which operates in the settled community, for example registration for free medical services with a named doctor, would not always suit a Traveller family. A Traveller Health Policy Unit has been established along with a Health Advisory Committee. Health Units for Travellers together with Primary Health Care Initiatives have also been established.

Traveller Accommodation

Until recently the approach to Travellers' accommodation problems was to house or settle them so that they would become absorbed into the mainstream society – **assimilation**. Sites were provided in areas where they would not be seen and often in unhealthy and unsanitary areas, for example close to public dumps. Much of what was provided in the past was also of poor quality and with few services. These policies were driven by assimilation objectives. They were also driven by a lack of respect for the Travellers and their way of life, coupled with a denial of their separate ethnicity.

Travellers live in the following types of accommodation, and almost three-quarters of Traveller families now live in houses.

▶ Standard housing (in mixed housing schemes)
▶ Group housing schemes (all Travellers)
▶ Official halting sites – permanent ones have full services, temporary ones often do not.
▶ Unofficial halting sites (on the roadside). About 800 families continue to live in this type of accommodation where there is no water supply, no electricity, no toilets or washing facilities and no rubbish collection. This substandard accommodation has been identified as the main contributor to lower life expectancy and the high rate of health problems experienced by the community.

Since the Task Force on the Travelling Community was established in 1995, the approach to meeting the accommodation needs has changed to take account of Traveller culture. The main issues addressed were: Travellers tend to have large families; extended families often live together or in close proximity; work and living space tends to be combined; and some element of nomadism is a feature for a large number of families. Official halting sites developed in recent years have been designed to take account of these needs, but the number of accommodation units has fallen far short of that recommended by the task force. Responsibility for the provision of official halting sites lies with the local authorities, but in the main they have failed to implement their 5-year plans for Traveller accommodation as required by the the Housing (Traveller Accommodation) Act 1998 because of the absence of any sanctions for this breach of the law and because of opposition from the settled community.

The availability of accommodation in local authority housing or group housing schemes has improved and provision has come close to meeting the target set out by the task force.

In 2002, the Housing (Miscellaneous Provisions) Act made trespassing on private or public lands a criminal offence punishable by 1 month in jail, a €3,000 fine and confiscation of property. This in effect criminalises the nomadic way of life.

Traveller Education

The Task Force on the Traveller Community (1995) identified poor and inadequate education as one of the greatest barriers to progress in the community. The main feature of the Traveller community in relation to education is that Travellers do not continue in education beyond primary school level. A 2006 Department of Education and Skills report found little change.

Recent figures indicate that while most Traveller children attend primary school, 63% of them have left school by age 15, compared to 13% nationally. Only a handful of Travellers currently attend third-level education. The first Traveller was called to the Bar in 2005, as was the first Traveller to become a member of the Gardaí.

The main reasons for the lack of participation by the Travelling community in education are:

▶ Their distinct cultural identity is ignored within the mainstream education system

▶ Discrimination and segregation such as exclusion from social activity by their peers and objections by settled parents.

This is being addressed to some extent in early education services. Pre-schools for Travellers have been in existence since 1984 and are grant-aided directly by the Department of Education and Skills. In addition, more Travellers are being trained to work in these early services, thus ensuring that the programmes provided are more appropriate and meaningful for the children. Segregation in early childhood services and at primary school level continues to be a major obstacle to progress (see Chapter 1). The main objective of the education strategy will be to ensure that Travellers are given the opportunity to benefit from an inclusive education system and gain equality of access, participation and outcomes.

General Discrimination

On an individual level Travellers are often viewed as scroungers, thieves and dirty. The practice of racism against Travellers by the general population is very serious and damaging. It is the power and therefore the racism of the settled community that labels the Traveller way of life as deviant and unacceptable and is the root cause of the social, economic and political exclusion of Travellers in Ireland today.

Most of the difficulties and problems already outlined are caused not by ignorance and lack of education on the part of the Traveller, but by ignorance, prejudice, discrimination and lack of education on the part of the settled community.

The effects of racism, prejudice and discrimination affect all areas of a person's life. The following give a flavour of the additional obstacles faced by the Traveller community.

▸ Resident groups and local authorities can prevent Travellers from coming into certain areas by preventing access to open spaces.

▸ Settled people can march on campsites and intimidate Travellers, often with the co-operation of the authorities.

▸ Racist and inflammatory articles can be printed in local and national newspapers.

Institutional racism also occurs in the actions and practices of our organisations and Government institutions. Examples include the following.

▸ A voting system that excludes anyone who does not have a fixed address.

▸ A legal system which does not facilitate minority ethnic representation on juries.

▸ A local authority system which empowers local authorities to place boulders and overhead barriers obstructing any area that might suit as a temporary halting site.

▸ A system which allows Travellers to be evicted or moved on without the provision of alternative suitable accommodation. Eviction in the settled community occurs usually only after a lengthy legal process and affects individual families rather than groups.

'TWENTY-YEAR-OLD HID FOUR STOLEN LOLLIPOPS IN HER BRA'
The Anglo-Celt, Thursday, 1 October, 2009

A 20-year-old Castleblayney woman who concealed four stolen lollipops in her bra was sentenced to three months when she pleaded guilty to the offence at Cootehill District Court.

Christina Ward, Drumcrew, Castleblayney, was charged with possessing a packet of biscuits and four lollipops, knowing them to have been stolen at Main Street, Castleblayney, on September 21.

Garda Grainne Gallagher said she received a report that members of the Travelling community had entered Carragher's Filling Station on the Shercock Road in Castleblayney and had taken some goods.

She stopped a vehicle and the defendant had a packet of biscuits and four lollipops in her bra. Garda Gallagher had spoken to Mr. Carragher's son who was in the store at the time the Travellers entered.

Judge Sean MacBride said: 'These people think they can come into a business and walk all over them.'

'No one can act like that,' he added. 'Young Mr. Carragher did the right thing by contacting the gardaí and informing them what happened.'

The judge accepted that the defendant was not the only one at it.

Business people deserve the protection of the law, he said. This was a serious crime where the defendant had worked in concert with her family. They were causing angst in the business community, where they are going into shops stealing what doesn't belong to them.

They were intimidating and breaking the law. Judge MacBride said he was sending the defendant away for three months to Dochas. He fixed recognisances in the defendant's own bond of €1,000 cash.

Conditions of the bail, if taken up, are that she resides at Drumcrew, Castleblayney, not to be up town between 11pm and 7am, sign on daily at Castleblayney between 6 and 9pm, abstain from intoxicating liquor and illegal drugs, commit no crime, surrender her passport and not to travel outside the jurisdiction.

Strategies for Change

There is no doubt that the voice of the Travelling community is growing and that they are being recognised as a distinct ethnic group, albeit one of many in modern Ireland. Recent positive developments include:

▸   The Traveller Education Strategy

▸   The Traveller Health Strategy and All-Ireland Traveller Health Report (2010)

▸   The National Action Plan against Racism

▸   The ongoing work of national and local Traveller groups and organisations.

Much more needs to be done in areas of combating prejudice and changing public attitudes towards Travellers and this will require not only willingness, but also resources. Many international and European bodies have identified the major obstacle to real progress as the hostility of the settled population and the unwillingness of the authorities to tackle this.

ACTIVITY

Aim: To investigate media coverage of Travellers by:

(a) *Looking at the media image portrayed*
(b) *Examining the use of language*
(c) *Questioning the views and assumptions underlying the report.*

Material: Collect current news articles from the daily papers or from magazines. Record a TV programme. If nothing is currently available, seek out recent coverage in your library.

Analyse the content of the article or programme using the following guidelines:

Media image	Language	Opinion
Is the article critical or supportive of Travellers? Is proof offered when claims or accusations are made? Are visual images positive or negative?	Is the title negatively or positively worded? What words are used to describe Travellers? Are these words negative or positive?	Whose opinions are given in the article? Have Travellers been given an opportunity to express their views? If this article was about you, your family or your community, how would you feel about it?

It is useful when doing this exercise to write down your results, taking note of relevant phrases and words used. If doing this in groups, then each group should discuss their findings and be encouraged to discuss their attitudes.

Race and Racism

In the biological/physiological sense it is not possible to divide human groups according to race. Attempts to do this are usually related to skin colour but are based on social attitudes. The term 'race' is commonly used to refer to groups who share distinctive cultural traits. It is more acceptable to use the term 'ethnic groups'. However, racism does exist. It seeks to justify and act upon ideas of inferiority and superiority based on characteristics ascribed to people who are supposedly biologically distinct.

Definitions

Racism is prejudice or discrimination in relation to a person's ethnic group. It is based on the claim that racial or ethnic groups are inherently superior or inferior, implying that one group would be entitled to dominate another.

Ethnic group is the term used to describe groups of people who share common cultural characteristics, e.g. language, dress, food, religion, customs, beliefs, traditions, etc. People in such groups perceive themselves and are perceived by others as having a distinct identity.

An ethnic minority group is a distinct ethnic group which makes up a small proportion of a particular society. In Ireland, Travellers are an ethnic minority group, as are different groups of immigrants.

Ethnocentrism occurs when one ethnic group (usually the largest one, but not always) sees its traditions and beliefs as the only important ones and therefore the only ones worth considering.

Xenophobia means a fear and dislike of strangers.

Asylum is a place of refuge for people in need of protection because of their beliefs, nationality, ethnic group, religion or political opinion. An asylum seeker is a person who is making an application to be granted refugee status.

Refugee is the term used universally to describe an individual who is fleeing persecution.

Programme refugees are groups of people who have been recognised as being in special need of protection. Usually this recognition is achieved in discussion with other countries, e.g. within the EU, and individual countries agree to take a certain number of refugees. The State plans for the arrival of programme refugees and should have accommodation, English classes and healthcare organised. On arrival, the programme refugee acquires the same rights as an Irish person and may apply for citizenship after 3 years living here.

Convention refugees are individuals whose applications are dealt with on an individual basis and judged according to criteria laid down in the 1951 Geneva Convention (see below). A person who has been granted refugee status is entitled to work, study and receive the same social welfare and health benefits as an Irish person.

Residency means that a permit is granted which allows a person to live in the country for a specified time. A child born in Ireland automatically becomes an Irish citizen. However, this does not transfer to her parents, and they may apply for residency, which has not been automatically granted in the past.

Leave to remain is granted to some people who cannot obtain refugee status and is granted totally at the discretion of the Minister for Justice, Equality and Law Reform.

Immigrants are people who choose to come live in Ireland for personal or economic reasons. They must apply to the State for permission to do so and should obtain the relevant visa and documentation in advance if they wish to work here. Until 2006 economic migrants from non-EU countries who were given leave to work had their permit attached to a specific employment. Because of the exploitation of migrant workers by unscrupulous employers, this has been changed and the permit is now the property of the worker, not the employer.

Illegal immigrants are people who arrive in the State without any documentation and who are not refugees or asylum seekers. Some illegal immigrants travelling from very poor circumstances are unofficially called economic refugees. Illegal immigrants can be deported immediately on being discovered or can be detained in prison. At present, there is no provision in Irish law for an explicit time limit on the detention, legal counselling is not free even when the person is destitute and there is no right to visitation.

Unaccompanied minors are children under the age of 18 years who arrive in Ireland unaccompanied seeking asylum.

Overview of the Legislation

The Universal Declaration of Human Rights 1948 assures people the right to look for and be granted asylum.

The Geneva Convention 1951 relating to the status of refugees sets down criteria and principles relating to war, famine and plague. It also states that no one should be returned to a country where the person's life or freedom would be at risk.

The Dublin Convention 1990 forces asylum seekers to seek asylum in the first safe country of the EU in which they land. The Convention also proposes to fingerprint all asylum seekers and refugees.

The Refugee Act 1996 places the arrangements and procedures in relation to refugees and asylum seekers on a statutory basis. The main elements of the Act are:

▶ The setting up of an independent body to assess applications.

▶ The inclusion of gender, sexual orientation and membership of a trade union as grounds under which people could apply for refugee status.

▶ The requirement that the media get written permission from the Minister for Justice, Equality and Law Reform before they can identify asylum seekers.

The **Immigration Acts 1999 and 2003** legislate for deportation from Ireland and include the appointment of the Refugee Applications Commissioner, the establishment of an Appeals Tribunal and the Refugee Advisory Board.

The **Illegal Immigrants (Trafficking) Act 2000** outlines penalties for trafficking, that is, carrying or arranging the transport of immigrants, and also deals with appeals, detention and deportation of asylum seekers. The 27th Amendment of the Constitution Act 2007 means that children whose parents are not Irish are no longer automatically entitled to citizenship.

Figure 13.1: Asylum Applications Made in Ireland, 1993–2010

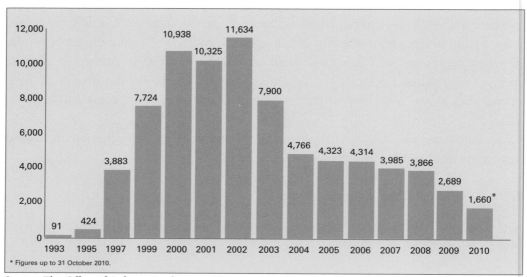

* Figures up to 31 October 2010.

Source: The Office of Refugee Applications Committee Report (2010).

Historical Perspective

Until recently Irish people have tended to think of themselves as a homogeneous group, but even a superficial glance over our history shows otherwise. Irish blood over the last few thousand years has been mixed with that of Celts, Normans, English, Scottish, Spanish, French, Jews and Huguenots, to name a few. After the Second World War most people who came to Ireland did so to further their education and many experienced prejudice and discrimination. A study carried out in the mid-1970s found that a 'severe' degree of racial prejudice existed in Ireland, with, for example, black people finding it extremely difficult to find accommodation.

In the latter half of the twentieth century Vietnamese, Hungarian, Czechoslovakian and Bosnian people came here as programme refugees. In the last 20 years, people of up to 100 different nationalities, but mainly from Eastern Europe and Africa, have sought refuge and/or employment in Ireland.

The number of refugees worldwide has increased from 5.7 million in 1980 to over 40 million today. The increasing sophistication of armed conflict means that ever-increasing numbers of people are experiencing horror and devastation in their lives, but over 80% of refugees only get as far as a neighbouring country. Less than 5% of refugees get as far as Europe and only one in 50 of these, or 0.06% of the total refugee population of the world, makes it to Ireland. Only a minority of those who apply for refugee status have their application granted.

The Experience of Racism in Ireland

Various surveys have found that most non-Irish people in Ireland have experienced some form of prejudice and discrimination and that the proportion is consistently higher if the person is black, whether that person is Irish or not. One survey found that 78% of asylum seekers generally had experienced racially motivated verbal or physical assaults. Ninety-eight per cent of Africans (compared to 14% of Eastern Europeans) had experienced verbal abuse. Verbal abuse, stereotyping, staring and ignoring are the most common forms of discrimination. The Association of Refugees and Asylum Seekers has documented scores of violent physical assaults, including murders, in recent years.

Other forms of racism are difficult to quantify and research in the area is lacking. Many people are fleeing oppressive regimes and are understandably reluctant to give information or to complain about the country that they hope will give them asylum.

Institutional racism is racism evident in the actions and practices of organisations, Government departments and State agencies. Examples of institutional racism are:

▸ On entering Ireland, people who do not appear to look Irish, European or white American may receive closer scrutiny from immigration officials.

▸ Care centres accommodating separated children (who are under the care of the Department of Health and Children) do not come under the Social Service Inspectorate and a number have been operating illegally, understaffed and unsafely. Around 300 children have gone 'missing' from these centres since 2001.

The policy of **direct provision** of accommodation and food to asylum seekers instead of money (as is given to all other social welfare recipients) is a clear example of discrimination. This limits the control and element of choice in their lives. **Dispersal**, which means that the State houses groups of asylum seekers in centres, segregated from the main community, is another clear example of whole groups being treated differently in terms of their accommodation requirements. In effect, these groups are living together in the same centre as others with whom they have little in common. In these centres people are not allowed to work or undertake training, recreational facilities are few and they are not allowed to cook their own food. Travelling is also restricted and an absence of more than 3 days means that they lose their place in the centre.

The main problems identified by the refugee/asylum population are:

▸ The long, slow process of decision-making in the Department of Justice, Equality and Law Reform. The Refugee Applications Commissioner and the Reception and Integration Agency are handling around 600 applications per month, but there is a considerable backlog and people may wait months and even years for a decision. Two-thirds go on to appeal against unfavourable decisions.

▸ Living in dispersal centres with nothing to do, little or no access to English classes and little chance to integrate.

▸ Lack of support services to enable children to access and participate in education.

▸ Experience of discrimination and prejudice, particularly for non-European people.

ACTIVITY

In the first instance, apply this exercise to yourself and ask yourself the questions listed below.

Talk to people casually about immigrants and take note (mental or written) of the attitudes and beliefs expressed. Follow this by attempting to probe how people formed their attitudes and where they got their information. You can do this by asking questions along the following lines.

▸ Have you ever had an immigrant as a friend?

▸ Have you ever been in an immigrant's home?

▸ Have you ever brought an immigrant to your home?

▸ Have you ever sought an immigrant's opinion about anything?

▸ Have you ever read a book about immigration?

▸ Have you ever had a conversation with an immigrant?

▸ Have you ever been in a group that included an immigrant?

▸ Where did most of your ideas come from?

Examine your findings to discover whether your interviewees were prejudiced and whether they had formed their attitudes and ideas based on direct experience or on labels and stereotypes.

These activities could be adapted to focus on any marginalised or disadvantaged group in our society, such as refugees, people who have a disability, people who have a mental illness or people who are homosexual.

The Way Forward

▸ Abandon discussion about whether an intercultural Ireland is a good thing or not; it is here to stay.

▸ Look at intercultural societies which are thriving and learn from them, e.g. Canada.

▸ Take a more proactive role in combating prejudice, stereotypes and discrimination.

▸ Speed up the processing of applications and differentiate completely between asylum seekers/refugees and immigrants.

▸ Abandon direct provision and long stays in dispersal centres.

▸ Facilitate access to education, training and employment.

Disability

Who Are Disabled People?

Disabled people are good, bad, ambitious, laid back, smart, silly, successful or unsuccessful. They are men, women, boys, girls, people of all ages, colours, religions or other kinds of beliefs, social class, political opinions or non-political.

They are mothers, fathers, children, young, middle-aged or old people, people who are unemployed, employed, unskilled or professional. In other words, they are the same people you would normally find in any society. They are ordinary people who happen to be disabled because of an impairment. It is estimated that in Ireland, these ordinary people account for around 10% of the population.

Historical Perspective

Until relatively recently, disabled people were fairly invisible in Irish society owing to the fact that they were mainly segregated into institutions which offered 'care' and 'special education', often run by religious orders. This involved separation from their families and communities, often at a young age, and had implications for their educational provision and future employability – rarely did disabled people get to actually sit the

Leaving Certificate and progress to higher education or to meaningful employment. Becoming institutionalised meant that they were unable for the challenge of mainstream employment and socialisation and often ended up in 'sheltered' employment, which paid an allowance rather than a wage or salary.

By the 1970s, however, an international movement for human and civil rights had sprung up. Women and black Americans were taking to the streets to demand their rights, and eventually disabled people began to demand the right to be treated as equal citizens in society. For them disability had become a social and an equality issue; they were no longer prepared to be treated as second-class citizens or to depend on charity, as had happened in the past.

In 1981 the United Nations proclaimed the United Nations Year of Disabled Persons, and following on from this the United Nations Decade of Disabled Persons was launched in 1983. This had important consequences for international, national and local developments. It put disability onto the political agenda, bringing about changes in the lives of disabled people.

Defining Disability

Disability is defined under The Employment Equality Acts 1998 and 2004 as:

(a) Total or partial absence of a person's bodily or mental functions, including the absence of a part of a person's body
(b) Body organisms causing or likely to cause chronic disease or illness
(c) Malfunction, malformation or disfigurement of a part of a person's body
(d) Condition of malfunction that results in a person learning differently
(e) Condition, illness or disease which affects a person's thought processes, perception of reality, emotions or judgement or which results in disturbed behaviour.

Examples of different types of disabilities include:

▸ Mobility and physical impairments, for example those that necessitate using a wheelchair or mobility aid, or those which affect a person's manual dexterity.

▸ Sensory impairments such as:

— Visual impairment, which can include partial or full blindness
— Auditory or hearing impairment, including deafness
— Speech or language impairment, including a complete inability to use spoken language.

▸ Intellectual disability, also known as 'learning difficulties'.

▸ Psychiatric illness or mental impairment.

While some forms of disability can be obvious, others are not readily apparent, for example epilepsy or a hearing impairment. Also, the same disability can vary and can affect people differently.

Approaches to Disability

There are two main models or ways of looking at disability: the **Medical Model** and the more recent **Social Model** of disability.

The Medical Model of Disability

In the Medical Model of disability, the focus is on the individual and the disability, which is seen as a **condition**. Once the condition is recognised and understood, treatment is sought. At the centre of the Medical Model are the notions of **condition** and **treatment**. The purpose of the treatment is to bring about some change in the individual. For example, a person with a visual impairment might undergo surgery to improve his vision and a child with a hearing impairment might be fitted with a hearing aid. The Medical Model can be helpful to us in working with disability, but it also has its disadvantages.

A person with a medical condition is not considered normal – she differs from other people because of the condition and will only become normal when her condition has been rectified or removed. This has a negative impact on the person's self-esteem and also significantly affects the way others perceive and relate to her.

The main characteristics of the Medical Model are:

▸ Focusing on the individual's medical condition, illness or absence of bodily functions.

▸ Locating the 'problem' in the individual, seeing it as a personal problem and an individual limitation.

▸ Based on a view of disability as a tragic occurrence in a person's life which the person cannot overcome or which can only be overcome through medical intervention or medication.

The Medical Model is likely to look for solutions to disability within the disabled person rather than in society. Such solutions could include:

▸ Cure of medical conditions.

▸ Requiring the disabled person to adjust to her environment (e.g. entering the building through the car park because you can't get up the front steps, or worse, having someone carry you up the steps).

▸ Rehabilitation in segregated institutions, rather than integration in mainstream environments.

The Social Model of Disability

In the Social Model, the focus is on the environment in which the disabled person lives and the acceptance by society that the environment can be changed to accommodate the needs of the person, rather than the other way around. The visually impaired person has every right to live a full life just the way she is – why should she have to change just because society would like her to be different? Her visual impairment is part of her identity. To facilitate her full participation in society, changes are made to her environment, both physical and human. For example, she can cross the road safely at a pedestrian crossing if there are paving slabs with raised dots to guide her and beeps to indicate when it is safe to cross. In this example, society has accepted the person as she is and made some changes so that she can participate equally, and with no suggestion that she is abnormal.

ACTIVITY

Aim: Medical Model or Social Model?

Divide the statements below into two lists, one containing the items that you think fit under the Medical Model (the problem lies with the individual) and the other containing the items that fit into the Social Model (the problem lies in the society or the world around us).

No parking spaces	Is sick
Has seizures	Has prejudiced attitudes
Is housebound	Cannot see or hear
Stairs instead of ramps	No sign language interpreters
Is isolated	Has low income
Is there a cure?	Is confined to wheelchair
Cannot use hands	No lifts
Needs help and carers	Poorly designed building
Has inaccessible transport	Cannot walk
Has segregated education	

Following the activity, discuss the following.

▶   What are the advantages and disadvantages of each model?

▶   Are there any barriers in your classroom and college that could cause discrimination?

▶   How could the situation be improved?

The main characteristics of the Social Model are:

▶ Focusing on disability as being socially created. This means that it recognises society must look to see how it can change that rather than expecting the disabled person or the impairment to change. For example, it is now quite common to see sign language interpreters at public events, a simple measure which enables deaf people to enjoy the event equally with everyone else.

▶ Recognising that disabled people should have power over their own lives.

The Social Model is likely to look for solutions to disability within society rather than within the disabled person. Such solutions could include:

▶ The removal of barriers for full inclusion and participation. This could include everything from physical and written barriers to attitudinal barriers, negative feelings and prejudices. This can only happen through the inclusion of disabled people in all aspects of community life, where meeting and interacting become commonplace and therefore normal.

▶ Education will also play a key role here, in that children need to encounter disabled people in their lives and live with images which depict disabled people participating fully in all aspects of our society.

Developments in Ireland

In Ireland, the disability movement developed in the late 1980s and 1990s, largely due to the changing political climate of the time, where equal rights for all were increasingly sought. The main milestones included the following.

1990   ▶ The establishment of the Forum of People with Disabilties. This brought disabled people together for the first time in a representative group to discuss issues relevant to disability and to chart a way forward. It was significant in that it recognised the right of disabled people for the first time to engage in a decision-making process about their own future.

1993   ▶ Building regulations were introduced which required that all new buildings should be fully accessible to disabled people.

▶ The establishment of the Commission on the Status of People with Disabilities, which set out to research disability in Ireland and make recommendations on the way forward.

1996   ▶ The Electoral Act was amended to give full voting rights to disabled people.

▶ A *Strategy for Equality*, the Report of the Commission on the Status of People with Disabilities, was issued, containing 402 recommendations to equalise the condition of disabled people in Ireland.

1998
  ▸ The Employment Equality Act made it illegal to discriminate against someone on the grounds of a disability.
  ▸ The Equality Authority and the Office of the Director of Equality Investigations were established.
  ▸ The Education Act provided the first legal definition of disability and special educational needs and outlined the responsibilities of the Government in relation to the provision of education for all.

1999
  ▸ The National Disabilities Authority Act was passed, which created the National Disability Authority (NDA) and defined its functions as a legal body responsible for overseeing all aspects of service provision to people with disabilities and to ensure that legislation related to disability is implemented properly.

2000
  ▸ The Equal Status Act was passed.
  ▸ The Education Welfare Act was passed, with the purpose of ensuring that every child in the State receives an appropriate education. It requires schools to ensure that all children, regardless of disability or special educational need, participate in and benefit from the entire life of the school.

2004
  ▸ The Equality Act makes specific mention of the rights of disabled people in the workplace and provides additional protection against unfair treatment and harassment. It outlines the duties of an employer of a disabled person to take practical measures which will enable the disabled person to enter employment and to advance in their employment.
  ▸ The Education for Persons with Special Educational Needs Act (EPSEN) was passed, to be fully implemented by 2009. The Act provides for the education of all children in an inclusive environment, defines 'special educational needs' and the content of the Education Plan, and recognises that the educational interests of all children should be taken into account when determining where a child with special educational needs will be educated.
  ▸ The National Council for Special Education (NCSE) was created under this Act.

2005
  ▸ The Disabilities Act was passed. Designed to protect the rights of disabled people, it provides for the assessment of health and educational needs and assures that appropriate planning and service delivery will be undertaken on the behalf those with disabilities by the Ministers concerned.

Living with Disability

Many disabled people face obstacles in their daily lives which make it difficult to access goods and services. These can include:

▶ **Communication obstacles** – inappropriate or disrespectful language, people speaking too quickly or unclearly, talking to a companion rather than directly to the disabled person ('Does he take sugar?').

▶ **Negative** or **patronising attitudes** which make assumptions about a person's ability or disability.

▶ **Poor access** to buildings, narrow doorways, steep staircases, cluttered layout, poor lighting, unclear signage.

▶ **Lack of thought** in how services are provided – staff uncertain about how to deal with the disabled person, over-complicated procedures, complex paperwork.

▶ Many **early childhood services** still do not accept disabled children. Early childhood services are not covered by the Education Act 1998, and unlike primary schools, are therefore not required to have a policy of open access for all children, whether disabled or not.

TASK
List some of the ways in which disabled people, including children, can experience discrimination because of their impairments.

Reasonable Accommodation

Under the Equal Status Act, providers of goods and services may not discriminate against a person on the grounds of disability. This includes mobility impairment, sensory impairment, intellectual impairment or mental health. The Act requires providers of goods and services to make reasonable accommodation for the needs of disabled people through making changes in what they do and how they do it. Without these changes it would be very difficult or impossible for disabled people to obtain these goods or services. Knowing what disabled people want helps in the provision of reasonable accommodation. Many kinds of reasonable accommodation cost little or nothing to implement, or in cases where a cost is incurred, grants are available to help offset the expense. Examples of reasonable accommodation for disabled people include:

▶ Making a building or classroom easier to get around by putting more thought into how the furniture is arranged.

▶ Making printed material such as brochures available on a website, CD, audio tape or in large print if requested.

Positive Action

There is no obligation to limit the changes to only those which are reasonable – it is now legal to actually discriminate in favour of a disabled person! This is known as positive action. Examples of positive action are:

▶ Reserving parking spaces for disabled drivers

▶ Reserving one or more places on a training course for a disabled participant.

Disability and Additional Needs

Increasing numbers of children in early education services are being identified as having attention-related disorders, autism or other socio-emotional difficulties, experiencing developmental delays, physical impairments, sensory impairments or emotional difficulties. All of these mean that there will be additional needs which need to be recognised and catered for when working with the child.

Working with Children with Additional Needs

A child is considered to have a special need or additional need if she is outside of the typical range of individual differences. Disability, or an additional need which arises as a result of a disability, is only one aspect of a child, not the whole child. The child with additional needs is a child first. Remember that children with disabilities have a wide range of abilities and needs, so it is not helpful to categorise them as a homogenous group – all children are individuals. Labels interfere with our understanding of the whole child instead of helping us.

For example, you may work with a child with a physical impairment who is developmentally advanced in another area such as language. It is necessary to reflect carefully when using labels like this because the label can obscure important information about the child.

The appropriate curriculum for the child with a disability is one which is planned in response to the observed developmental stages, interests and needs of the child – in other words, it is offered in the same way as for all children in the group. It is based on observation, it focuses on what the child can do and it builds on her strengths. This curriculum provision occurs in a well-planned environment, where active learning is promoted and where respect and choice are the norm. (See Chapter 1, Aistear: The Early Childhood Curriculum Framework.)

Children with Exceptional Ability/Giftedness

Remember that additional needs can also become apparent when a child is developmentally ahead of her peers. She may use more complex language, show advanced understanding of concepts or ask a lot questions. She may also become bored easily as she does not find the work or play materials stimulating or challenging enough. Children may be developmentally ahead in a number of areas such as music or athletics as well as the traditional areas. It is important to remember that this rarely extends across all the domains of development, so a child who is advanced in reading skills may still need lots of support in her social or other areas of development.

ACTIVITY

Aim: To evaluate an early childhood care and education environment in terms of how it can accommodate children with additional needs, with specific reference to physical impairment.

Using your workplace or work placement as a model, and in consultation with the supervisor, examine the physical environment to find out how it would accommodate a child with a physical disability.

▸   Draw up a checklist which you could use to help you in this assessment.

▸   Include aspects such as access, space, layout, arrangement of furniture and play materials, eating arrangements, etc.

▸   Carry out your assessment, draw conclusions and make recommendations for improvements.

▸   Suggest areas where reasonable accommodations could be made to facilitate access.

When working with a child who has an additional need, remember to:

▸   Observe and reflect on the child's strengths, interests, talents, background, learning style and temperament. All good planning and provision is based on observation and knowledge of the individual child.

▸   Ask yourself what the additional needs are:
   —   What behaviours is the child exhibiting?
   —   Are they interfering with her learning?
   —   Are they interfering with other children's learning?

▸   What adjustments do you need to make to the environment and to the provision that would support her additional need and make it easier for her to learn and develop?

▸   Develop strategies based on what you have observed while taking account, where appropriate, of the child's specific condition.

CASE STUDY

The Wheels Community

The Wheels Community is a purpose-built residential estate which is geographically isolated and inhabited only by people in wheelchairs.

All the buildings are single storey, with ramped entrances and low, wide doorways. Ceilings are set at 5 feet high, as nobody living here needs more than that. All switches, handles and other controls are at a sensible height for the users. The same is true of counters, tables, work surfaces and so on. None of the cafés and restaurants has chairs, as all their customers provide their own. The same is true of the cinema and concert hall.

Many other facilities are drive-in, such as banks, supermarkets, fast food outlets, etc. in order to cater for the large number of vehicles specially adapted for the townspeople. Most of these vehicles are not equipped with seats, but with clamps to anchor the wheelchairs into position.

The system works well, and the first generation of residents continued to refine their environment to suit their needs. The community developed, and as is the nature of things, romances developed and marriages took place in the church without pews and the drive-in registry office.

Being moral and upstanding citizens, it was only after these marriages that children began to appear on the scene. It was not at first apparent, but as the children grew, the parents began to notice that things were not as they should be. These children only needed wheelchairs for the first year or two of life. While this new generation remained small, their problems could be managed at home and within the community. As they grew up, however, they suffered frequent bruising to the head as they tried to walk through the low doorways or to stand up in the low-ceilinged rooms. There was also an increasing amount of toe damage as they would get their feet underneath some of the thousands of wheels about the town. Many also complained of back problems from having to bend down all the time.

Communication became difficult, as eye contact was lost with the children's increasing height and distance from the speaker. They began to be marginalised as they could not use the facilities at the youth club or join the basketball teams, or even sit in the coffee bar with their wheelie friends.

It became increasingly obvious that special provision would need to be made for them. Residential hostels were built, and social workers employed to counsel both them and their parents about their obvious differences from the mainstream of society. Areas were set aside especially to cater for them, with chairs available in cafés and the cinema, and separate entrances to allow for their greater height being built where possible.

Some parents even went as far as providing protective headgear for their children; charities were set up to help these poor able-bodied people who needed help. Money was raised to send them off to special schools where their problems could be catered for. Many suffered psychological problems, however, and there was an element in the community who shunned them and insisted that they should live a separate life. These people would give to the charities, but not let their daughter marry one (not their wheelie daughter anyway). An extremist group even went as far as raising money to be used for the amputation of the lower limbs of the able-bodied, but this was always a minority view.

Some of the 'able-bodied handicapped' reacted to this attitude and set up their own pressure group, organising marches demanding equal rights, adapted buildings suitable for their needs as well as everybody else's, and a guaranteed 'able-bodied' allowance from the town council.

They came to be seen as troublemakers, and the wheelie townspeople did not know how to deal with them. They came to feel uneasy in their presence, and then to avoid them if they saw them about, sometimes even crossing the street so that they did not meet.

(Source: Skelt, A., 1993, *Caring for People with Disabilities*, London: Pitman.)

- ▸ Recognise that parents are your partners in working with the child; you may also form partnerships with other specialists.

- ▸ Don't try to change a child's impairment. Your task is to seek the child underneath and work with her.

- ▸ Observation is the key which will help you to unlock and reveal the child behind the disability and the additional need.

The ultimate goal for a child is the same, whether disabled or non-disabled or whether or not there is an additional or special need. This is the goal of enabling and empowering the child to develop to her full potential in an environment which is free from prejudice and discrimination.

The Way Forward

It is absolutely essential that we as a society become aware about disability, how we have dealt with it, how we deal with it in the future and its effect on people's lives.

Disabled people have an absolute right to experience independence, access, inclusion, opportunity and an equal life chance – in short, equality. This would have a positive outcome not only for disabled people, but for society as a whole.

Equality and the Law

Martin Luther King, US civil rights leader of the 1960s, reflected on the fact that laws cannot change what is in a person's heart, but they can change what she is able to do about what is in her heart. The law is there to protect people. It also serves a purpose in demonstrating society's opposition to intolerance and discrimination: it should also promote positive action. The enforcement of laws may help to bring about some changes in attitudes, as enforcement demonstrates a commitment to the values and concepts underpinning the laws.

Laws were often passed in response to pressure from certain sections of Irish society and were piecemeal in their efforts to eliminate prejudice and discrimination. When we examine Irish legislation closely and the order in which it came into force, it becomes evident that a lot of the changes to our laws were EU/internationally driven. Some Irish individuals went directly to Europe to appeal to the courts to have their human rights upheld, e.g. the Norris action in relation to the decriminalisation of homosexuality. Also, it is worth noting that in the absence of comprehensive equal status legislation, individuals and groups had to use other laws to try to defend their rights and to fight discrimination. An example of this would be when members of the Traveller community invoked the Incitement to Hatred law to try to protect themselves, although this law is not strictly relevant to equal status at all.

Another aspect of this piecemeal approach to equality legislation without a full commitment to the basic ideal of equality is that the laws often act as stopgaps but do not address the fundamental problems. For example, equal pay for men and women is of little use in addressing problems of low pay for women in occupations that are predominantly female, as is the case in the childcare profession. Nor is it of any value to the many women who have to stay out of employment because of the lack of affordable childcare.

The basic principle underlying equality legislation today is that in general, people should be judged on their merits as individuals rather than by reference to irrelevant characteristics over which they have no control.

Currently, the two principal pieces of legislation are:

▶   The Employment Equality Acts 1998 and 2004
▶   The Equal Status Acts 2000 to 2004.

(The Equality Act 2004 provides for the implementation of EU directives regarding aspects of the above Acts.)

Both pieces of legislation prohibit discrimination on the following nine grounds:

1.   Gender
2.   Marital status

3.   Family status
4.   Sexual orientation
5.   Religious belief
6.   Age
7.   Disability
8.   Race
9.   Membership of the Traveller community.

▸   **Gender:** 'Gender' and 'sex' are now often used interchangeably, but there are important differences relevant to equality and diversity in the meaning of the two words. Sex refers to biological differences, which are used to distinguish males from females. Gender relates to society's ideas about appropriate masculine and feminine roles and characteristics. While the biological differences between men and women are the same the world over, gender differences may vary from society to society and in different eras.

   Sexism means prejudice or discrimination in relation to a person's gender. **Discrimination** against transsexual people is also covered by the gender ground.

▸   **Marital status:** Refers to whether a person is single, married, separated, divorced or widowed.

▸   **Family status:** Refers to whether a person is pregnant, has or does not have children under 18 or is the resident primary carer of a person with a disability.

▸   **Religion:** Refers to one's religious belief, affiliation or lack of it.

▸   **Age:** Refers only to a person over 18 years, except for the provision of car insurance. The Child Care Act 1991 is the relevant legislation in relation to persons under 18 years.

   Prejudice or discrimination in relation to a person's age is called **ageism.**

▸   **Sexual orientation:** Refers to whether a person is attracted to men, women or both in their choice of sexual partner. A **homosexual** is one who is attracted to a person of the same sex as himself or herself (gay men, lesbian women). A **heterosexual** is one who prefers partners of the opposite sex. A **bisexual** is a person who is attracted to both.

▸   **Homophobia** is the fear and dislike of homosexuality and homosexual people. While sexual orientation in itself may not be an issue in early years work, attitudes towards homosexual people can be formed before children even hear the word. Negative attitudes which indicate homophobic reactions are shown, for example, in the name 'sissy' conferred on boys who cry or in shock-horror reactions to boys who like to dress up in girls' clothing.

Employment Equality Acts

▶   Prohibit discrimination by employers, collectives, advertising, employment agencies, vocational training authorities and by vocational bodies (i.e. professional associations and trades unions) in advertisements and in recruitment.

▶   Define sexual harassment for the first time in Irish law.

▶   Support positive action regarding age, disability, gender and Travellers.

▶   Established a statutory Office of the Director of Equality Investigations.

ACTIVITY

Aim: This activity aims to highlight the derogatory nature of some of the language relating to homosexuality and to explore underlying homophobic attitudes and beliefs.

Many of the names used to describe gay or lesbian people are extremely hurtful and derogatory.

▶   **Brainstorm all the terms/statements that you have heard used about gay men, lesbian women and bisexual people.**

▶   **List everything on a chart under the following three headings – gay men, lesbian women and bisexual. Spend some time in the group discussing the attitudes and myths that are associated with these terms/statements.**

Equal Status Acts

▶   Prohibit discrimination in relation to the provision of goods and services, the obtaining and disposal of accommodation and access to and participation in education. All services that are generally available to the public, whether statutory or private, are covered.

▶   Prohibit sexual harassment or victimisation.

▶   Require reasonable accommodation of people with disabilities.

▶   Allow for positive action to promote equality of opportunity and to cater for people who have additional needs.

The weakness of the legislation is that it does not state clearly and unequivocally rights for minority groups, nor does it recognise that discrimination on the grounds of social class is widespread. Sufficient resources have not been allocated to ensure the effective enforcement of the legislation.

The Equality Authority

The Equality Authority is an independent body with five main functions:

1. To combat discrimination in the areas covered by the Acts
2. To promote equality of opportunity in matters which the legislation applies to
3. To provide information to the public through a range of formats and media
4. To monitor and review the operations of the Acts outlined above
5. To make recommendations to the Minister for Justice, Equality and Law Reform as appropriate.

The Equality Authority has an in-house legal service which may, at its discretion, provide a free confidential advisory service.

The Equality Tribunal

The purpose of the Equality Tribunal is to investigate, mediate and decide in claims of unlawful discrimination. Where it has been established that there has, in fact, been discrimination, an equality officer may order one or more of the following: compensation, equal pay, arrears of wages, equal treatment or a specified course of action. This order is legally binding.

SUMMARY

▶ Prejudice and discrimination are widespread in Ireland and are particularly experienced by some sections of the population.

▶ Change has come about through the efforts of pressure groups who raised awareness and lobbied for change; the change is limited.

▶ Laws have been passed which have helped to combat discrimination, but much more needs to be done. Most of this legislative change has occurred since Ireland joined the European Union.

▶ The Employment Equality Acts 1998 and 2004 prohibit discrimination on nine grounds in relation to employment.

▶ The Equal Status Acts 2000 to 2004 prohibit discrimination in relation to the provision of goods and services.

▶ The Equality Authority and the Equality Tribunal promote and enforce the equality agenda.

14

WHY FOCUS ON CHILDREN?

AREAS COVERED

▸ Developmental Issues and Equality

▸ Empowering Children

▸ Goals of an Environment Committed to Equality and Anti-bias

▸ Adults as Role Models

▸ Materials and Activities

Introduction

The UN Convention on the Rights of the Child 1989 (see Chapter 3 and Appendix 1) sets out the right of all children to grow up in an environment that is free from prejudice and discrimination and one which enhances each child's self-image. It is in the valuing of differences and diversity that we embrace the real principles of fairness and justice for all regardless of gender, class, race, religion, age, marital status, ethnic group, ability and sexual orientation. This chapter raises equality issues in relation to development, care and education in early childhood. It explores how an environment committed to equality promotes an all-round positive attitude to oneself and others. The role of the adult is explored as it is central to the existence of such an environment. Finally, a range of activities and materials for use in early years settings is suggested.

Developmental Issues and Equality

Children are aware of differences from a very early age.

▸ **By the age of 2**, most children will have a sense of their own gender identity and will be able to distinguish girls from boys. This is not surprising because in most cultures, including ours, one of the first things asked about a new baby is whether it is a boy or a girl. From then on, children are socialised according to their gender identity and they constantly see men and women in their families and communities behaving according to set social roles.

▶ **By the age of 3,** children are able to recognise colours and different skin colour. They may also be aware of how different skin colour is perceived by people in the society in which they live. Between 3 and 4 years children also begin to recognise the different abilities and different roles that people have. They will ask factual questions about these.

▶ **By the age of 5,** children are strongly influenced by social norms in how they behave toward others in relation to gender, race and ability. Additionally, their cognitive development is such that they are ready for more complex explanations. They are also able to question attitudes and behaviour. (See Chapter 10 for information on roles and norms.)

ACTIVITY

Aim: To help you become aware of how children perceive gender differences.

Copy and enlarge the pictures on pages 292 and 293 and give them to a boy and a girl aged approximately 5–6 years old.

▶ Ask the child to colour in the pictures.

▶ Observe the child during the activity.

▶ Record the following.

— Which picture does the child colour first?

— What colours are chosen for each picture?

— What is the child saying while doing the activity?

▶ Comment on:

— Which picture was chosen to be coloured first and why you think this might be.

— What colours were chosen for each picture. Are they typically 'masculine' and 'feminine'? On what do you base this opinion?

— What language the child used, if any, during the activity.

— Whether the child appears to be developing rigid ideas about what is appropriate for boys and for girls.

With the children's permission you could borrow the pictures and include them as part of an observation on social development.

This page may be photocopied

Empowering Children

To empower children means to:

▶   Develop their confidence, autonomy, independence and competence

▶   Develop their skills and strategies for coping with discriminatory behaviour.

Young children's learning is experiential and exploratory and it is their right to learn in an atmosphere that is free from prejudice and discrimination and fosters an ethos which is anti-bias. How we relate to others is shaped by our life experiences. We can be encouraged to question and to challenge what we have learned. One of the aims of early childhood education should be to enable children to develop their awareness and understanding, to question false and unfair assumptions about the world and people around them and to challenge damaging attitudes and practices.

A child who feels inferior will fail to reach his full potential. A child who feels superior will fail to appreciate differences in a positive way and will not benefit from the richness inherent in the world. He will also be less able to cope with change. If his situation alters, for example, as a result in a change in the family's financial status or as a result of becoming disabled, he will be less able to adjust in a healthy and positive way.

Children are empowered when they feel good about themselves and their identity. Children will feel good about themselves and they will be comfortable in the early years environment if they feel:

▶   **Valued:** Adults know their names, their likes and dislikes, listen to them and show them respect.

▶   **Liked:** Adults give time to them, showing affection, smiling and generally showing that they (the adults) like being with them.

▶   **Secure:** Security comes from being accepted, the provision of routines and consistency, the setting of limits and being given some privacy.

▶   **Supported:** The child needs to know that nobody is allowed to put him down, tease or exclude him on the basis of a perceived difference such as size, hair colour, skin colour or gender.

▶   **That their family type is included in the resources of the setting:** Visual images such as books and posters should show all types of families – large ones, small ones, one-parent families, extended families.

▶   **That their ideas and skills are used:** Offer to display all work, not just that which the adult considers 'good'. Give all children an opportunity to help regularly with different tasks suited to the ability of each child; all children should have an opportunity to speak and have a choice about giving their opinions or news.

▶ **That assumptions are not made about them:**

— Boys as well as girls like to be complimented on their appearance; both are equally good at cleaning and tidying if they get guidance and support.

— Girls as well as 'big strong boys' can help with fetching and carrying.

— A child who comes from a poor family may be hurt if not asked to bring in the same as everyone else, even though the adult may feel that it would put too much pressure on the parents.

— A child may or may not want to participate in Christmas or Easter because of his religious background.

▶ **That their emotions are acknowledged:**

— Encourage children to recognise and acknowledge their feelings; go beyond sad, happy and angry to other emotions such as pleasure, frustration, fear, dislike, loneliness, pride, shame, embarrassment.

— Facilitate them in learning words to describe what they are feeling by drawing pictures, reading stories, using charts and naming their feelings and your own.

— Acknowledge your own feelings and be a positive role model on how feelings can be dealt with.

▶ **That they are allowed to take some control in their lives:** Appropriate to their age and stage of development and without endangering their health and safety, children can be:

— Given choices and allowed to make some decisions for themselves.

— Encouraged and facilitated to choose activities within the nursery/pre-school setting.

— Consulted about their likes and dislikes.

ACTIVITY

SCENARIO 1

A pre-school group is busy making Father's Day cards. The early years worker notices that one little boy is not participating very enthusiastically. When encouraged to do so, he says, 'I have no daddy at home.' The worker says, 'We'll just write Mammy instead.'

▶ How might the worker have avoided the situation arising in the first place?
▶ How would you have handled the situation as it arose?

ACTIVITY

SCENARIO 2

It is Caitlín's first day at pre-school; she has cerebral palsy and has some difficulty with fine motor tasks. At the end of each day the children change to outdoor shoes and put on their coats to go home.

Jenna is a very capable child and the early years worker says to Caitlín as Jenna is standing beside her, 'Jenna is able to get herself ready really quickly and then she will help you with your shoes and jacket.' She says to Jenna, 'Caitlín has some special problems and will need some help.' Afterwards the worker says, 'Well done Jenna, that can be your job every day; isn't that nice, Caitlín?'

In terms of feeling good:

▶   How might Jenna feel in this scenario?
▶   How might Caitlín feel?
▶   How would the children feel valued/supported?
▶   What could the worker have done differently?
▶   What could the worker have said differently?

Goals of an Environment Committed to Equality and Anti-bias

Responding to the individuality of each person is the cornerstone principle in the provision of an environment committed to equality and anti-bias practice. This approach supports and affirms the child, the child's family, home background and community. It stretches the experiences of children to take account of the diversity that exists in their group, community and country.

An environment committed to equality aims to do the following.

1. Free children from limiting stereotypical definitions which may close off aspects of their development.

A child who needs to use a wheelchair for mobility will increase his self-esteem and independence by being facilitated to fully participate in all activities, but will be undermined by having everything done for him.

2. Promote the self-esteem of individual children by enabling them to feel positive about themselves.

Effort should be appreciated rather then results rewarded; what might seem like a mess to an adult may be the result of intense effort and concentration with paint and a brush by a small child.

3. Promote and value individual development by facilitating each child's participation in activities necessary for physical, cognitive, social and emotional growth.

The individual should be catered for within the group. While some children will enjoy settling down to do jigsaws, a child who dislikes this activity or is unable to concentrate may be wrongly labelled uncooperative or disruptive.

4. Develop each child's skill in questioning and challenging stereotypes.

Men and women, girls and boys, whatever their ability, colour or ethnic group, should be shown in a variety of activities and roles. When involved in role play, children should be encouraged to take on non-stereotypical roles. Girls can be brave and protective, boys can be caring. Questioning and challenging should be encouraged.

5. Foster children's curiosity, enjoyment and awareness of cultural differences and similarities.

Resources should be provided which will broaden children's knowledge and awareness of the world in which we live. Different religious festivals can be acknowledged/celebrated at appropriate times throughout the year. At Christmastime children could be introduced to the idea that not all people celebrate Christmas. Likewise, not all children make First Communion. Children can also be introduced to different foods, clothing, music and languages.

6. Enable children to stand up for themselves and resist and handle discriminatory behaviour.

Children will only do this if they feel supported. A clearly defined and implemented anti-bullying policy agreed by parents, children and the setting is an essential element of this type of support. Children should be encouraged to come up with their own ideas on change, as they are in the Danish project mentioned in Chapter 3. In mixed schools, for example, boys often tend to dominate the open space in the school playground and girls tend to play games like hopscotch and skipping on the periphery. Although girls may feel this to be unfair and will comment upon it, they are unlikely to try and even less likely to succeed in gaining equal access to this space unless backed up by school authorities.

7. Imbue children with a sense of fairness and justice for all.

The stage of cognitive development is important here. Children are acutely aware of fairness at around 5 to 7 years. However, adults need to be aware of it at all times. If children are co-operating in 'turn taking' it is important to ensure that there is enough

Here the adult is saying that the child's fears are silly and unimportant.

Here the adult is taking the child seriously and acknowledging his feelings.

time/resource for each one to have a turn; if you do not do this then you cannot expect the child who has been left out to be so patient next time.

Young children love to take responsibility for doing jobs like setting the table or giving out biscuits – lists are a good way for the adults to ensure that no child is overlooked. This helps the group as a whole to appreciate the idea of fairness.

Adults as Role Models

The adults are the single most important resource in any environment. It is they who have the power to structure the environment, to buy the toys and books, to plan the activities and to organise the play space. If they are not aware of and are not committed to equality and diversity, then all the equipment in the world will be of little use. In other words, the success or failure of an anti-bias curriculum depends on the adults involved.

 Do

Focus on differences and similarities that are, first of all, within the children's daily experience and that make sense to them. For example, in a group of 5-year-old children, an activity on hair could be used to highlight many differences within the group – colour, texture, curly or straight, short or long. The activity could be extended to focus on hair in the wider community, on styles in different cultures, fashions and many more topics.

Respond to questions, giving information, vocabulary and opportunities for discussion. Always try to be factual and if you do not know then say so, but make a point of finding out, including the child/children in the process if possible. Anti-bias education happens best in the context of interactions and experiences.

Provide challenging experiences for children so that they can learn about and explore the world through play.

Respond to each child's individuality and to each child's individual needs.

Use praise and affirmation to reinforce behaviour and attitudes that are desirable.

Provide a rich, varied and inclusive learning environment even if the group appears to be homogeneous, e.g. all white and able-bodied. Be careful not to add insult to injury here by having a token picture or book full of the very stereotypes you are trying to challenge (see the Resources section at the end of this book).

Intervene when difficult or hurtful incidents arise.

Set limits. It is never OK to be hurtful about another's characteristics.

Challenge sexist, racist and any offensive language or behaviour. If someone is hurt, insulted or discriminated against in any way, the adult should step in immediately and let the offending person or child know that his behaviour/language is not acceptable. Explain what was offensive and give correct information. However, support for the offended child comes first; support and encourage the child to express his feelings and to speak for himself if he wishes to do so. An apology may also be appropriate. Depending on the age and size of the group, these issues can also be addressed in the larger group through project work, discussion, role play and puppets.

Model respect toward everyone, adults and children alike.

Constantly examine your own attitudes.

Draw up a policy and code of practice in relation to equality. This should include admission procedures, professional practice and what to do in the case of discriminatory behaviour. The basic premise of such a policy should be that every person is deserving of respect and the service should aim to facilitate each and every one to reach his full potential. No one should be discriminated against on the basis of social class, age, disability, gender, ethnic group, religion, marital or family status, sexual orientation or membership of the Travelling community. Parents and children should be involved in drawing up such a policy and it should be reviewed regularly.

Don't

Use hurtful or exclusionary language or behaviour.

Excuse such behaviour or language in others – 'She didn't realise what she was saying.'

Leave it to someone else to take action – 'The manager should be the one to deal with this.'

Materials and Activities

Contact addresses and numbers are given in the Resources section at the end of the book to help you locate some appropriate resources. Much improvement is required in relation to equality in commercially available materials; many of the better materials are presently only available abroad or on the internet. However, no one should be discouraged by the lack of appropriate and affordable materials – you can always make your own! (See Chapter 5.)

ACTIVITY

SCENARIO 1

John is 3 years old and has just started attending an early years setting. He was born in Ireland of Chinese parents. He is exposed to the English language, Irish culture and festivals. His immediate family also continues to honour and celebrate Chinese culture, so John has a wide experience spanning both cultures.

SCENARIO 2

The Tashita family moved to Ireland just 3 months ago. Their daughter, Akane, is 3 years old and has just started attending an early childhood centre. Her mother, who speaks no English, brings her and collects her each day. Akane tends to observe what is going on or plays on her own. A trainee early childhood worker has begun a work experience placement and when she asks, 'What nationality is Akane?' she is told, 'Chinese or Japanese.'

Discuss the following.

▸ Would it help to know where a child is from? Why?

▸ How could you improve communication with Akane's mother?

▸ What difficulties might you encounter in your work with both children/families?

Exercise

▸ Make a list of ways in which you could help both children reach their potential, acknowledging all aspects of their background.

▸ Plan some activities that would help Akane to learn English.

▸ Plan activities that would help each of the children to settle in their environment.

▸ Plan activities to expose the children in your place of work to some words from another language.

Posters and Pictures

▸ Visual material should reflect the diverse community in which we live.

▸ Posters and pictures should depict one-parent as well as two-parent families.

▸ Flats, apartments, trailers and farmhouses as well as semi-detached houses should appear in visual and play materials.

▸ A variety of religions and ethnic groups should be portrayed.

▸ Gender stereotypes should be challenged by pictures of men and women in a broad variety of roles.

TASK
Find posters and pictures that you could use in your place of work.

Books and Stories

Books should be available to children in all age groups and not just to the child who can read. Picture books, if carefully selected, can be used at all ages to introduce the richness and diversity in society. Pictures of people with different skin colours eating a variety of foods, using household objects as well as expensive shop items, should be on display.

In selecting books, you should look for those that:

▸ Build positive images, particularly of people who may not usually be portrayed in a positive manner

▸ Challenge stereotypes

▸ Show children and families in a world context

▸ Help to develop children's autonomy and self-esteem

▸ Depict children from a range of backgrounds and cultures playing leading roles.

Books or stories which present stereotypical images (and there are no shortage of these) can be used to help children explore various issues and develop their critical thinking, if the adult is aware of what the issues are. For example:

▸ In the story of *Pocahontas*, children are introduced to a Native American girl.

▸ In *Beauty and the Beast* or *The Hunchback of Notre Dame* they are introduced to people with a disability. With their interest already engaged, many other books and resources can be used to correct and broaden their view and to explore the many issues that are brought up in these very popular cartoon classics which children may see frequently.

▸ In many traditional children's stories, the stepmother gets a very bad press (*Cinderella*, *Children of Lir* and *Snow White*). With many families breaking down today, it is of the utmost importance to present alternative views of the stepparent.

▶ For some children, their only exposure to disability may be through reading *Peter Pan*, where Captain Hook is the 'baddie'.

▶ Witches are invariably depicted as old women.

▶ The poor parents in *Hansel and Gretel* abandoned their children in the woods.

The list is endless and these classics will probably remain favourites for many years to come.

However, there are many new books coming on the market and these should be selected carefully in order to combat some of the stereotypes and present a more balanced picture to children.

The checklist on page 304 can be used to assess books (and other materials) with reference to equality and anti-bias content.

TASK
Use the Equality and Difference checklist on page 304 to evaluate a selection of books that are available to the children where you work. Include books suitable for all ages.

Key for Filling in the Checklist

Key to Equality Categories		Symbols for Equality Rating	
G	— Gender	++	Very positive images
M	— Marital Status	+	Positive
F	— Family Status	o	Neutral
S	— Sexual Orientation	-	Negative Stereotype
R	— Religious Belief	=	Extremely Negative
A	— Age	If area is not covered, leave blank	
D	— Disability		
E	— Ethnic Group		
T	— Traveller Community		

Figure 14.1: Sample of an Equality and Anti-bias Checklist

Equality and Difference
Checklist for Assessing Books

A	Title	Suitable for: Age Range	Equality Categories									Comments
			G	M	F	S	R	A	D	E	T	
Civardi, A. & S. Cartwright	Going to the Dentist	1–6 years	–	+	=	–						Middle class only All carers – female One token black child

ACTIVITY

Devise a similar checklist and use it to equality-proof resources in your work placement.

Songs, Music and Games

Most children love activities in this area and simple enjoyment can increase each child's sense of well-being and self-esteem.

▸ Learn songs in different languages and accents; this will lead to an appreciation of different languages and dialects.

▸ Use various musical instruments; the percussion variety can be easily made from an assortment of household objects.

▸ CDs are relatively cheap and children usually enjoy folk songs and music regardless of where they come from. At the pre-school stage it is not necessary for the children to be able to identify the language of the song or where the instrument comes from; it is important that the children enjoy the variety. Later on, children can learn about the origins and history.

▸ Make puzzles and games from laminated pictures pasted onto lightweight cardboard and cut into pieces.

▸ Use photographs of children or their families to make jigsaws. This presents an ideal opportunity to bring up the whole area of difference and similarity. Keep a copy of the original picture stored with the puzzle.

▸ An added value here is that parents and children can become aware that you do not need to spend a lot of money to develop talents or enjoy yourself.

Dramatic Play

The imaginary play area should be as diverse as possible and boys and girls can be encouraged to explore a broad range of roles through dressing up. Arrange and stock this area so that it can be a home, a shop, an airport, a submarine or any number of scenes that children may opt to play.

▸ Provide large sheets of material and lacy bits and pieces in addition to dresses, suits and briefcases in the dressing-up box. This helps develop children's imagination and creativity.

▶ Provide clothing from different cultures – these should be linked to visual material so children will connect them in a realistic way. However, remember that some pictures can themselves promote stereotypes instead of the opposite. Would a picture of a child in an Irish dance costume be typical of what Irish children wear every day?

▶ Provide a variety of dolls, male and female, and dolls with different hair, skin colour and features. These can be used to help children explore a variety of issues.

▶ Use dolls or puppets to tell stories and act out scenes. This can be an ideal way to introduce and explore a broad range of topics. They can also be used to help children learn how to cope with different and difficult situations, for example, how to be assertive rather than rude or aggressive.

▶ 'Persona' dolls are used increasingly in early years work with children. For details about how to use these, see the Resources section.

In Ireland today, many children will already have been exposed to different types of food; to add to their experience, they could prepare some of these foods using the proper utensils. The Chinese wok and chopsticks are readily available in shops. Vegetables on the nature table could include okra and squash as well as potatoes and carrots. Organise outings to shops which sell Asian or African food.

CASE STUDY

We often think of access solely in terms of children/people who have a disability, but limitations on access are wider and more far-reaching, as the case study below demonstrates. This is an important issue in the provision of equality and opportunity to all children.

Jane, who is a lone mother, has one 3-year-old daughter, Amy. They live in a small apartment. The family income comes solely from Jane's earnings from her part-time job as a nurse. There is no support or contact from Amy's father. Jane's own mother gives some emotional and practical support, although this is limited.

Jane is anxious for Amy to get the best possible chance for a good start in education. She has put Amy on the waiting list for the local funded nursery but she is unlikely to get a place. Meanwhile, Amy attends a private nursery while Jane is at work and Jane pays the fees out of her earnings.

Jane brings her daughter to the nursery each day. Absences are infrequent but tend to occur when there are parties or outings. Jane depends on public transport and is often late collecting her daughter. Jane does not attend parent meetings although she always seems interested at other times to discuss her child's progress with staff.

In the nursery setting Amy is a very obedient child who is very willing to please. She tends to be a loner and does not mix easily with the other children. She also has on occasion taken toys belonging to other children and this has caused friction with both the children and their parents.

On the physical side she is often tired and sometimes comes to the nursery having had no breakfast.

Read the case study above carefully and in a group, identify the following.

▸   What are the main issues of access for Amy and Jane?

▸   What are Amy's additional needs?

▸   How can the nursery team best meet all of Amy's additional needs?

▸   What frictions might arise regarding the child's and the parent's participation in the nursery?

Colour

Many toys and equipment today tend to come in bright blues, greens, reds and yellows for older children and in pastel shades for babies. Various shades of blacks, greys and browns are rarely seen in toys, giving the subtle message that these colours are less desirable. It may sound far-fetched to state that this idea transfers itself to darker shades of skin colour, but children as young as 3 have learned to think that black is not a good colour! All colours should be used and face paints should include darker shades.

SUMMARY

▸   Children learn attitudes and ways of behaving through the socialisation process.

▸   Diversity is all around us. Children become aware of differences and they learn to respond to those differences at a very young age.

▸   Prejudice and discrimination affect *all* children.

▸   The adult role is of crucial importance in the provision of an environment which is supportive to all and which celebrates diversity.

▸   Adults must be able to take action when offensive language or behaviour is used.

▸   Materials, resources and activities should be inclusive.

▸   A written policy on equality and associated procedures should be a fundamental part of any early learning establishment.

Appendix 1

UN Convention on the Rights of the Child – Unofficial Summary of Main Provisions

Article 5
Parental guidance and the child's evolving capacities

The State's duty to respect the rights and responsibilities of parents and the wider family to provide guidance appropriate to the child's evolving capacities.

Article 6
Survival and development

The inherent right to life and the State's obligation to ensure the child's survival and development.

Article 7
Name and nationality

The right to have a name from birth and to be granted a nationality.

Article 8
Preservation of identity

The State's obligation to protect and, if necessary, re-establish the basic aspects of a child's identity (name, nationality and family ties).

Article 9
Separation from parents

The child's right to live with his/her parents unless this is deemed incompatible with his/her best interests; the right to maintain contact with both parents if separated from one or both; the duties of States in cases where such separation results from State action.

Article 12
The child's opinion

The child's right to express an opinion and to have that opinion taken into account in any matter or procedure affecting the child.

Article 13
Freedom of expression

The child's right to obtain and make known information and to express his or her views, unless this would violate the rights of others.

Article 14
Freedom of thought, conscience and religion

The child's right to freedom of thought, conscience and religion, subject to appropriate parental guidance and national law.

Article 18
Parental responsibilities

The principle that both parents have joint primary responsibility for bringing up their children and that the State should support them in this task.

Article 19
Protection from abuse and neglect

The State's obligation to protect children from all forms of maltreatment perpetrated by parents or others responsible for their care and to undertake preventive and treatment programmes in this regard.

Article 20
Protection of children without families

The State's obligation to provide special protection for children deprived of their family environment and to ensure that appropriate alternative family care or institutional placement is made available to them, taking into account the child's cultural background.

Article 25
Periodic review of placement

The right of children placed by the State for reasons of care, protection or treatment to have all aspects of that placement evaluated regularly.

Article 26
Social security

The right of children to benefit from social security.

Article 27
Standard of living

The right of children to benefit from an adequate standard of living, the primary responsibility of parents to provide this and the State's duty to ensure that this responsibility is first fulfillable and then fulfilled, where necessary through the recovery of maintenance.

Article 37
Torture and deprivation of liberty

The prohibition of torture, cruel treatment or punishment, capital punishment, life imprisonment and unlawful arrest or deprivation of liberty. The principles of appropriate treatment, separation from detained adults, contact with family and access to legal and other assistance.

Appendix 2

Doing a Research Project

Glossary of Terms

Administer: To direct or conduct an interview, questionnaire or test.

Atypical: Irregular, not usual.

Bias: A slant or point of view. A study is said to be biased if the researcher has been subjective and influenced the outcome. To prejudice the outcome.

Bibliography: A list of all books, articles and other sources that the researcher has read or consulted which has informed the author.

Case study: A detailed profile of a person, a group, an organisation or even a country, usually used to illustrate a point of view or a theory.

Checklist: A list which shows at a glance items that are arranged in a logical order, and against which the researcher can check.

Citation: A passage referred to or words quoted from the work of another author.

Classify: To arrange in sets according to common characteristics.

Closed questions: Have pre-set answers. The researcher limits the range of answers. (See also **questionnaire** and **open questions**.)

Confidentiality: Adherence to principles of trust and privacy; every individual has a right to privacy regarding information that is collected about them.

Content analysis: An examination and classification of the subject and approach of a piece of communication such as an individual document, media article or programme, book, letter or report.

Data: Facts, quantities or conditions which are given or known.

Ethics: Relating to morals and obligation.

Experiment:

A trial where the researcher sets up conditions in order to study the effects of one or more factors on a subject(s).

Hypothesis:

A theory; a speculation on what might be.

Interview:

A conversation between a researcher and a respondent, the purpose of which is to elicit information on a certain topic/area.

Longitudinal survey:

A study undertaken over a period of time; it could be weeks or years.

Methodology:

The research techniques used to collect information for the research project.

Non-participant:

No involvement with or influence on the subject.

Objective:

External to the researcher's own mind, feelings or values.

Official statistics:

Facts and figures contained in authorised public sources.

Open questions:

Allows respondents to give a broad, informative and in-depth answer if they wish to do so.

Opinion poll:

A survey of people's opinions.

Participant:

The researcher is part of the group.

Primary research/source:

All the information and data that the researcher has found out for himself/herself.

Qualitative research:

Pertaining to quality, it aims to gain insight through the study of individuals.

Quantitative research:

Pertaining to quantity; it aims to study the relationship of one set of facts to another using scientific methods.

Questionnaire:

A list or series of questions designed to elicit certain information. (See also open questions and closed questions.)

Quotation:

The use of an author's exact words.

References:

A list and description of all the works (e.g. books, articles, websites) which have either been quoted or mentioned in a text.

Reliability:	The research method used will produce the same or similar results every time it is carried out in the same conditions.
Representative sample:	A section of the population which is typical of the general population.
Respondent:	A person who replies to questions or who allows himself/herself to be interviewed.
Response rate:	The number or percentage of people who participate in the research.
Sample:	The numbers of people/groups about whom facts are gathered.
Secondary sources:	All sources of information, other than primary sources, which may be used to support primary research or may be used exclusively in a study.
Structured interview:	A very tightly organised interview with set questions. (See also **interview** and **unstructured interview**.)
Subjective:	Relating to the researcher's own opinions, feelings and thoughts.
Survey:	To gain information from a representative selection of the population. Questionnaires, interviews or checklists are common tools used.
Unstructured interview:	An open interview with the interviewer given scope to rephrase questions or to ask extra ones. (See also **interview**, **structured interview** and **open questions**.)

Doing a Research Project

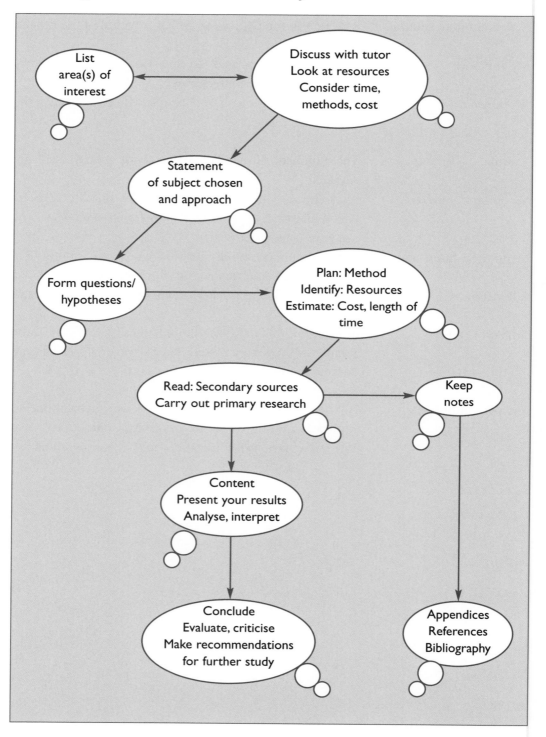

Choosing a Topic

Choose your topic early and avoid the urge to keep changing. List your areas of interest.

Several exercises and tasks are set throughout this book which would be ideal to take on as a project, but you may prefer to choose a topic about which you know absolutely nothing or a topic about which you feel very strongly or have a particular interest. The choice should be an individual one. If a group undertakes a project together, careful planning, close co-operation and regular reviews are required. It is also important in the introduction to outline clearly the role and tasks undertaken by each member of the group.

Narrowing the Subject Area

Discuss your choice of topic with your tutor. Your tutor will pose many questions which will help you to narrow your focus.

Inevitably, whether you are doing a school project or a PhD, you will begin with a broad idea which then has to be narrowed down. For example, you might be interested in considering the impact of television on children; the following questions would help to narrow the focus of the topic:

▶   Which programmes am I going to consider?
▶   What age group will I focus on? There will be a vast difference between the content of a study that has 2- to 3-year-olds rather than teenagers as a focus.
▶   What slant will you take?
    —   Effects of violence
    —   Effects on general knowledge
    —   Effects on social interaction
    —   Effects on literacy

Statement of Subject Chosen

Write down a broad outline of the topic you are going to cover, your aims and your hypotheses.

Identify Sources

Where and how are you going to get your information? Be realistic. Start with your textbooks (secondary research). List all other possible sources – local libraries, facilities, services, newspapers, TV, local representatives, tutors, other students, staff at your work placement, children, etc. Do not be discouraged if there appears to be a lack of secondary material on your chosen topic. If there is very little already, then your project will be all the more interesting.

Using the Library

In a library it is useful to be familiar with the arrangements and divisions. All libraries are divided into three main areas:

▸ Fiction: This is usually arranged by author in alphabetical order; it may also be subdivided into different categories, e.g. romance, adventure, science fiction.

▸ Non-fiction.

▸ Reference – dictionaries, thesaurus, etc.

If you know the name of the book or the author you can locate it using the author or subject index.

All libraries now use a computerised catalogue and you will be shown how to locate the books on this system.

If a particular title is not available in the library, the librarian will be able to tell you in which library it is available.

When you have located a book, use the following approach to find out if it contains material which might be relevant or useful in your research. Check the:

▸ Contents page

▸ Date of publication

▸ Introduction

▸ Conclusion

▸ Index.

What Research Methods to Use?

If you are going to do some primary research, decide what primary method suits your purpose. For example, if you are doing a survey:

▸ Are you going to use a questionnaire/interview/checklist?

▸ What questions will you ask?

▸ How many people will be included in your research and how will you select them?

▸ Are you going to approach organisations?

▸ How much is it going to cost?

▸ How much time will you need for your primary research?

▸ Is all this possible?

Designing and Using a Questionnaire

▸ **Decide** what information you want.

▸ **Design** the questions that will help obtain the information.

▸ **Write** the questions down in logical sequence on a form.

▸ **Select** the people that you are going to question.

▸ **Ask** these people the questions.

▸ **Record** the answers, using tick boxes, graphs or other suitable methods which make them easy to read.

▸ **Present** the findings in an appropriate way.

▸ **Conclude** with statements drawn from the analysis.

Writing Up Your Report

Your project will contain the following sections.

▸ **Title page and contents page.**

▸ **Introduction.** Your introduction should be brief and clear. It should give a broad overview of the general area, which might include a definition of subject area identifying size and context. For example, if you are going to do a study on Traveller children and their participation in early education, your introduction would include a definition of 'Traveller', how many Travellers there are, percentage of the population as a whole, percentage that are aged 5 or under, an overview of Traveller participation in education generally and a comment on literacy levels.

Your introduction should then state clearly what you are going to examine in your project and what you expect or hope to find out; in the example above: *'I am going to look at the participation levels of Traveller children of pre-school age in integrated early education settings. Participation levels have always been very low so I will try to identify the main barriers and difficulties as well as identifying the factors which contribute to successful integration.'*

▸ **Methodology.** This can be fairly brief. You should outline how you conducted your study. State what type of research you used (primary/secondary) and include a brief description of this, giving numbers covered and time spent if applicable. What did you read? You should point out the strengths and weaknesses in your methodology.

▸ **Content.** This is the main part of your written project in which you:

   ▸ Present

   ▸ Analyse

   ▸ Relate to theory.

Experiment with different ways of presenting your findings. Data taken from surveys or questionnaires need to be put into categories and groups so that the reader will easily be able to see patterns of difference or similarity and be able to extract significant information. Numerical data can be presented in many ways, such as tables, bar charts, histograms and graphs. These are the simplest methods of presenting your data; if you have access to a computer then you may be able to produce very elaborate presentations. Photographs, video or audio recordings may be used. When you have presented your findings it is important to describe what you have found, drawing attention to significant points, what surprised you or which results were predictable. How did your findings relate to the literature? For example, if you study a group of 5-years-olds playing with construction toys, then you should be able to relate this to what is said about children's development in your textbooks.

Example of Table: **Local Authority Assessment of Social Housing Needs: Comparison with Previous Return by Category of Need (Net Need)**

Category of need	2002	2005	2008	Change
Homeless	2,468	2,399	1,394	−41.9%
Travellers	1,583	1,012	1,317	30.1%
Unfit accommodation	4,065	1,725	1,757	1.9%
Overcrowded accommodation	8,513	4,112	4,805	16.9%
Involuntary sharing	4,421	3,375	4,965	47.1%
Leaving institutional care	82	262	715	172.9%
Medical or compassionate reasons	3,400	3,547	8,059	127.2%
Elderly	2,006	1,727	2,499	44.7%
Disabled	423	480	1,155	140.6%
Not reasonably able to meet the cost of accommodation	21,452	25,045	29,583	18.1%
Total	**48,413**	**43,684**	**56,249**	**28.8%**

Source: The Department of the Environment, Heritage and Local Government.

Example of a Graph: **Applications to the Office of Refugee Applications, 1991 to March 2010**

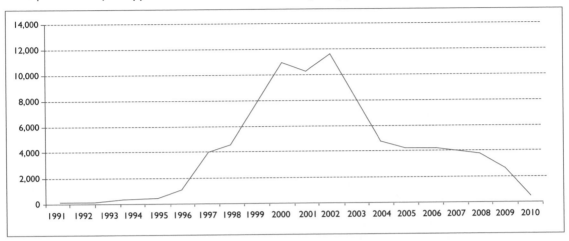

Example of a Pie Chart: **Children's Residential Services Classified by Service Type**

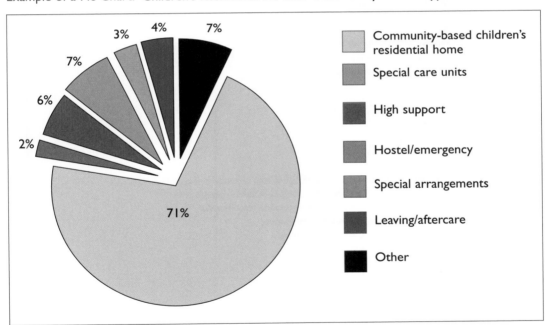

Source: *National Children in Care Report* (HIQA 2008).

Example of Bar Chart: **Proportion of Women in National Parliaments, Single/Lower House** (% of Total)

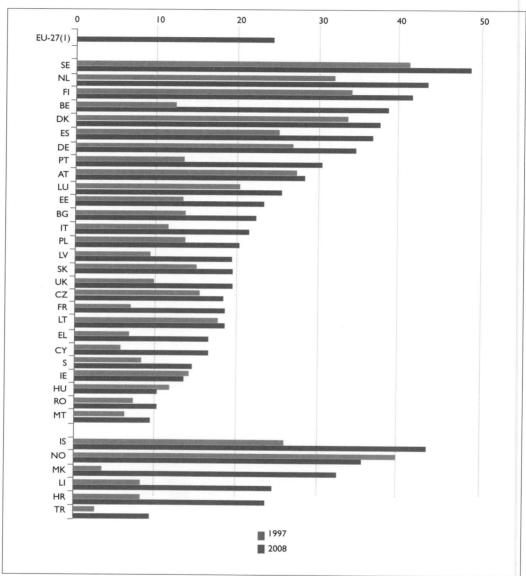

Source: Eurostat (EU-SILC) (2010).

Conclusion

- ▶ Summarise
- ▶ Clarify
- ▶ Evaluate
- ▶ Recommend.

In simple language, '*What was I looking for, what did I find and what does it mean?*' Summarise and clarify the main points but do not go into long repetitions of what you have already said. Do not be tempted to include opinions and hunches here that were not evident in your research.

Be critical of yourself and your methodology and indicate improvements you could make if undertaking the project again. Were you surprised by anything you discovered while doing your project? Comment on bias and any ethical issues that have arisen. Suggest ways that you feel the research area could be extended. In your evaluation, do not be afraid to be negative, e.g. admitting 'In my questionnaire, answers given to No. X revealed nothing material to the study because I had phrased the question badly.' You will demonstrate by admitting this that you have acquired an insight into the skill of devising questions. However, if you try to cover up the fact that some part was not a success or if you do not mention it, hoping that it will not be noticed, you will be showing that you have gained little skill or that you are a dishonest researcher!

Appendices

In the appendices, include material not suitable for the main part of your study, for example, newspaper cuttings, an observation, the questionnaire that you used, a copy of a table of statistics. Number them clearly, as the purpose of appendices is that you can refer to them in the main text.

Keep a record of all your planning notes. This is part of the research. Sometimes you will do a lot of background work, which will not be evident in your written submission, and it is recommended to provide evidence of all your project work. This can go in an appendix.

References and Bibliography

An outline of the Harvard system of referencing is given below. There are other systems and this is why you will notice that references and bibliographies may be presented differently. All methods are broadly similar, but whatever one you adopt you should stick to it, or both you and your readers will be totally confused.

- ▶ Quotations must be taken word for word from the original text.

▶ Short quotations begin and end with a single inverted comma, e.g. 'A third – and now very powerful – factor in the development of early services and the need for more has been the changing structure of the family' (Hayes, 2005: 17).

▶ Longer quotations (three or more lines) are set out separately from the enclosing paragraph; they are usually indented and do not have quotation marks:

> The child's individuality is the basic building block of diversity among children. Individuality and diversity are companion concepts in the child's life experience. The concern of the significant adults in the child's life must be to make both individuality and diversity a celebration . . . (Fallon/CECDE, 2005: 23)

▶ If you do not quote a sentence in full you indicate this by use of an **ellipsis**, as in the example above.

▶ Please note in the example that the reference is placed in brackets at the end of the quote and consists of the author's surname and the year of publication, followed by the page number.

▶ **Citations:** If the author's name is part of the sentence you should put the year of publication in brackets (parentheses): 'Lesovitch (2005) argues that referring to Roma as nomads is perpetuating a myth as most of them were forced to settle under communist rule and have lived a settled lifestyle since that time.'

▶ If there are more than three authors, the citation lists the first surname followed by 'et al.', e.g. Byrne et al. (2010).

▶ At the end of your project, essay or report, you should list the references by author surname alphabetically.

For books:
Author's surname, Initials, Year of publication, *Title*, Place of publication: Publisher.
Example:
O'Toole, F., 2009, *Ship of Fools*, London: Bloomsbury.

For journal articles:
Author's surname, Initials, Year of publication, 'Title of article', *Name of journal*, Volume number, Issue number, Pages.
Example:
McMinn, J., 2006, 'Eliminating Poverty Is a Women's Rights' Issue', *Poverty Today*, Vol. 34, No. 12, pp. 43–7.

For edited collections:
Surname of editor, Initials (ed.), Year of publication, *Title*, Place: Publishers.

To reference a chapter in edited collections:

Example:
Peeters, J., 2005, 'Promoting Diversity and Equality in Early Childhood Care and Education Training – Men in Childcare' in Schonfeld, H., S. O'Brien and T. Walsh (eds), *Questions of Quality: International Conference*, Dublin: CECDE.

For electronic sources:
Website information: Author, Year, Title, Medium, Location URL, Access or cited date in brackets. Note: It is important to also print out the first page, as web pages change frequently or indeed may disappear altogether. You may put these pages in an appendix.

Example:
Jowett, A., 2010, Referencing Using the Harvard Method, available at www.nhgs.co.uk/technology/harvard.pdf [cited on 22 June 2010].

DVD source: Author, Year, *Title*, Type of medium, Place: Publisher.

Example:
Evanescence, 2006, *Anywhere But Home* (DVD), NYC: Sony Music Studios.

Please note:
▸   Punctuation marks are used specifically – commas, full stops, colons and quotation marks (the latter in relation to journal articles).
▸   The second line of the reference is indented so that the surname of the first author is easily identified.
▸   Second and subsequent author's initials come before the surname.

There are many finer points to be learned about referencing; only the basics are included here. Probably the best way to learn is to note how references are handled in your textbooks and other books that you will read. Detailed guildelines on the complete Harvard system are given by A. Jowett (see above) or many other websites.

It is important that whenever you use the ideas of other writers or quote from their works that you acknowledge them in your text and at the end of your essay/project. This is important so that others who may want to follow up on the ideas will have detailed and accurate information about your sources. If you do not reference or acknowledge your sources, then that is called **plagiarism**. Plagiarism is a serious offence and is basically academic fraud. It is akin to stealing – stealing someone else's intellectual property.

Appendix 3
Sample Narrative Observation

Observation of a Child's Physical Development

Observation no.: 1

Observation date: 12.01.11

Method used: Narrative

Media used: Pen and paper

Start time: 14.20

Finish time: 14.30

Number of children present: 8

Number of adults present: 3

Permission obtained from: Supervisor

Setting: The observation took place in the early years service of a large third-level college. The service is open from 8.00 a.m. until 6.00 p.m., Monday to Friday and it caters for 85 children age range 6 months to 5 years. The groups are divided according to their age groups and this includes a Montessori class for the older age group. All the staff are female and a number are from different countries. A number of staff are qualified, but not all. The service is situated on campus in an old building but inside is bright and cheerful and it has been fitted out in a purposeful way. The service was last visited by the HSE at the end of last year.

Immediate context: The observation took place in the 'wobbler' room. The children have just woken up and a free play session has commenced. TC is pushing a buggy at the beginning of the observation session.

Name of child: TC

Brief description of the child observed: TC is a female aged 2 years and 5 months. She is the only child in the family and has been attending the service since she was 10 months old. She has asthma and has had frequent ear infections — grommets were inserted 3 months ago and according to the record an improvement has been evident.

Aim and rationale: The aim of the observation is to observe TC for a short time as she involves herself in various activities during free play in order to assess what stage of physical development she is at.

Observation:

TC is holding the handle of a buggy with both hands and is pushing it at a run from one side of the room to the opposite side. She is now standing with the buggy in front of her, still holding it with both hands and for about 30 seconds she remains still, looking in the direction of a worker who is dressing a doll. She is again running with the buggy and turns around dragging the buggy after her with her right hand. The buggy falls over. She is grasping it with both hands and stands it upright. She now lets go of the buggy and is walking over to the worker. She is holding her arms out and the worker is offering her the doll. She is taking the doll, rolling it into her arms and holding it close to her for a few seconds, looking towards it all the time. She is now putting it into the buggy using only her right hand, palmar grasp and bending down from the waist. She is taking it out again using the same hand and grasp and is placing it carefully on the ground again bending from the waist. She is picking it up with both hands and is holding it close to her body. Now using her left hand, palmar grasp she is placing the doll back in the buggy. After a few seconds with her right hand and a tripod grasp she is lifting the doll up by its hair. She is pulling the buggy over to lie on its side and then bending her knees to the ground, right knee first. She lies down beside the buggy, hugging the doll close to her and faces a mirror to the left side of her. Now she releases the doll, rolls over onto her tummy and pushing herself up with her right hand on the floor she begins to crawl. She is crawling on all fours around in a complete circle, then putting her right foot on the floor first she is getting up into a standing position.

Dropping down on both knees she gets into a crawling position again and is crawling towards some open cupboards. She is crawling into one of the cupboards. She is crawling from one side of the cupboard to the other (she does this twice) and then she lies down looking out towards the room. She is saying 'ab ap lee'. She gets into crawling position again and is crawling out of the cupboard, saying 'ubba, ubba' and right foot under her first she gets to her feet. Again she is getting down on her knees, left knee first and is crawling back into the cupboard. This time she turns over into sitting position and sits with both feet flat on the floor and her knees drawn up, legs slightly apart. After about 20 seconds she is bending over, places her right hand on the floor and bending her right knee under her she is shuffling out of the cupboard and getting into a standing position, saying 'ab see, ab see'. She is walking over towards the buggy and grasps it around the handle with both hands.

Observation ends

Evaluation:

The aim of this observation was to observe TC and assess her stage of physical development — both fine and gross motor skills. Throughout the observation TC was very active and was using her whole body and gross motor skills for the most part. My observation of fine motor skills on this occasion was limited.

Fine motor skills

Fine motor skills are 'the skills which involve the co-ordination of eye and hand movements'(Donohoe and Gaynor, 2011: xx). While TC is holding the buggy she is using a whole hand or palmar grasp around the handles. When she takes the doll from the buggy she uses a tripod grasp picking it up by the hair. According to Meggitt(2006) these skills are present by the age of 12 months. This does not mean that TC has not mastered more advanced fine motor skills, but they were not evident in this observation.

Gross motor skills

'Gross motor skills are whole body and limb movements, co-ordination and balance'(Donohoe and Gaynor, 2011: xx). Throughout the observation TC used a variety of gross motor skills. First she runs and then walks with the buggy; she moves safely and confidently without bumping into anything or falling over. According to Bruce and Meggit (2006), by 3 years a child can walk and run forward and walk and tip toe.

She was also demonstrating her gross motor skills in getting into crawling, sitting and standing positions, rolling over and pushing herself up. She also bends over to pick things up holding her balance. According to Bruce and Meggitt (2006), these skill begins to develop from the age of 18 months.

Summary

The overall view of TC's physical development is that she is an active child and is able to move, balance and manoeuvre herself confidently. Although she is skilfull at running as well as walking, she also seems to like to crawl. She is building her confidence in skills attained at an earlier age and is using these to completely and thoroughly investigate her surroundings.

Personal learning gained:

- Through observing TC I learned how children explore and how they move in small and large spaces.

- According to Piaget, active learning is very important at this sensory motor stage and in doing this observation I realised how important physical skills are in facilitating the investigation and exploration of the child's environment and surroundings.
- I did not observe very much fine motor skills on this occasion and I think that in future I would plan to do observations at a time when a child is doing activities where the relevant skills being observed are being used — if I had observed TC at the sand tray, for instance, I think I would have observed more fine motor skills as well as the large body movements.
- Although I thought that I had managed to get great detail into my observation I realised when it came to the evaluation that even more detail would have helped towards a more thorough assessment of skills.
- In researching the textbooks I have also learned a great deal about the physical development of 2-3-year-olds generally.

Recommendations:

- TC has great confidence and ability to move around and the provision of more space would help her build on these skills, e.g. plenty of outdoor play and also indoor climbing equipment and obstacle courses.
- She also likes to explore and a variety of items of different textures and sizes would introduce new experiences to her.

References:

Bruce, T. and C. Meggitt, 2006, Child Care and Education, 2nd edn, London: Hodder Arnold.

Donohoe, J. and F. Gaynor, 2011, Education and Care in the Early Years, 4th edn, Dublin: Gill & Macmillan.

Meggitt, C., 2006, Child Development: An Illustrated Guide, 2nd edn, Oxford: Heinemann.

Signatures

Learner ——————————— Date ———————————

Supervisor ——————————— Date ———————————

Tutor ——————————— Date ———————————

Appendix 4

Sample Child Record Form
CONFIDENTIAL

Please use **BLOCK CAPITALS.**

Name of Child _____Pronounced _____

Date of Birth _____Male/Female _____

Address _____

_____

Telephone No. _____ Mobile No. _____

Mother's Name _____

Mother's Workplace/College _____Telephone No. _____

Address _____

_____

Father's Name _____

Father's Workplace/College _____Telephone No. _____

Address _____

_____

Emergency Contacts

Details of two persons who may be contacted in an emergency. Contact with these persons will only be required when parents cannot be contacted.

1. Name _____ Telephone No. _____

   Address _____

_____

Relationship to Child _____

2. Name _____   Telephone No. _____

Address _____

_____

Relationship to Child _____

Persons to Collect Your Child

Details of persons (other than parents) who are allowed to collect your child under normal circumstances.

1. Name _____   Telephone No. _____

Relationship to Child _____

2. Name _____   Telephone No. _____

Relationship to Child _____

Medical Details

Family Doctor _____Telephone No. _____

Address _____

_____

_____

_____

See also form in Appendix 5.

Vaccination		Usual Age for Immunisation	Date Received
BCG		Birth to 1 month	
5 in 1	Diphtheria Tetanus Whooping Cough Hib Inactivated Polio	2 months	
Meningococcal C		2 months	
5 in 1		4 months	
Meningoccocal C		4 months	
5 in 1		6 months	
Meningoccocal C		6 months	
MMR (Mumps, Measles, Rubella)		12–15 months	
Hib		12–15 months	
4 in 1	Diphtheria Tetanus Whooping Cough Inactivated Polio	4–5 years	
MMR (Mumps, Measles, Rubella)		4–5 years	

Does your child suffer from any chronic illness? Please give details. _____

_____

Is your child on any prescribed treatment for the above? Please give details. _____

_____

Has your child been hospitalised for any reason? Please give details. _____

_____

Does your child suffer from any allergies? Please give details. _____

_____

I give my permission for childcare centre management to arrange medical assistance or obtain emergency hospital treatment for my child, if deemed necessary, in my absence.

Signed: _____ Date: _____

Parent/Guardian ....

Centre use only: Attendance from _____to _____

Adapted with permission from Child Record Form, The Willows, Dún Laoghaire VEC Childcare Centre, Sallynoggin, Co. Dublin.

Appendix 5
Standard Form for Reporting Child Protection and/or Welfare Concerns to a HSE Region

PRIVATE AND CONFIDENTIAL

In case of Emergency or outside Health Board hours, contact should be made with An Garda Síochána.

A. To Principal Social Worker/Designate: _____

This will be printed as relevant to each Community Care Area.

1. **Details of Child:**

Name: _____   Male: ☐   Female: ☐

Address: _____

_____   Age/D.O.B.: _____

_____   School: _____

1a. Name of Mother: _____   Name of Father: _____

Address of Mother if different to Child: Address of Father if different to Child:

_____   _____

_____   _____

_____   _____

Telephone Number: _____   Telephone Number: _____

1b. Care and Custody arrangements regarding child, if known: _____

_____

1c. Household Composition:

Name	Relationship to Child	Date of Birth	Additional Information e.g. School/Occupation

Note: A separate report form must be completed in respect of each child being reported.

2.   **Details of concern(s), allegation(s) or incident(s) dates, times, who was present, description of any observed injuries, parent's view(s), child's view(s) if known.**

3.   **Details of person(s) allegedly causing concern in relation to the child:**
Name: _____   Age: _____   Male: ☐   Female: ☐
Address: _____
Relationship to Child: _____
Occupation: _____

4.   **Name and Address of other personnel or agencies involved with this child:**
Social Workers: _____   School: _____
_____   _____

Public Health Nurse: _____   Gardaí: _____
_____   _____

G.P.: _____   Pre-School/Crèche/Youth Club: _____
_____   _____

Hospital: _____   Other (Specify e.g. Youth Groups etc.): __
_____   _____

5.   **Are Parents/Legal Guardians aware of this referral to the Social Work Department?**
Yes   ☐   No   ☐
If Yes, what is their attitude? _____

6.   **Details of Person reporting concerns:**
(Please see Guidance Notes re. Limitations of confidentiality)
Name: _____   Occupation: _____
Address: _____
_____   Telephone Number: _____
Nature and extent of contact with Child/Family: _____
_____

7.   **Details of Person completing form:**
Name: _____   Date: _____
Occupation: _____   Signed: _____

Appendix 6

International Standard Classification of Occupations (ISCO-88)

Class	Occupations
1	Legislators, senior officials and managers
2	Professionals
3	Technicians and associate professionals
4	Clerks, administrative and secretarial occupations
5	Service workers and shop and market sales workers (early years and care workers)
6	Skilled agricultural and fishery workers
7	Craft and related trade workers
8	Plant and machine operators and assemblers
9	Elementary occupations
0	Armed forces

National Children's Nurseries Association, *Minimum Quality Standards in a Nursery*, Dublin: NCNA.

National Children's Resource Centre, 2004, *Child and Family Directory*, Dublin: Barnardos.

National Economic and Social Forum, 2005, *Forum Report No. 31: Report on Early Childhood Care and Education*, Dublin: NESF.

NCCA, 2006, *Aistear: The Early Childhood Curriculum Framework*, Dublin: NCCA.

O'Doherty, A. and P. O'Doherty, 2000, *A Career in Childcare?*, Dublin: National Children's Nursery Association.

Organisation for Economic Co-operation and Development (OECD), 2004, *Thematic Review of Early Childhood Care and Education Policy in Ireland*, OECD Directorate of Education, Paris: OECD.

Pavee Point, 2002, *Éist: Respect for Diversity in Early Childhood Care, Education and Training*, Dublin: Pavee Point Travellers' Centre.

Purcell, B., 2001, *For Our Own Good: Childcare Issues in Ireland*, Cork: Collins Press.

Riddall-Leech, Sheila, 2009, *Heuristic Play: A Practical Guide for the Early Years*, Leamington Spa: Step Forward Publishing Ltd.

Schonfeld, H., Dr G. Keirnan and T. Walsh, 2004, *Making Connections – A Review of International Policy Practices and Research Relating to Quality in Early Childhood Care and Education*, Dublin: CECDE.

Schonfeld, H., S. O'Brien and T. Walsh (eds), 2004, *Questions of Quality – Conference Report*, Dublin: CECDE.

Síolta, 2006, *The National Quality Framework for Early Childhood Education*, Dublin: CECDE.

Treoir, 2009, *Information Pack for Unmarried Parents*, 2nd edn, Dublin: Federation of Services for Unmarried Parents.

Yeo, A. and T. Lovell, 2002, *Sociology and Social Policy for the Early Years*, London: Hodder and Stoughton.

USEFUL ADDRESSES

All the organisation and departments listed below have extensive information on their websites, publications free for download and forward links to numerous other sites.

Most of the contact numbers are for the Dublin area and for this the authors apologise; however, head offices of services and organisations tend to be located in the capital. Where services and organisations are nationwide, the telephone numbers and contact addresses can be obtained in local directories or on the relevant website.

AIM Family Services, Family Law Information, Mediation and Counselling Centre, 64 Dame Street, Dublin 2. Tel: 01-670-8363, www.familyservices.ie.

Amnesty International, 1st Floor, Ballast House, 18–21 Westmoreland Street, Dublin 2. Tel: 01-863-8300, www.amnesty.ie.

Barnardos National Children's Resource Centre, Christchurch Square, Dublin 8. Tel: 01-453-0355, www.barnardos.ie.

Childminding Ireland, 9 Bulford Business Campus, Kilcoole, Co. Wicklow. Tel: 01-287-8466, www.childminding.ie.

Children's Rights Alliance, 4 Upper Mount Street, Dublin 2. Tel: 01-662-9400, www.childrensrights.ie.

Citizens Information Board, Ground Floor, George's Quay House, 43 Townsend Street, Dublin 2. Tel: 01-605-9000, www.citizensinformation.ie.

City and County Childcare Committees, www.pobal.ie.

Department of Education and Skills, Marlborough Street, Dublin 1. Tel: 01-889-6400, www.education.ie.

Department of Health and Children, Hawkins House, Dublin 2. Tel: 01-635-4000, www.dohc.ie.

Department of Justice and Law Reform, 94 St Stephen's Green, Dublin 2. Tel: 01-602-8202, www.justice.ie.

Department of Social Protection, Áras Mhic Dhiarmada, Store Street, Dublin 1. Tel: 01-704-3000, www.welfare.ie.

Department of the Environment, Heritage and Local Government, Head Office, Custom House, Dublin 1. Tel: 01-888-2000, www.environ.ie.

Equality Authority, 3 Clonmel Street, Dublin 2. Tel: 01-417-3333, www.equality.ie.

Equality Tribunal, 3 Clonmel Street, Dublin 2. Tel: 01-477-4100, www.equality.ie.

Family Mediation Service, 4th Floor, St Stephen's Green House, Earlsfort Terrace, Dublin 2. Tel: 01-611-4100, www.fsa.ie.

Forbairt Naíonraí Teo, St Patrick's Hall, Marino Institute of Education, Griffith Avenue, Dublin 9. Tel: 01-853-5101, www.naionrai.ie.

Further Education and Training Awards Council (FETAC), East Point Plaza, East Point Business Park, Dublin 3. Tel: 01-865-9500, www.fetac.ie.

Health and Safety Authority, The Metropolitan Building, James Joyce Street, Dublin 1. Tel: 01-614-7020, www.hsa.ie.

Integration Ireland: The Immigrant Network, 18 Dame Street, Dublin 2. Tel: 01-645-3070, www.integratingireland.ie.

IMPACT (Trade Union for Early Childhood Workers), Nerney's Court, Dublin 1. Tel: 01-817-1500, www.impact.ie.

IPPA, Playgroups and Daycare, Broomhill Business Complex, Broomhill Road, Tallaght, Dublin 24. Tel: 01-463-0010, www.ippa.ie.

Irish Congress of Trade Unions (ICTU), 31–32 Parnell Square, Dublin 1. Tel: 01-889-7777, www.ictu.ie.

Irish Society for the Prevention of Cruelty to Children (ISPCC), 29 Lower Baggot Street, Dublin 2. Tel: 01-676-7960, www.ispcc.ie.

National Children's Nurseries Association (NCNA), Unit 12C, Bluebell Business Park, Old Naas Road, Bluebell, Dublin 12. Tel: 01-460-1138, www.ncna.net.

National Economic and Social Forum, 16 Parnell Square, Dublin 1. Tel: 01-814-6300, www.nesc.ie.

Office of the Minister for Children and Youth Affairs, Hawkins House, Dublin 2. Tel: 01-635-4000, www.omc.gov.ie.

Ombudsman for Children's Office, Millennium House, 52–56 Great Strand Street, Dublin 1. Tel: 01-865-6800, www.oco.ie.

One Family, Tel: 01-662-9212, www.onefamily.ie.

Parental Equality, 15A Clanbrassil Street, Dundalk, Co. Louth. Tel: 042-933-3163, www.parentalequality.ie.

Pavee Point Travellers' Centre, 46 North Great Charles Street, Dublin 1. Tel: 01-878-0255, www.paveepoint.ie.

Start Strong: Advancing Children's Early Care and Education, www.startstrong.ie.

Treoir (National Federation of Services for Unmarried Parents and Their Children), 41 Gandon House, Custom House Square, IFSC, Dublin 1. Tel: 01-670-0120, www.treoir.ie.

UN High Commissioner for Refugees (UNHCR), 1–3 Lower Fitzwilliam Street, Dublin 2. Tel: 01-631-4614, www.unhcr.ie.

Women's Aid, Everton House, 47 Old Cabra Road, Dublin 7. Tel: 01-868-4721, Helpline: 1800-341-900, www.womensaid.ie.

DISABILITY ORGANISATIONS

Association for Children and Adults with Learning Difficulties (ACLD), 1 Suffolk Street, Dublin 1. Tel: 01-679-0276.

Department of Education and Skills, Special Education Section, Cornamaddy, Athlone, Co. Westmeath. Tel: 0506-21363, www.education.ie.

Irish Deaf Society, 30 Blessington Street, Dublin 7. Tel: 01-860-1878, www.deaf.ie.

National Children's Resource Centre, Barnardos, Christchurch Square, Dublin 8. Tel: 01-453-0355, www.barnardos.ie.

National Council for Special Education, 1–2 Mill Street, Trim, Co. Meath. Tel: 046-948-6400, www.ncse.ie.

National Disability Authority (NDA), 25 Clyde Road, Dublin 4. Tel: 01-608-0400, www.nda.ie.

People with Disabilities in Ireland (PwDI), 4th Floor, Jervis House, Jervis Street, Dublin 1. Tel: 01-872-1744, www.pwdi.ie; email info@pwdi.ie.

SPECTRUM (umbrella organisation comprising Dyslexia Association of Ireland, Brainwave – The Irish Epilepsy Association, ASPIRE – Aspergers Syndrome Association of Ireland, HADD [Hyperactive Attention Deficit Disorder] Family Support Group, Irish Association for Gifted Children, Dyslexia Awareness), Tel: 01-874-8349.

ADDRESSES FOR PRACTICAL RESOURCES SUCH AS TEACHING MATERIALS AND CHILDREN'S BOOKS MAINLY IN RELATION TO EQUALITY AND DIVERSITY

Amnesty International, www.amnesty.ie.
    Education resources for primary and post-primary teachers on human and children's rights.

Futa Fata, An Spidéal, Co na Gaillimhe, www.futafata.com (English–Irish books).

Letterbox Library, 71–73 Allen Road, Stoke Newington, London N16 8RY. www.letterboxlibrary.com
    Books, posters and resources for all ages on a broad range of topics.

Mantra Lingua, Global House, 303 Ballards Lane, London N12 8NP. www.mantra lingua.com
    Books, CDs and DVDs (bilingual).

Pavee Point Travellers' Centre, 46 North Great Charles Street, Dublin 1. www.paveepoint.ie
    Posters, pictures, jigsaws, cards. Also a CD-ROM 'Éist – Respect for Diversity in Early Childhood Care and Education'.

Trócaire, www.trocaire.ie.
    Resources for teachers on citizenship and rights.

CHILD PROTECTION: BOOKS SUITABLE FOR 3–6-YEAR-OLDS

Berenstain, S. and J. Berenstain, 1985, *The Berenstain Bears Learn about Strangers*, New York: Random House.

Elliot, M., 1991, *Feeling Happy, Feeling Safe*, London: Hodder & Stoughton. (colouring book)

Klevan, S. and J. Bergsma, 1999, *The Right Touch*, Worthington: Illumination Arts.

Mayer, M., 1991, *There's a Nightmare in My Cupboard*, London: Methuen. (fears)

Index